≫ An ≪

AFRICAN
AMERICAN
COOKBOOK

An
AFRICAN AMERICAN
COOKBOOK

Exploring Black History and Culture
Through Traditional Foods

Phoebe Bailey

with the special assistance of
Christina G. Johnson and Kesha M. Morant

Good Books
New York, New York

Acknowledgments

A special thank-you to the congregation of Bethel African Methodist Episcopal Church, ChurchTowne of Lancaster, Pennsylvania.

Thank you, too, to Saints Memorial Community Church, Willingboro, New Jersey, and to Mr. Jerald and Mrs. Dawn Davis.

Good Books books may be purchased in bulk at special discounts for sales promotion, corporate gifts, fund-raising, or educational purposes. Special editions can also be created to specifications. For details, contact the Special Sales Department, Good Books, 307 West 36th Street, 11th Floor, New York, NY 10018 or info@skyhorsepublishing.com.

Good Books is an imprint of Skyhorse Publishing, Inc.®, a Delaware corporation.

Visit our website at www.goodbooks.com.

10 9 8 7 6 5 4 3

Library of Congress Cataloging-in-Publication Data is available on file.

Print ISBN: 978-1-68099-645-6

Printed in China

Photo Credits:
Merle Good: all black-and-white photographs by Merle Good, except those on page 268.

Abigail Gehring: Collard greens with ham hocks; collard greens; red cabbage; Wild rice, chicken, and broccoli bake; Parmesan baked chicken legs; Chicken cobbler; Cajun chops; Spareribs; Fried cabbage and bacon; Corn pudding; Dill potato salad; red potatoes; Sweet potato pone

Cover photo by Bonnie Matthews. Recipe pictured is Turnip Greens and Cornmeal Dumplings, page 14.

All other food photography by Shutterstock

Cover design by Daniel Brount
Interior design by Laura Klynstra

To **MRS. MARGARET M. BAILEY,**
my mother,
a designer of recipes,
who gave her family and
all who knew her
a wealth of wisdom and
a strong example of faith.

The royalties from the
sale of this book go to
Bethel Harambee Historical
Services and the Hopkins Research
and Study Center. These two orga-
nizations are committed to the pres-
ervation, stories, and living history of
African American traditions and culture in
ChurchTowne of Lancaster, Pennsylvania.

CONTENTS

INTRODUCTION

Welcome reader! Here are mouthwatering recipes that are easy to prepare and that will make every meal a delight. And with the recipes comes a look into our family and cultural traditions and some lessons we've learned. You will find quotes from some famous and some not-so famous people. We heard about many of them for the first time while sitting at the dinner table. Some of our songs are here. We heard them while preparing meals—for they're more than church songs. They were born out of the enslaved Africans' battle for freedom.

This book is about more than just food. We believe that, as important as food is to our being, it is what happens around a meal that actually sustains us. It is in preparing a meal that we discover "If you do not have what you want, use what you have." And when we work within that attitude, we find that God sufficiently provides for all our needs. It is at mealtimes that we learn family traditions, manners, how to share, how to wait our turns, how to listen to others, and many other important life lessons.

We use this book ourselves at home. And we share it within our congregation, which is a part of the African Methodist Episcopal Church. We are known as AMEs. I have discovered that AME also stands for "always eating and meeting." I can attest to the fact that this is true. So if you are in the neighborhood of ChurchTowne of Lancaster, Pennsylvania, please stop in and stay awhile. For at Bethel, it is always mealtime.

A special thanks to God for His many blessings, and to Phoebe, Christina, and Kesha, who helped to make this cookbook a reality. Thanks to the Bethel African Methodist Episcopal Church family for their recipes, stories, prayers, support, and the down-home meals that inspired this book. Thanks to all the wonderful African American cooks who contributed their traditional and favorite recipes to create a cornucopia of dishes. Thanks to the Goods who patiently worked with us to bring this book to press, and to all and anyone else who helped us.

Thank you to whose "who had so little but did so much with the little they had." These are those who toiled in the heat of the day and complained not about their lot, who bore their crosses and marched on in Jesus' name. These are those who when they looked to the future they saw us. These are our heroes, our elders, our parents, our support. We bless your spirits and He who gave you the strength to provide us hope.

—REVEREND EDWARD M. BAILEY
Bethel African Methodist Episcopal Church, ChurchTowne of Lancaster, Pennsylvania

WADE IN THE WATER

Wade in the water,
Wade in the water children.
Wade in the water,
God's gonna trouble the water.

See that host all dressed in white,
God's gonna trouble the water;
The leader look like the Israelite,
God's gonna trouble the water.

See that band all dressed in red,
God's gonna trouble the water;
Looks like the band that Moses led,
God's gonna trouble the water.

See that band all dressed in black
God's gonna trouble the water;
They come this far, and ain't turning back.
God's gonna trouble the water.

Spirituals carried code language for enslaved Africans. In this one, runaways are directed to go to the river. The water will cover the fleeing Africans' scent and tracks, to make it difficult for the bloodhounds to track them. The water also connects towns, cities, and states, leading the hearers to the conductor who will lead them to their next station or safe house. The song mentions three colors: red, white, and black. Fleeing Africans would look for someone wearing these colors at their next stop.

MAIN DISHES

Some of my fondest memories of my mother surround her ability to create a meal out of anything. Having to prepare supper for 15 children every evening required a lot of creativity and patience. Thankfully, my mother never ran short of either. She could make a simple meal a gourmet experience. I thank God that my mother had the ability to plan and prepare meals as she wanted to for us children.

Our ancestors who lived on plantations, however, did not have this luxury. Many mothers were in the fields working from sunup to sundown, planting and preparing the fields for harvest. These mothers' young children were often left back at the slaves' quarters, usually with an elder enslaved African, who because of illness or feebleness could no longer offer free field labor for the Massa.

Those mothers who worked in the Big House, the great house, the house that offered comfort—these mothers who were separated from their babies—would try to sneak down to the slave quarters with some small morsel of food for their children, praying every step of the way not to be discovered.

—PHOEBE BAILEY

MAIN DISHES *Traditional*

—◆—

GUMBO FEAST

Mary Alice Bailey

MAKES 10 SERVINGS

1½ pounds chicken legs and thighs

salt to taste

pepper to taste

1½ teaspoons red pepper flakes

3 tablespoons oil

1 pound smoked pork sausage, kielbasa, or turkey sausage, cut into ½" pieces

1 large onion, chopped

3 cloves garlic, minced

2 quarts chicken stock

1 whole bay leaf

½ teaspoon dried thyme leaves

1 bell pepper, chopped

2 ribs celery, chopped

¼ cup cornstarch

¼ cup cold water

1 bunch green onion tops, chopped

⅓ cup fresh chopped parsley

1. Season the chicken with salt, pepper, and red pepper flakes. Brown quickly in oil. Remove chicken from skillet and set aside.

2. Brown sausage in drippings. Remove sausage from skillet and set aside.

3. Add onion and garlic and stir into drippings. Cook, stirring constantly for about 4 minutes.

4. Add stock, seasonings, chicken, and sausage. Bring to a boil. Cook for 40 minutes, skimming the broth as needed.

5. Stir in chopped green pepper and celery ribs. Continue simmering another 20 minutes.

6. Make a smooth paste by mixing together cornstarch and cold water. Remove ½ cup stock from cooking pot and stir into paste. When smooth, stir into gumbo in stockpot. Continue stirring until broth thickens. Stir in green onion tops and parsley. Heat for 5 minutes.

7. Serve over rice.

SEAFOOD GUMBO

2 quarts beef stock or canned beef broth

1 cup chopped smoked ham

2 bay leaves

2 tablespoons crushed red pepper

2 teaspoons salt

6 tablespoons bacon drippings

¼ cup flour

3 tablespoons vegetable oil

3 cups frozen or fresh okra

2 large onions, chopped

1 green bell pepper, minced

2 stalks celery, chopped

2 cloves garlic, minced

16-ounce can whole tomatoes

¼ cup ketchup

1 tablespoon hot pepper sauce

1 tablespoon Worcestershire sauce

½ teaspoon dried thyme

1 pound raw shrimp, shelled and deveined

1 pound crabmeat or 6 hard-shell crabs, cooked
    and cleaned

12 oysters, shucked, with liquid

1 bunch scallions, chopped

1 tablespoon gumbo filé

6–8 cups cooked rice

1. Combine the stock, ham, bay leaves, red pepper, and salt in a large kettle. Bring to a boil over high heat. Reduce to simmer. Cover and cook for 60 minutes.

2. Meanwhile, heat bacon drippings in a skillet over medium heat. Stir in flour. Cook over very low heat, stirring constantly, until flour is dark brown and the roux smells nutty, about 25 minutes. Then stir into simmering beef stock until smooth and thickened.

3. Heat oil in skillet. Sauté okra, onions, green pepper, celery, and garlic for 10 minutes, until vegetables are almost tender. Stir in tomatoes, ketchup, and seasonings and bring to a boil.

4. Add vegetables to thickened stock.

5. Stir shrimp, crabmeat, oysters, scallions, and gumbo filé into stew. Simmer, covered, for 5 minutes, or until shrimp are pink.

6. Serve immediately over 1-cup individual servings of rice.

{ We used to roast sweet potatoes in the fireplace before we had dinner. The only heat we had was from the fireplace and the cooking stove. Mother had made several quilts, so after getting ourselves situated and our feet warm, we were fine. }

—ELIZABETH McGILL,
a member of Bethel AMEC, Lancaster, PA

MAIN DISHES & *Traditional*

NEW ORLEANS GUMBO

MAKES 8-10 SERVINGS

2 cups diced cooked chicken
2 cups diced cooked ham
2 cups diced cooked hot sausage
¼ cup margarine
28-ounce can tomatoes
⅓ cup chopped onion
1 teaspoon dried thyme
2 teaspoons dried rosemary
1 teaspoon dried basil
1 teaspoon dried oregano
2 tablespoons gumbo filé
1 pound jumbo shrimp, shelled and deveined
1 pound crabmeat
2 tablespoons chopped parsley

1. Place chicken, ham, and sausage in large pot.

2. Add margarine, tomatoes, onion, thyme, rosemary, basil, oregano, and gumbo filé.

3. Cover and simmer for 30 minutes.

4. Add shrimp and crabmeat. Continue to cook another 5 minutes.

5. Stir in parsley. Serve over hot rice.

OKRA GUMBO

Lisa Jacobs
MAKES 5-6 SERVINGS

4 slices bacon
1 medium onion, sliced thin
1 green pepper, chopped
2 celery ribs, sliced
2 (10-ounce) boxes frozen sliced okra, thawed and drained
16-ounce can sliced or stewed tomatoes, undrained
2 tablespoons Worcestershire sauce
½ teaspoon sugar
¼ teaspoon salt

1. Fry bacon until crisp. Drain and set aside.

2. Pour off half of drippings. Sauté onion in drippings over medium heat until golden.

3. Stir in green pepper and celery. Sauté until crisp-tender.

4. Add remaining ingredients, except bacon. Cover. Cook over low heat for 60 minutes, stirring every 15 minutes.

5. Crumble bacon over top before serving in soup bowls. Ladle into soup bowls or serve over rice.

BRUNSWICK STEW

Mattie Mae Roche
MAKES 6-8 SERVINGS

1 hog's head
1 pound boneless stewing beef
1 pound onions
3 pounds white potatoes
1 quart stewed tomatoes
1 quart cream-style corn
1 pint peas
2 tablespoons salt
black pepper to taste
1 pint lima beans
4 cups ketchup
½ cup Worcestershire sauce
½ cup apple cider vinegar
¼ cup lemon juice
1 teaspoon Tabasco sauce

1. In large stockpot cook hog's head and beef in water to cover until meat is tender and leaves the bone. Debone meat and reserve broth. Chop meat into small pieces and set aside.

2. Chop onions and cube or slice potatoes. Add to broth. Cook until just tender.

3. Stir in meat and other ingredients. Cook on low heat until vegetables are tender and stock thickens, about 2–3 hours.

COLLARD GREENS

Betty Jean Joe, Carrie Alford
MAKES 12 MAIN-DISH SERVINGS
OR 20 SIDE-DISH SERVINGS

large ham hock, 1 pound bacon, or 2 pounds
    neckbones
4 bunches collard greens
2 sticks butter
1 teaspoon salt
1 tablespoon sugar
½ cup vinegar

1. Cook meat. (Simmer ham hocks and neckbones until they are half-cooked or fry bacon.) Place in large stockpot.

2. Wash collard greens. Cut out stems. Cut greens into pieces. Wash again. Add to meat. Cover entirely with water.

3. Add butter, salt, sugar, and vinegar. Let boil 4–5 hours, or until meat and greens are tender.

{ Africans who found themselves on the shores of Pennsylvania at the beginning of the seventeenth century, with few exceptions, were not here to explore land or to practice the innovative sociopolitical ideology espoused by the end of the eighteenth century—"life, liberty, and the pursuit of happiness." These early forced African immigrants were transatlantic human cargo and became the foundation of the economic foothold in America.

—DR. SHIRLEY PARHAM }

MAIN DISHES & *Traditional*

9

COLLARD GREENS

Ann Beardan, Mrs. Dana Beardan Frierson

MAKES 6-8 MAIN-DISH SERVINGS
OR 10-12 SIDE-DISH SERVINGS

2 smoked ham hocks, large turkey wings, or
   1 pound thickly sliced bacon
1½ quarts water
5 pounds fresh collard greens
1 onion, chopped
1 teaspoon salt
1 teaspoon pepper
1 tablespoon vinegar
1 pinch baking soda
hot pepper pods or hot sauce, optional

1. Place ham hocks in Dutch oven or large stockpot. Add water. Cook for 1½–2 hours. (If using bacon, fry until crisp, then add to stockpot with drippings. Add water and continue.)

2. Break off and discard collard green stems. Wash leaves thoroughly. Slice into bite-size pieces by rolling up several leaves together and slicing in ¼" strips.

3. Add collards, onion, salt, pepper, vinegar, baking soda, and hot pepper pods to pot. Cover and cook on medium heat for an hour, or until vegetables are tender.

COLLARD GREENS WITH HAM HOCKS

MAKES 5 SERVINGS

1 smoked ham hock
4 cups water
2 pounds collard greens
1 teaspoon salt
1½ teaspoons crushed red pepper flakes
1 tablespoon sugar
¼ cup bacon drippings

1. Place ham hock in 5-quart pot. Add water. Bring to a boil. Cover. Reduce heat and simmer for 45 minutes. Skim foam from broth several times.

2. Cut away thick part of collards' stems. Wash greens thoroughly. Drain. Chop into small pieces. Add to ham hock and broth.

3. Stir in salt, red pepper, sugar, and bacon drippings. Cover. Cook at a lively simmer for 20 minutes, or until greens are tender.

4. Turn off heat. Cover pot and let sit a few minutes before serving.

QUICK(ER) COLLARD GREENS

MAKES 4–6 MAIN-DISH SERVINGS

2 ham hocks
3 cups water
1-pound bag frozen collard greens
1 tablespoon sugar
1 teaspoon salt
½ teaspoon pepper

1. Place ham hocks in stockpot. Add water. Bring to a boil over medium heat. Cover and simmer for 60 minutes, adding more water as needed.

2. Add collards, sugar, salt, and pepper to ham hocks and broth. Simmer for 30–45 minutes, or until meat and vegetables are tender

3. Remove meat from bone, stir into broth and vegetables, and serve.

MUSTARD GREENS AND HAM HOCKS

MAKES 8–10 SERVINGS

3 smoked ham hocks
3 quarts water
2 pounds mustard greens
1 teaspoon salt
1 teaspoon freshly ground black pepper
1 teaspoon sugar
1 teaspoon dried thyme leaves
2 pounds green cabbage
4 medium potatoes, peeled and cut into chunks

1. Place ham hocks in 4-quart saucepan. Cover with water. Cover pan and bring water to a boil. Reduce heat to simmer and cook for 90 minutes, or until meat is almost tender.

2. Wash mustard greens thoroughly. Drain. Remove thick part of stems. Coarsely chop leaves. Add to ham hocks.

3. Stir in salt, pepper, sugar, and thyme. Cook 30 minutes.

4. Cut cabbage into quarters. Remove core. Chop coarsely. Add cabbage and potatoes to pot. Cook 30 minutes, or until all vegetables are tender.

{ I love collard greens and rice. The way my mother cooked collard greens with fat back and cornbread . . . it was delicious.

—HATTIE McFADDEN,
a member of Bethel AMEC,
Lancaster, PA

MAIN DISHES & Traditional

CABBAGE AND
SMOKED NECKBONES

MAKES 3-4 SERVINGS

3–4 smoked pork neckbones
1 head cabbage, chopped
½ teaspoon salt
½ teaspoon black pepper

1. Crack neckbones into pieces. Cover with water in large stockpot and cook slowly until done. Drain, leaving enough juice in pot to keep cabbage from sticking.

2. Add cabbage to pot with neckbones and broth.

3. Stir in seasonings. Cook slowly until cabbage is tender.

TURNIP GREENS
AND CORNMEAL DUMPLINGS

Carrie Alford

MAKES 6-8 SERVINGS

1 ham hock
2 quarts water
1 bunch (about 3 pounds) turnip greens
    with turnips attached
1 teaspoon salt
1 cup cornmeal
½ teaspoon salt
¾ cup boiling water
1 egg, beaten

1. Place ham hock in Dutch oven. Add water and bring to a boil. Cover. Reduce heat and simmer for an hour, or until meat is tender. Remove hock from oven and cut meat off bone. Set meat aside. Discard bone.

2. Peel turnips and cut in half. Clean greens and remove stems. Add turnips, greens, and 1 teaspoon salt to ham broth.

3. Bring to a boil. Cover. Reduce heat and simmer for 2 hours, or until greens and roots are tender. Stir ham back into greens and broth.

4. Combine cornmeal and 1/2 teaspoon salt in mixing bowl. Stir in boiling water. Add egg. Mix well.

5. Drop dumpling batter by spoonfuls into boiling greens-ham broth. Cover. Boil for 20 minutes (don't lift the lid to look or stir). Reduce heat so that mixture simmers another 10 minutes.

BUTTER BEANS WITH HAM HOCKS

MAKES 4–6 SERVINGS

3 large ham hocks or 1 meaty ham bone
3 cups water
1½ pounds fresh butter beans or
    2 (16-ounce) cans butter beans, drained
1 tablespoon sugar
½ pound okra, thinly sliced
1½–2 teaspoons salt
½–1 teaspoon freshly ground pepper

1. Place ham hocks and water in large stockpot. Cover and bring to a boil. Reduce heat and simmer for 45 minutes.

2. Remove hocks from the cooking pot. Cut meat from bone and shred it. Return meat and bone to stockpot.

3. Add beans to pot. Heat to simmering.

4. Stir in remaining ingredients. Simmer for 25 minutes, or until beans and okra are tender. Discard bones and serve hearty soup.

BLACK-EYED PEAS WITH HAM

MAKES 4–6 SERVINGS

¾ cups dried black-eyed peas
2 cups water
⅓ cup chopped, fully cooked, smoked ham
1 cup sliced okra
1 small onion, chopped
½ teaspoon salt
2 cloves garlic, crushed
¼ teaspoon red pepper sauce
1 tablespoon vegetable oil
1 tablespoon chopped fresh cilantro
1 small tomato, seeded and chopped

1. Combine peas and water in saucepan. Boil uncovered for 2 minutes. Reduce heat.

2. Add ham. Cover. Simmer for 30–40 minutes, stirring occasionally, until beans are tender. Drain.

3. Sauté okra, onion, salt, garlic, and pepper sauce in oil for 5 minutes, or until onion is soft.

4. Stir in cilantro, tomato, peas, and ham. Heat until heated through.

{ The free African community, especially the churches, took leadership in the Underground Roadway. The Underground Railroad attests to the intellect, leadership, stamina, determination, and diligence of Africans in their efforts to attain freedom.
— Dr. Shirley Parham }

MAIN DISHES & Traditional

BOILED STRING BEANS WITH HAM

MAKES 4 SERVINGS

1 meaty smoked ham bone or 8 pigs' tails
2⅓ pounds fresh string beans
1 tablespoon salt
1 teaspoon freshly ground black pepper
1 teaspoon sugar

1. Place meat in 6-quart stockpot. Fill pot half-full of water. Bring to a boil. Cover. Simmer for 45 minutes.

2. Snap stem end off each bean and gently pull along length of bean to remove string. Rinse under cold running water. Drain.

3. Add beans, salt, pepper, and sugar to meat. Simmer for 15–30 minutes until beans are very tender.

4. Remove meat from bone. Stir ham back into vegetables and broth before serving.

RED BEANS, SAUSAGE, AND RICE

MAKES 8 SERVINGS

1 pound dried red beans
1 medium onion, chopped
4 garlic cloves, minced
8-ounce can tomatoes, drained
½ pound salt pork, diced
1 pound smoked sausage, sliced
red pepper or Tabasco sauce, optional

1. Cover beans with water and soak overnight in large stockpot.

2. When ready to cook, add more water if needed so that beans are covered. Slowly bring to a boil.

3. Add onion, garlic, and tomatoes. Simmer until beans are tender, about 1½–2 hours.

4. Add salt pork, sausage, and red pepper or Tabasco. Simmer until liquid is thickened.

5. Serve over rice.

NOTE: If you prefer a more tomatoey sauce, add 3 more cups tomatoes or tomato juice in Step 3. If adding juice, remove stockpot lid for Step 4.

RED BEANS
AND RICE

MAKES 12 SERVINGS

1 cup dried red kidney beans
10 cups water, divided
1 smoked ham hock
2 tablespoons salt
½ teaspoon crushed red pepper flakes
½ teaspoon crushed dried thyme
2 cups dry long-grain rice

1. Pour 5 cups water over beans. Soak in refrigerator overnight.

2. Drain beans and place in 5-quart pot. Add ham hock, salt, red pepper, thyme, and 4 cups water. Heat to boiling. Reduce to a low simmer. Cover and cook for 60 minutes, or until beans are almost tender

3. Stir rice and 1 cup water into beans. Heat to boiling. Reduce to simmer. Cover and cook about 25 minutes, until rice and beans are tender and liquid is absorbed.

4. Remove meat from ham hock. Chop and return to rice and beans.

CAROLINA
RED RICE

MAKES 8 SERVINGS

¾ cup diced onion
⅓–½ cup diced green pepper
2 tablespoons vegetable oil
1½ pounds cooked ham, finely chopped
2 (8-ounce) cans tomato sauce
2 cups water
1⅓ tablespoons sugar
½ teaspoon salt
¼ teaspoon pepper
2 cups uncooked long-grain rice

1. Sauté onion and green pepper in oil in a Dutch oven until tender.

2. Stir in ham. Cook over medium heat for 3 minutes.

3. Add tomato sauce, water, sugar, salt, and pepper. Stir well. Bring to a boil.

4. Add rice. Reduce heat. Cover and simmer over low heat for 15 minutes.

5. Cut a circle of brown paper, 2 inches bigger around than the circumference of the Dutch oven. Remove lid from Dutch oven and place paper over pot. Replace lid over paper. Continue to simmer over low heat for 15–20 minutes.

{ We lived in a house with no ceiling and no water. It was normal to look at the stars at night. My mother used flour and parts of an old catalog to make patches for cracks in the walls, trying to keep out the bitter cold air.

—ELIZABETH MCGILL,
a member of Bethel AMEC, Lancaster, PA }

NEW ORLEANS
RED BEANS AND RICE

Michelle Akins
MAKES 6 SERVINGS

6 slices bacon, cut into 1" pieces
2 onions, cut into ½" wedges
garlic clove, minced
14-ounce can beef broth
1 cup uncooked long-grain rice
1 teaspoon dried thyme
1 teaspoon salt, optional
½ cup diced green bell pepper
2 16-ounce cans red kidney beans

1. Fry bacon in skillet over medium heat until browned but not crisp. Remove from skillet. Reserve 2 tablespoons drippings in pan.

2. Sauté onions and garlic in drippings until onions are tender but not brown.

3. Add enough water to beef broth to make 2½ cups. Add to skillet. Bring to a boil.

4. Stir in rice, bacon, thyme, and salt. Cover tightly and simmer for 15 minutes.

5. Add green pepper. Cover and continue cooking for 5 minutes. Remove from heat.

6. Stir in beans. Cover and let stand for 5 minutes, or until all liquid is absorbed.

DIRTY RICE

MAKES 8 SERVINGS

1 pound chopped chicken livers or giblets
1 pound bulk sausage, crumbled
½ cup butter or margarine
1 cup chopped onion
½ cup chopped celery
1 bunch green onions, chopped
2 tablespoons chopped fresh parsley or dried parsley flakes
1 clove garlic, minced
½ teaspoon dried thyme
½ teaspoon dried basil
3 cups cooked rice
salt to taste
pepper to taste
hot sauce to taste
10¼-ounce can chicken broth

1. Sauté livers and sausage in butter until browned. Remove meat from skillet, reserving drippings.

2. Sauté onion, celery, green onions, parsley, and garlic in butter until tender.

3. Stir in thyme, basil, rice, livers, and sausage. Mix well.

4. Add salt, pepper, hot sauce, and chicken broth.

5. Cook over medium heat until rice is hot, stirring frequently to avoid sticking.

{ Food was a part of a lot that we did together at church. The woman's auxiliary used to have bake sales, and as part of our Christmas parties we gave out turkey baskets. We had chicken and waffle dinners and coffee klatches after the service. We had fashion shows along with mother-daughter banquets and teas. Every Christmas we had the candlelight service and food after that. We made Easter candy and we worked! We worked!

—MARY BOOTS,
a member of Bethel AMEC, Lancaster, PA }

GRITS SOUFFLE

Rebecca Carter
MAKES 10–12 SERVINGS

1½ cups grits
1½ teaspoons salt
4 cups boiling water
12 tablespoons (1½ sticks) butter, at room
    temperature
6 eggs
1½ cups whole milk
1 cup grated sharp cheese, divided

1. Stir grits and salt into boiling water. Cook until very thick.

2. Add butter. Mix well.

3. Beat eggs in mixing bowl. Add milk and ½ cup cheese. Stir into hot grits.

4. Pour into greased 3-quart casserole dish. Top with remaining ½ cup cheese.

5. Bake at 350°F for 45 minutes.

THE ORIGINS OF THE UNDERGROUND RAILROAD are hidden in the midst of time but a tradition persists that places its point of origin in Lancaster County. About the year 1804, a prominent resident of Lancaster named Col. Thomas Boude purchased the services of a young boy named Stephen Smith from a family named Cochran in Paxtang (today's Harrisburg). While Africans born before March 1, 1780 were to be enslaved for life, their children were made indentured servants whose term of service could extend until their twenty-eighth year. Col. Boude brought young Stephen to his house in Columbia Boro. Stephen's mother was not involved in the transaction and she missed her son, so she decided to go to Columbia and join him. Pursued by the daughter of the Cochran family, Mrs. Smith found support from the concerned residents of Columbia and that, according to one of the more reliable histories of Lancaster County, was the beginning of the Underground Railroad locally.

This story was told by Samuel Evans, a magistrate for many years in Columbia and personally acquainted with Stephen Smith and William Whipper. Unlike later narrators, Evans emphasized the role that free Africans played in helping and protecting freedom seekers who came to Columbia. Thomas Bessick, a native of Maryland, lived in Columbia, and before the Civil War he met freedom seekers who had arrived in Columbia and escorted them to the train that would take them to Philadelphia and to William Still. This occurred frequently under the noses of the authorities who came into the borough to recapture the enslaved. Robert Loney was also an agent of the Underground Railroad who ferried freedom seekers across the Susquehanna to temporary safety in Columbia. From 1830 to 1860, Columbia had a Black population of about 1,000 and could afford cover to freedom seekers who came into town. Black Columbians were largely formerly enslaved persons from Virginia who had arrived on the banks of the Susquehanna before 1822.

Many Black Columbians lived in a section known as "Tow Hill." Sometime before 1850 an incident occurred that underlines the role that free Africans played in their own liberation. A freedom seeker was apprehended by deputized men in Columbia and taken to Lancaster, where he would have been surrendered to an agent of his alleged owner. A group of women led by Tow Hill residents Julia Miller and Mary Jane Turner ambushed the party on the road and freed the freedom seeker, who continued on his way to Canada.

MAIN DISHES *Other Favorites*

MACARONI AND CHEESE, HOME-STYLE

Brothers and Sisters Cafe
MAKES 4-6 SERVINGS

1 pound dry macaroni
1 pound sharp or extra sharp cheese, grated
1 stick (¼ pound) butter or margarine, at room temperature
12-ounce can evaporated milk
2 eggs, slightly beaten
salt to taste
pepper to taste

1. Cook macaroni according to package directions, until just soft. Drain.

2. Gradually stir in cheese and butter until well mixed.

3. Fold in milk, eggs, and seasonings until well blended. Pour into greased baking dish

4. Bake at 350°F for 45 minutes. Let set 10 minutes before serving.

———◆×◆———

NOTE: You can use ½ pound sharp yellow cheddar cheese and ½ pound sharp white cheddar cheese and save a bit of each for garnishing the top of the casserole before baking it.

—CREGG CARTER

FEATHER-LIGHT CHEESE CASSEROLE

Nancy C. Hill
MAKES 6-8 SERVINGS

2 tablespoons margarine or butter
15 saltine crackers, crushed
1½ cups (6 ounces) shredded cheddar cheese
1½ cups milk
3 eggs, beaten
½ cup sliced fresh mushrooms or canned mushrooms, drained

1. Melt margarine in 1½-quart casserole.

2. Combine crushed crackers, cheese, milk, eggs, and mushrooms. Mix well. Pour into casserole dish.

3. Bake at 350°F for 45-50 minutes, or until puffy and set.

———◆×◆———

Africans forced into American slavery came from various African specialty crafts and skills—griots (African oral tradition), weavers, silversmiths, bricklayers, glassmakers, potters, seafarers, astronomers, physicians, and mathematicians.

—DR. SHIRLEY PARHAM

FETTUCINE AND MIXED FRESH VEGETABLES

Carol Grassie
MAKES 6–8 SERVINGS

¾ cup finely chopped onion
3 tablespoons olive oil
1 large red bell pepper, cut into strips or minced
12 ounces (5 cups) shiitake, or similar, mushrooms, trimmed and thinly sliced
½ teaspoon salt
⅛ teaspoon pepper
1 pound fettucine
¼ cup (½ stick) unsalted butter, cut in small pieces, at room temperature
½ cup finely chopped fresh parsley

1. Sauté onion in oil, stirring occasionally, for 5 minutes or until softened.

2. Add red pepper, mushrooms, salt, and pepper. Cook, stirring occasionally, for 5–7 minutes, or until mushrooms are tender yet firm and have begun to give off liquid. Set aside.

3. Cook fettucine according to package directions. Drain. Toss with butter.

4. Add vegetable mixture and parsley. Toss.

PASTA PRIMAVERA

Gwen Jones
MAKES 4 SERVINGS

1 large onion, diced
1 cup broccoli florets
½ cup diced carrots
½ cup fresh or frozen peas
1 cup diced zucchini
1 cup diced yellow squash
8–10 cups water
½ pound whole wheat dry spaghetti
2 tablespoons cornstarch
1 cup chicken stock or broth
¼ cup grated Parmesan cheese
1 small tomato, peeled and diced

1. Steam onion, broccoli, and carrots until crisp-tender. Set aside.

2. Steam peas, zucchini, and yellow squash until crisp-tender. Add to rest of cooked vegetables.

3. Boil spaghetti in water for 8–10 minutes. Drain.

4. Combine cornstarch with ¼ cup chicken stock and stir until smooth. Add remaining stock. Bring to a boil. Reduce heat and stir constantly until thickened.

5. Add Parmesan cheese. Mix well. Pour over spaghetti, tossing thoroughly.

6. Add steamed vegetables. Garnish with diced tomato.

PRIMAVERA PIZZA

2 tablespoons olive oil
1 teaspoon garlic, minced
1 cup zucchini, thinly sliced
¾ cup mushrooms, sliced
1 cup broccoli florets
¼ cup black olives, sliced
1 pizza crust
2 cups provolone cheese, grated
8 tomato slices
3 tablespoons fresh chopped basil
2 teaspoons dried oregano
2 cups mozzarella cheese, grated

1. Heat oil in heavy skillet. Add garlic, zucchini, mushrooms, and broccoli. Cook until just soft.

2. Add olives. Set aside.

3. Top crust with provolone cheese. Top with tomatoes. Sprinkle on basil and oregano. Cover with cooked mixture. Top with mozzarella cheese.

4. Bake at 425°F for 20–25 minutes, or until cheese begins to melt.

LINGUINE WITH ASPARAGUS AND PESTO

Rina Mckee
MAKES 3–4 SERVINGS

8 ounces dry linguine
1 teaspoon olive oil
1 pound fresh asparagus, cut into 1" lengths
3 fresh basil leaves
¼ cup grated Parmesan cheese
¼ cup chopped pecans or walnuts
1 small garlic clove
¼ teaspoon salt
3 tablespoons olive oil

1. Cook and drain linguine. Add 1 teaspoon oil. Toss. Set aside and keep warm.

2. Steam asparagus lightly until just tender. Set aside and keep warm.

3. Combine remaining ingredients in blender. Blend until smooth.

4. Stir asparagus into pesto sauce. Serve over linguine.

FETTUCCINE ALFREDO

MAKES 4 SERVINGS

12-ounce package fettuccine noodles
1 cup half-and-half
4 tablespoons butter or margarine
½ cup grated Parmesan cheese
¼ teaspoon salt
¼ teaspoon coarsely ground black pepper

1. Cook fettuccine according to package directions. Drain.

2. Return fettuccine to saucepan. Add remaining ingredients. Mix well. Heat over low heat and serve.

NOTE: To make this a complete meal, add cooked chicken breast and broccoli to the cooked fettuccine. Add remaining ingredients, heat through, and serve.

I loved Arco Starch. You wanted to get the really big hunks. I remember the little blue box said something about starch for clothing, but Arco Starch you could eat. I always wondered why all the adults had white mouth, but it was the Arco Starch.

— BARBARA MCFADDEN ENTY, a member of Bethel AMEC, Lancaster, PA

SPINACH MANICOTTI

Rina Mckee
MAKES 8–10 SERVINGS

1 quart and 1 cup spaghetti sauce with meat
1½ cups water
15-ounce box ricotta cheese
10-ounce package frozen chopped spinach, thawed and squeezed dry
1½ cup shredded mozzarella cheese, divided
¼ cup grated Parmesan cheese + ½ cup shredded Parmesan cheese, divided
1 egg
2 teaspoons minced fresh parsley
½ teaspoon onion powder
½ teaspoon pepper
⅛ teaspoon garlic powder
8-ounce package manicotti shells

1. Combine spaghetti sauce and water. Spread 1 cup diluted sauce in ungreased 9" x 13" pan.

2. Combine ricotta cheese, spinach, 1 cup mozzarella cheese, ¼ cup grated Parmesan cheese, egg, parsley, onion powder, pepper, and garlic powder.

3. Stuff uncooked manicotti with spinach-cheese mixture. Arrange over sauce in pan.

4. Pour remaining sauce over manicotti.

5. Sprinkle with ½ cup mozzarella cheese and ½ cup shredded Parmesan cheese.

6. Cover and refrigerate overnight.

7. Remove from refrigerator 30 minutes before baking.

8. Bake uncovered at 350°F for 40–45 minutes.

NOTE: To add zest to the flavoring, add 2 cloves minced garlic and 1 small chopped onion to the mixture in Step 2.

RISOTTO WITH SPRING VEGGIES

Rina Mckee
MAKES 8 SERVINGS

8 tablespoons (1 stick) butter, divided butter
2 leeks, thinly sliced
½ cup chopped onion
2 cups arborio rice, uncooked
2 quarts vegetable stock
1 jar artichoke slices, drained
salt to taste
pepper to taste
⅔ cup fresh or frozen peas
⅔ cup peeled fava beans
1 tablespoon finely chopped parsley
Parmesan cheese, optional

1. In large saucepan, sauté leeks and onion in 4 tablespoons butter until onion is transparent.

2. Add rice. Stir to coat grains. When rice glistens and becomes opaque, add a ladleful of stock over high heat, allowing the rice to absorb the liquid. Stir rice and broth constantly so rice doesn't stick to bottom of pot. After stock is absorbed, add another ladleful, continuing to stir so the rice does not dry out.

3. After 5 minutes, fold in artichoke slices. Add salt and pepper.

4. A ladleful at a time, add as much of the rest of the simmering stock to the rice as is needed to make it tender but not mushy. Stir constantly.

5. When rice has become tender and creamy, add peas, fava beans, parsley, and 4 tablespoons butter. Toss gently.

6. Shave Parmesan cheese over each serving.

STUFFED YELLOW SQUASH WITH CHEESE SAUCE

Marlene Clark
MAKES 6 SERVINGS

3 medium-sized yellow squash
2 cups water
1 teaspoon salt
1 clove garlic, crushed
½ pound ground beef
1 tablespoon oil
½ cup raw, long-grain rice
1 teaspoon salt
pepper to taste
16-ounce can stewed tomatoes
½ cup water
2 tablespoons butter or margarine
2 tablespoons flour
1 cup milk
1 cup shredded sharp cheddar cheese

1. Wash squash. Cut off stems and discard. Cut squash in half lengthwise. Scoop out seeds.

2. In medium skillet, bring water and salt to a boil. Add squash, cut-side down. Cover. Cook over medium heat for 5 minutes, or until vegetables are tender but not mushy. Drain well.

3. Sauté garlic and beef in oil until beef is no longer pink, about 10 minutes.

4. Add rice, salt, and pepper. Cook for 2 minutes, stirring constantly.

5. Add tomatoes and water. Cook, tightly covered, over low heat for 20 minutes, or until rice is cooked and liquid is absorbed.

6. Fill squash with rice mixture. Bake at 375°F for 20–25 minutes.

7. Meanwhile, melt butter in saucepan. Stir in flour over low heat, continuing to cook and stir for about 3 minutes to take away raw flour taste.

8. Whisk in milk and continue cooking and stirring until mixture comes to a boiling point and begins to thicken.

9. Stir in grated cheese until smooth.

10. Pour cheese sauce over baked stuffed squash before serving, or pass cheese sauce separately so that your diners can serve themselves.

ITALIAN EGGPLANT PARMIGIANA

Mrs. Margaret Bailey
MAKES 8 SERVINGS

2 medium eggplants (about ½ pound each), washed and stemmed
salt
1 cup chopped onion
2 tablespoons oil
6-ounce can tomato paste
2¼ cups water
1 teaspoon dried basil
½ teaspoon dried oregano
1 teaspoon salt
¼ teaspoon pepper
1 cup flour
3 eggs, beaten
1 cup oil
¾ pound mozzarella cheese, sliced
1 cup grated Parmesan cheese

1. Cut eggplants crosswise into ¼"-thick slices. Place in colander. Sprinkle with salt. Leave to drain for 30 minutes. Wipe dry with paper towel.

2. Sauté onion in oil until tender.

3. Stir in tomato paste, water, basil, oregano, 1 teaspoon salt, and pepper. Cook slowly, uncovered, for 20 minutes, stirring occasionally. Remove from heat.

4. Dust each eggplant slice with flour. Dip in beaten eggs. Fry on both sides in hot oil until soft and golden. Add more oil as needed. Drain.

5. Line a 2½-quart baking dish with a little of the tomato sauce. Arrange a layer of eggplant slices over it. Cover with a layer of mozzarella cheese. Add more sauce and a sprinkling of Parmesan cheese. Repeat layers until all ingredients have been used.

6. Bake at 350°F, uncovered, for 30 minutes, or until eggplant is tender and golden on top.

SPANISH RICE

Rina Mckee
MAKES 2-4 SERVINGS

1 cup uncooked, long-grain rice
1 cup chopped onion
2 tablespoons oil
2½ cups water
1½ teaspoons salt
¾ teaspoon chili powder
⅛ teaspoon garlic powder
½ cup chopped green pepper
8-ounce can tomato sauce

1. Sauté rice and onion in oil for 5 minutes, stirring frequently, until rice is golden brown and onion is tender.

2. Stir in remaining ingredients.

3. Heat to boiling. Reduce heat to low. Cover and simmer for 30 minutes, stirring occasionally, until rice is tender and liquid is absorbed.

SPANISH RICE

Michelle Akins
MAKES 6–8 SERVINGS

6 slices bacon, chopped
¼ cup chopped onion
¼ cup chopped green pepper
2 cups canned tomatoes
3 cups cooked rice
1 teaspoon salt
⅛ teaspoon pepper
¼ cup grated cheese

1. Fry bacon until crisp. Remove from skillet and reserve drippings.

2. Add onion and pepper to drippings. Cook until onion is soft.

3. Add tomatoes, rice, salt, pepper, and bacon.

4. Pour into greased casserole. Sprinkle with cheese.

5. Bake at 350°F for 30 minutes.

We had nothing to eat but yams, which were thrown amongst us at random—and of these we had scarcely enough to support life.

—CHARLES BALL

PASTA MEXICANA

MAKES 4–6 SERVINGS

2 medium onions, coarsely chopped
5 chili peppers, chopped
28-ounce can Italian-style plum tomatoes
2 cups of your favorite beef or turkey chili
    or see Two-Bean Beef Mix on page 30.
½ pound dry linguine, cooked

1. Place onion and chili peppers in heavy skillet or roasting pan. Cover. Cook over high heat for 8–10 minutes, until onions are browned and chili skins are charred.

2. Remove fresh chilies. Peel. Discard skin and seeds. Chop and return to pan.

3. Stir in tomatoes and beef or turkey chili. Cook over medium heat, stirring occasionally, for 15–20 minutes.

4. Serve sauce over linguine.

NOTE: You may substitute 2 4-ounce cans chopped green chilies for the 5 chili peppers. Stir them into the skillet (in Step 1) after the onions begin to brown. Skip Step 2 and go on to Step 3.

BAKED LASAGNA

Willie Jean Murray
MAKES 10–12 SERVINGS

3 (12-ounce) cans tomato puree
1 (12-ounce) can + ¼ cup water, divided
1½ teaspoons salt, divided
¼ teaspoon + ⅛ teaspoon pepper, divided
garlic powder to taste
1 pound bulk sausage
1 pound ground beef
2 eggs, beaten
1 pound ricotta cheese
1½ pounds cottage cheese
1-pound box lasagna noodles
3 tablespoons oil
1 pound mozzarella cheese, thinly sliced
⅓–½ cup Parmesan cheese

1. Combine tomato puree, 1 can water, 1 teaspoon salt, ¼ teaspoon pepper, and garlic powder in large saucepan. Bring to a boil, then reduce heat to simmer.

2. Form sausage into small balls. Sauté in skillet until slightly browned. Add to tomato mixture in saucepan.

3. Form ground beef into small balls. Sauté in oil until lightly browned. Remove from pan and add to tomato-sausage mixture in saucepan.

4. Simmer for 1 hour over low heat, stirring occasionally.

5. Combine eggs, ricotta cheese, cottage cheese, ¼ cup water, ½ teaspoon salt, and ⅛ teaspoon pepper. Mix well and set aside until ready to assemble lasagna.

6. While tomato-meat sauce is simmering, cook lasagna noodles until al dente.

7. Grease baking dish (or a 9" x 13" baking pan) and cover bottom with a thin layer of tomato-meat sauce. Add a layer of noodles, a layer of cheese mixture, a layer of mozzarella cheese, and another layer of sauce. Repeat layers until all ingredients are used. Sprinkle with Parmesan cheese. Cover with foil.

8. Bake at 350°F for 1 hour.

STUFFED SHELLS

MAKES 6 SERVINGS

1 pound ground beef
1 small onion, chopped
1 tablespoon oil
dash of garlic powder
salt to taste
pepper to taste
8 ounces mozzarella cheese, shredded
¼ cup dry bread crumbs
¼ cup chopped fresh parsley
1 egg, slightly beaten
⅓ cup water
18–20 giant shells, uncooked
1 quart spaghetti or pizza sauce
½ cup grated Parmesan cheese

1. Brown beef and onion in oil. Drain.

2. Add garlic powder, salt, and pepper. Cool.

3. Stir in mozzarella cheese, bread crumbs, parsley, egg, and water.

4. Cook shells in boiling water for 15 minutes. Drain.

5. Stuff shells with meat mixture.

6. Spread half jar of sauce over bottom of greased 9" x 13" pan.

7. Add shells. Cover with remaining sauce. Sprinkle with Parmesan cheese.

8. Bake at 400°F for 25 minutes.

EGGPLANT-BEEF MEDLEY

Marlene Clark
MAKES 6–8 SERVINGS

3 tablespoons bacon drippings
1½ pounds ground beef
⅓ cup chopped onions
⅓ cup chopped green peppers
3 small hot peppers, chopped
1 teaspoon garlic, minced
1½ teaspoons salt
¼ teaspoon pepper
2 medium eggplants, peeled and chopped
1½ cups rice, cooked
2 teaspoons lemon juice

1. Heat drippings in skillet.

2. Stir in ground beef, onions, peppers, garlic, salt, and pepper. Stir constantly, cooking over medium heat for 5 minutes, or until the vegetables begin to become tender and the beef browns. Then stir in eggplant and continue cooking for about another 5 minutes, until the eggplant softens but does not lose its shape.

3. Stir in rice. Pour into greased baking dish.

4. Bake at 375°F for 30 minutes. Remove from oven. Sprinkle with lemon juice.

TWO-BEAN BEEF MIX

Cormylene Williams
MAKES 10 SERVINGS

1 pound ground beef
½ cup chopped onion
28-ounce can whole tomatoes
15-ounce can chili beans
15-ounce can kidney beans
15-ounce can tomato sauce
2 teaspoons chili powder
¼ teaspoon garlic powder
⅛ teaspoon red pepper
shredded cheddar cheese

1. Brown beef and onion in large stockpot. Drain.

2. Stir in remaining ingredients except cheese. Simmer for 20–25 minutes.

3. Garnish with cheese.

4. Serve in soup bowls with sturdy bread alongside, or over cooked brown rice.

BAKED BEANS BREWSTER-STYLE

Debbie Brewster
MAKES 10 SERVINGS

½ pound ground beef
1 large onion, chopped
1 (28-ounce) can baked beans
2 cups barbecue sauce
1 teaspoon brown sugar
hot sauce, optional
½–¾ cup shredded cheddar cheese

1. Brown ground beef and onion together in skillet.

2. Mix beef and onion with remaining ingredients, except cheese, in large mixing bowl.

3. Pour into greased casserole dish.

4. Bake at 350°F for 30–40 minutes, or until heated through and bubbly.

5. Garnish with shredded cheese and return to oven until cheese melts and browns.

HAMBURGER CASSEROLE

Cregg Carter
MAKES 6 SERVINGS

1 green pepper, chopped
1 cup diced onion
1 pound ground beef, browned
2 cups dry macaroni
10¾-ounce can cream of chicken soup, undiluted
½ cup ketchup
1 cup grated cheese

1. Sauté pepper, onion, and ground beef together in large skillet.

2. Meanwhile, cook macaroni until al dente.

3. In large mixing bowl combine ground beef, vegetables, and cooked macaroni.

4. Add soup and ketchup and blend well.

5. Pour into greased baking dish.

6. Sprinkle cheese over top.

7. Bake at 350°F for 20–30 minutes, or until casserole bubbles.

{ When I came to Bethel African Methodist Episcopal Church, I heard a sermon about the Queens of Farica and how beautiful and wise they was—Queen of Jeni, Queen of Sheba, Queen Mother Dira. Then I realized that my skin was not black, but sun-kissed, my lips weren't big, they's luscious, and my hair, my hair is naturally beautiful. That sermon helped me to love myself!
—*Living the Experience* }

SHEPHERD'S PIE TO FEED A CROWD

MAKES 30-35 SERVINGS

10 pounds ground beef
2 jumbo onions, chopped
1 quart brown gravy
1 pound 10-ounce box instant mashed potatoes
3 pounds frozen peas
ground black pepper
paprika
½–1 cup butter, melted
3–4 cups brown gravy

1. Sauté ground beef and onions in batches in large skillet until browned. Place browned meat and onions in large mixing bowl. Drain drippings from skillet after each batch is browned and discard.

2. Stir 1 quart gravy into browned meat and onions. Pour into large greased casseroles or baking pans.

3. Make mashed potatoes according to directions on package. Spread on top of hamburger.

4. Spoon frozen peas over mashed potatoes.

5. Sprinkle with black pepper and paprika.

6. Top with melted butter.

7. Bake at 350°F for 30–40 minutes.

8. Serve with additional gravy.

CORNED BEEF AND CABBAGE

Mary Alice Bailey
MAKES 10 SERVINGS

5-pound corned beef brisket
1 large onion, coarsely chopped
6 whole cloves
6 carrots, peeled and sliced
8 potatoes, peeled and cubed
1 teaspoon dried thyme
1 small bunch of parsley
2 pounds cabbage, cut into wedges
freshly ground black pepper

SAUCE:
½ pint whipping cream
2 tablespoons horseradish

1. Place beef in large pot. Cover with cold water and bring to a boil. Reduce heat to simmer and cook for 2 hours. Skim fat as it rises to the top.

2. Add onion, cloves, carrots, potatoes, thyme, and parsley. Cook for another hour.

3. Remove parsley and whole cloves.

4. Add cabbage. Simmer for 20 minutes.

5. Remove meat and slice. Place on center of large platter.

6. Strain vegetables. Season heavily with black pepper. Arrange vegetables around meat on platter.

7. Whip cream until it stands in peaks. Fold in horseradish. Serve with meat.

GROUND BEEF AND CABBAGE

MAKES 6–8 SERVINGS

1 medium onion, sliced
1 tablespoon oil
1 pound ground beef
salt to taste
pepper to taste
1 medium head cabbage, shredded
2 tablespoons oil
14½-ounce can stewed tomatoes
8-ounce can tomato sauce

1. Sauté onion in oil until soft.

2. Add ground beef, salt, and pepper. Brown meat. Remove from pan but reserve drippings.

3. In pan, sauté cabbage in drippings and oil until crisp-tender.

4. Add beef mixture, stewed tomatoes, and tomato sauce. Cover.

5. Simmer for 10 minutes.

—◆•◆•◆—

NOTE: Add 2–3 tablespoons brown sugar in Step 4, if you wish.

CHINESE BEEF WITH BROCCOLI

Linda Maison
MAKES 4 SERVINGS

1 pound round steak, thinly sliced
1 envelope dry meat marinade mix
1 cup water
½ teaspoon ground ginger
1 pound broccoli, peeled and cut up
2 tablespoons oil

1. Place steak in bowl.

2. Combine meat marinade mix, water, and ground ginger. Pour over steak. Let stand 15 minutes.

3. Stir-fry beef and broccoli in oil in large skillet or wok for 5–8 minutes, until broccoli is crisp-tender.

4. Pour marinade over meat and vegetables and heat through. Serve over rice.

{
The front door of a white family's house was off-limits, unless you were cleaning that area. When you were doing housework in the South, you ate your food on the porch if there was a screen, or in the corner of the kitchen. You ate whatever was left over. You did not use the same dishes they used, unless it was a "good" white lady.

Young white children called grown Black folks by their first names, but you had to call them "Mr." or "Miss."

—ELIZABETH MCGILL,
a member of Bethel AMEC, Lancaster, PA
}

MAIN DISHES & Other Favorites

SUCCULENT VEAL STEW

Doris Kelly
MAKES 4 SERVINGS

1 teaspoon salt
¼ teaspoon ground ginger
¼ teaspoon garlic powder
3 tablespoons flour
1 pound boneless veal shoulder, cut in
    1" cubes
2 tablespoons vegetable oil
1¼ cups chicken broth
1 tablespoon cornstarch
2 tablespoons water
1 tablespoon dry sherry

1. Place salt, ginger, garlic powder, and flour
   in clean paper bag. Add veal cubes. Shake
   vigorously until all pieces are coated.

2. Heat oil in large skillet. Add seasoned veal and
   brown on all sides. Reduce heat.

3. Add broth. Cover and simmer over low heat for
   60 minutes, or until veal is tender.

4. Combine cornstarch and water. Stir into
   mixture. Cook for several minutes, until liquid
   thickens and clears.

5. Stir in sherry.

6. Serve over pasta or rice.

HAM AND CABBAGE DINNER

Edna Hardrick
MAKES 6–8 SERVINGS

½ cup light brown sugar
1 cup prepared mustard—brown, spicy, or plain
4–5 pounds precooked ham
½ pound bacon, cut into 1" squares
half a head of cabbage, sliced
2 medium onions, sliced
1½ cups water
4–5 medium-sized potatoes, sliced or cut into
    small chunks
red pepper to taste
salt to taste

1. Dissolve brown sugar in mustard to make glaze.

2. Brush portion of glaze over ham.

3. Bake ham in 350°F oven, uncovered, for
   25 minutes per pound, brushing with glaze
   periodically.

4. Meanwhile, brown bacon in Dutch oven.

5. Add cabbage, onions, and water to bacon. Stir
   and cook for 5 minutes.

6. Layer potatoes over cabbage. Steam until
   potatoes are done.

7. Sprinkle with red pepper and salt.

8. Slice ham and wedge into Dutch oven or
   serving platter, alongside vegetables. Spoon
   juices over all.

PORK FRIED RICE

1 small onion, chopped
1 green pepper, sliced
2 tablespoons oil
1½ pounds pork strips
4-ounce can bean sprouts, drained
2 cups cooked rice
2 tablespoons soy sauce
salt to taste
2 eggs, beaten

1. Sauté onion and green pepper in oil until browned. Remove vegetables from oil.

2. Sauté pork in oil just until cooked.

3. Add onion, green pepper, bean sprouts, and rice to pork.

4. Stir in soy sauce and salt.

5. Add eggs and cook until eggs are set, stirring often, about 5–10 minutes.

PORK MU SHU BURRITOS

MAKES 4 SERVINGS

1½ cups canned chop suey vegetables
1½ tablespoons oil
6 ounces boneless pork chops, beef tips, or chicken or turkey breast, cut into ¼" x 1½" strips
half a jar of hoisin sauce, divided
4 large flour tortillas, warmed

1. Drain vegetables. Rinse with cold water. Drain. Cover with cold water for 10 minutes. Drain very thoroughly.

2. Heat oil in wok or heavy skillet over high flame. Add meat. Sauté for 3 minutes, until just done.

3. Add vegetables. Heat.

4. Add 4 tablespoons hoisin sauce to pork-vegetable mixture. Heat through.

5. Spread 1 tablespoon hoisin sauce on each tortilla. Fill with meat mixture. Roll up like a burrito.

{ I can give but little hope that the infamous Slave Law will be declared unconstitutional. I can advise nothing better than that the subjects of it put themselves beyond reach.

—THADDEUS STEVENS, ESQ., referring to the Fugitive Slave Law of 1850 }

MAIN DISHES & Other Favorites

CAJUN CASSOULET

Nancy Perkins
MAKES 6-8 SERVINGS

¼ pound bacon
1 medium onion, diced
1 green bell pepper, diced
3 cloves garlic, minced
1 rib celery, diced
2½ cups red beans, cooked from dried beans, or canned
1 tablespoon tomato paste
2 cups chicken broth
½ pound andouille or smoked sausage, sliced and lightly browned
1 cup bread crumbs
2 tablespoons melted butter
1 teaspoon Cajun seasoning

1. Sauté bacon in heavy skillet. Remove bacon but reserve drippings. Crumble and set bacon aside.

2. Sauté onion, pepper, garlic, and celery in bacon drippings. Cook until soft.

3. Stir in beans, tomato paste, broth, and bacon. Simmer for 15 minutes.

4. Place sausage in greased casserole dish. Top with bean mixture. Cover. Bake at 350°F for 30 minutes.

5. Toss together bread crumbs, butter, and seasoning. Sprinkle over casserole. Bake uncovered for 20 minutes, or until lightly browned.

CORNBREAD SAUSAGE STUFFING

Nanette Akins
MAKES 6 SERVINGS

3 cups water
2 cups chopped celery
1 cup grated carrots
1 cup chopped onions
1 teaspoon poultry seasoning
salt to taste
pepper to taste
1 pound bulk sausage, browned and drained
3 cups crumbled cornbread
1 egg, lightly beaten

1. Make cornbread one day before you make stuffing. (See page 162 for Cornbread recipe.)

2. Combine water, celery, carrots, onions, poultry seasoning, salt, and pepper in saucepan. Cook over medium heat for 20 minutes. Remove from heat.

3. Stir in browned sausage, crumbled cornbread, and egg. Mix well.

4. Pour into greased casserole dish. Cover.

5. Bake at 350°F for 1½–2 hours. Uncover during last 20 minutes of baking time to brown.

CORNBREAD DRESSING

MAKES 4–6 SERVINGS

10-ounce box cornbread mix
8 ounces bulk pork sausage
¾ cup (1½ sticks) butter
1 cup chopped onion
1 cup chopped celery
1 cup sliced fresh mushrooms
1 tablespoon poultry seasoning
3 cups herb-seasoned croutons
¼ cup chopped parsley
¾ cup chicken broth or milk

1. Bake cornbread according to directions on box. Break into pieces. Set aside.

2. In skillet, cook sausage until lightly browned. Transfer to large bowl.

3. Sauté onion, celery, and mushrooms in butter until tender. Stir in poultry seasoning. Add to sausage. Mix well.

4. Toss cornbread, croutons, parsley, and chicken broth with sausage mixture.

5. Spoon into buttered baking dish. Cover with foil.

6. Bake at 325°F for 30 minutes.

I remember my mother would sit down at the table in the wealthiest mansions and be asked what the menu should be for an upcoming affair. My mother would skillfully draft out a 12-course menu for the evening's event.

—MARGARET JAMISON

SAUSAGE AND CHEESE OMELET

MAKES 2–3 SERVINGS

8 turkey sausage links, removed from casings
6 eggs
freshly ground pepper
1 tablespoon cold water
1 tablespoon vegetable oil
⅓ cup shredded sharp cheddar cheese
3-ounce can chopped mushrooms, drained

1. Crumble sausage and cook in large skillet. When browned remove meat from skillet and set aside. Keep drippings in pan.

2. Beat together eggs, pepper, and water until combined but not frothy.

3. Pour egg mixture into meat drippings in skillet. Sprinkle with sausage, cheese, and mushrooms.

4. Cover. Cook until cheese starts to melt and omelet is golden brown. Fold in half. Serve immediately.

HEARTY SAUSAGE BAKE

MAKES 4 SERVINGS

1 pound bulk sausage
8 potatoes
½ cup chopped celery
⅓ cup chopped onions
14½-ounce can diced tomatoes, undrained

1. Brown sausage in skillet and set aside.

2. Cook and mash potatoes.

3. Mix together sausage and mashed potatoes. Add remaining ingredients.

4. Pour into greased baking dish.

5. Bake at 325°F for 1½–2 hours.

CHICKEN AND VEGETABLES

Sonya Gibson
MAKES 8-10 SERVINGS

2 medium onions, chopped
¼ cup chicken broth
2½ pounds chicken breast, cut in pieces, skin
    removed
1½ teaspoons salt
½ teaspoon pepper
½ teaspoon curry powder
water
1 sweet red pepper, sliced
1 green pepper, sliced
6 medium tomatoes, peeled and coarsely
    chopped
½ pound French-style fresh green beans or
    19-ounce package frozen French green beans
    thawed to room temperature
½ pound fresh mushrooms, sliced
2 leeks, sliced
half a medium cucumber, peeled and cubed
1 clove garlic, crushed
chopped fresh parsley

1. Cook onions in broth until soft.

2. Add chicken. Sprinkle with salt, pepper, and
   curry powder. Add water until covered. Simmer
   for 30 minutes.

3. Add peppers, tomatoes, beans, mushrooms,
   leeks, cucumber, and garlic. Add more water
   if needed.

4. Cook 10-15 minutes, or until vegetables are
   tender.

5. Sprinkle with parsley just before serving.

6. Serve over rice.

WILD RICE, CHICKEN, AND BROCCOLI BAKE

Channie Tyson
MAKES 4-6 SERVINGS

2 cups cooked wild rice
1 pound fresh broccoli, lightly steamed and
    drained
3–4 cooked chicken breast halves, cooked and
    cubed
1 can cream of chicken soup
1 cup milk
¼ pound mushrooms, sliced
1 teaspoon lemon juice
½ teaspoon curry powder
1 cup shredded sharp cheddar cheese

1. Place rice in greased casserole dish.

2. Arrange broccoli over rice.

3. Spread chicken over broccoli.

4. Combine soup, milk, mushrooms, lemon juice,
   and curry powder. Pour over chicken.

5. Sprinkle cheese over top. Cover.

6. Bake at 375°F for 30 minutes.

CHINESE POT-AU-FEU

Doris Kelly
MAKES 6-8 SERVINGS

2 cups water
8 dried shiitake mushrooms
3½-pound chicken with giblets, cut into 8 or
    more pieces
2 leeks, cut in 2" pieces
4 carrots, sliced thin
2 cloves garlic, minced
4 slices fresh ginger
¼ cup dry sherry
1 tablespoon light soy sauce
1 head Napa cabbage (Chinese celery), cored and
    cut in 2" pieces
1 pound fresh spinach, washed, with stems
    discarded
salt to taste
pepper to taste

1. Bring water to a boil. Remove from heat. Add
   mushrooms and soak for 15 minutes. Drain,
   reserving liquid.

2. Remove mushroom stems. Thinly slice
   mushrooms.

3. In large saucepan, combine chicken, giblets,
   mushrooms, leeks, carrots, garlic, ginger, sherry,
   and soy sauce. Add mushroom liquid and enough
   water so that all ingredients are covered.

4. Bring to a boil. Skim off froth and fat.

5. Lower heat. Partially cover saucepan and simmer
   until chicken is tender, 45-60 minutes.

6. Add cabbage, spinach, salt, and pepper. Simmer
   for 5 minutes. Discard ginger. Skim fat from
   liquid.

7. Serve chicken and vegetables on platter,
   accompanied by a tureen of stock and another
   of boiled white rice.

CHICKEN DIVAN

MAKES 8 SERVINGS

4 large whole chicken breasts, cooked
2 pounds broccoli, cooked until just tender
2 tablespoons butter or margarine
2 tablespoons flour
1 cup chicken stock
1 egg yolk
¼ cup Parmesan cheese
1 tablespoon cooking sherry

1. Place chicken in shallow pan. Cover with
   broccoli.

2. Melt butter over low heat. Add flour. Stir in
   chicken stock and bring to a boil.

3. Add a bit of hot chicken stock mixture to egg
   yolk. Then add egg mixture to the rest of the
   hot chicken stock mixture. Mix well. Bring entire
   mixture to a boil until slightly thickened.

4. Remove from heat. Stir in Parmesan cheese and
   cooking sherry. Mix well.

5. Spread over chicken and broccoli. Place under
   broiler until slightly brown, about 8-10 minutes.

ROAST TURKEY WITH OYSTER CORNBREAD STUFFING

Willie Jean Murray

MAKES 10–14 SERVINGS

2 cups white, water-ground cornmeal
water
peanut oil
1 stalk celery, chopped
4 tablespoons (½ stick) margarine or butter
1 large white onion, chopped
half a large loaf bread (about 12 slices), slices toasted
½ pound (2 sticks) butter, melted
3 eggs
1½ teaspoons salt
½ teaspoon pepper
½ teaspoon dried thyme
2 teaspoons poultry seasoning
½ teaspoon paprika
1 pint oysters, drained and diced
liquid from oysters
12-pound turkey

1. Combine cornmeal with enough water to make the consistency of a stiff biscuit dough.

2. Heat small amount of peanut oil in frying pan over low heat. Pat cornmeal dough over the entire bottom of pan. Cook over low heat until light brown. Turn and cook other side. (Don't worry if the cornmeal mixture crumbles as you turn it over.) Remove from pan. Cool in large mixing bowl. Crumble when cool.

3. Sauté stalk of celery in 4 tablespoons margarine. Add onion and cook until tender.

4. Combine cornmeal mixture, celery, onion, bread, ½ pound butter, eggs, salt, pepper, thyme, poultry seasoning, paprika, oysters, and liquid. Stuff into turkey.

5. Bake in large roaster at 325°F for 20–30 minutes per pound. Tent with foil if turkey begins to become too brown or dry. Bake any extra stuffing that wouldn't fit into the bird in a greased casserole at 325°F for 30 minutes.

SMOKED TURKEY AND BLACK-EYED PEAS

Jean Townsend

MAKES 10–12 SERVINGS

2 (14½-ounce) cans black-eyed peas
16-ounce can stewed tomatoes, undrained
1 medium onion, sliced
2 teaspoons seasoned salt
1½ teaspoons dried basil leaves
½ teaspoon dried oregano
½ teaspoon dried thyme leaves
½ teaspoon ground cayenne red pepper
3 pounds smoked turkey drumsticks
½–1 cup water, optional

1. Combine all ingredients in a 6-quart stockpot. Cover. Bring to a boil. Reduce heat and simmer for 30 minutes. If mixture seems to become dry, stir in water.

2. Remove drumsticks and slice meat from bones. Stir turkey back into vegetable mixture.

3. Serve over rice.

JAMBALAYA

Sonya Gibson
MAKES 6–8 SERVINGS

½ cup chopped celery
¼ medium-sized green pepper, chopped
¼ cup chopped onions
2 tablespoons oil
14-ounce can tomatoes
4 cups cooked rice
½ teaspoon salt
¼–½ teaspoon black pepper, according to your preference
1 cup chopped cooked ham
1 cup chopped cooked chicken
1 cup chicken stock
1 pound fresh, medium-sized shrimp, shelled and deveined

1. In large stockpot sauté celery, green pepper, and onion in oil until tender.

2. Stir in tomatoes and rice.

3. Season with salt and pepper.

4. Stir in ham, chicken, and stock.

5. Add shrimp. Stir gently.

6. Pour into greased 3–4-quart casserole.

7. Bake at 325°F for 30 minutes.

NOTE: To create a spicier stew, add 2 chopped hot chili peppers in Step 1 and add 1 cup thinly sliced andouille or hot Italian sausage in Step 4.

STUFFED BELL PEPPERS

Mrs. Margaret Bailey
MAKES 12 SERVINGS

¼ cup finely chopped parsley
1 medium onion, finely chopped
1 rib celery, finely chopped
½ cup (1 stick) butter or margarine
½ pound ground beef
2 pounds shrimp, cooked, peeled, and deveined
1 loaf stale French bread, torn into ½" pieces
6 eggs
1 teaspoon dried thyme
salt to taste
pepper to taste
6 large green bell peppers, cleaned and cut in half
¼ cup (½ stick) butter or margarine, melted
bread crumbs

1. Sauté parsley, onion, and celery in ½ cup butter. Simmer for 20 minutes.

2. Add ground beef. Cook 15 minutes longer, stirring constantly. Stir in shrimp and cook an additional 5 minutes, continuing to stir.

3. Place bread in large baking pan. Pour water over until bread is dampened. Squeeze dry.

4. Add eggs. Mix well.

5. Add beef/shrimp mixture. Mix well.

6. Season with thyme, salt, and pepper.

7. Bake at 325°F for 2 hours, stirring well every 30 minutes. Remove from oven. Cool and refrigerate.

8. Stuff peppers with cooled mixture. Top with bread crumbs. Brush with ¼ cup melted butter or margarine. Brown under broiler.

GREEN PEPPER SURPRISE

Michelle Akins
MAKES 4–6 SERVINGS

4 green peppers
½ cup chopped celery
2 tablespoons chopped onion
½ cup (1 stick) butter
1½–2 cups herb-seasoned stuffing
½ cup water
1 cup fresh or canned crabmeat
6-ounce can tomato sauce

1. Cut green peppers in half. Remove stems and seeds. Cook in boiling water for 2 minutes. Drain.

2. Sauté celery and onion in butter until golden brown.

3. Add stuffing, water, and crabmeat. Mix well.

4. Fill pepper halves with crabmeat mixture.

5. Place in greased shallow baking dish.

6. Bake at 350°F for 30 minutes.

7. Heat tomato sauce to boiling point. Serve separately to pour over peppers.

SHRIMP STIR-FRY

Nanette Akins
MAKES 6–8 SERVINGS

1 large onion, sliced or chopped
1 garlic clove, minced
¼ jar sliced pimentos
1 green pepper, sliced or chopped
1 rib celery, sliced
8 ounces fresh or canned mushrooms, sliced
3 tablespoons margarine or oil
1 pound shrimp, cleaned and deveined
8 ounces snow peas
8 ounces fresh bean sprouts
1 tablespoon Old Bay Seasoning
soy sauce to taste
8-ounce can water chestnuts

1. Stir-fry onion, garlic, pimentos, pepper, celery, and mushrooms in margarine for 2 minutes. Push vegetables aside.

2. Add shrimp and cook until just pink. Stir together all ingredients.

3. Add snow peas, bean sprouts, seasoning, and soy sauce. Stir in water chestnuts. Cook for 2 minutes.

4. Serve over rice.

SHRIMP FRIED RICE

8 cups cooked rice
¼ cup Italian dressing
1½ pounds frozen shrimp, cooked
¼ cup (½ stick) butter
3 medium onions, chopped
3 cans small shrimp
7 eggs, lightly scrambled
14-ounce can bean sprouts, drained
3 tablespoons soy sauce

1. Sauté rice, dressing, and frozen shrimp in butter in large wok until rice browns. (If you don't have a wok, use a large iron skillet, working in batches.)

2. Stir in onions and canned shrimp. Sauté lightly.

3. Add eggs, bean sprouts, and soy sauce. Mix well and heat just until warmed through.

⟡

NOTE: This recipe can be easily divided to serve a smaller group.

HERRING AND RICE

Allen Mitchell
MAKES 6 SERVINGS

5–6 pieces fresh herring, about 3 pounds total
half green pepper, chopped
1 small onion, chopped
1 teaspoon vegetable oil
2 cups long-grain rice, uncooked
5 cups water
salt to taste
pepper to taste

1. Soak herring in cold water overnight.

2. Sauté green pepper and onion in vegetable oil in skillet.

3. Place rice and water in large stockpot, along with sautéed vegetables and cut-up herring. Cover. Cook slowly until rice is tender, about 45–60 minutes. Do not allow to cook dry.

4. Season with salt and pepper before serving.

{ I was lying in a room, and this woman came in. She had new clothes in her hand, and I thought theys couldn't be for me, I ain't never had anything like them before. The touch of the soft cotton against my skin, made me think I done died and went to heaven.

—*Living the Experience* }

MAIN DISHES & Other Favorites

STEAL AWAY!

Steal away, steal away, steal away to Jesus!
Steal away, steal away home, I have not long to stay
here.

My Lord calls me.
He calls me by the thunder.
The trumpet sounds within my soul;
I have not long to stay here.

Green trees are bending,
Poor sinners are a trembling;
The trumpet sounds within my soul;
I have not long to stay here.

My Lord calls me,
He calls me by the lightning;
The trumpet sounds within my soul;
I have not long to stay here.

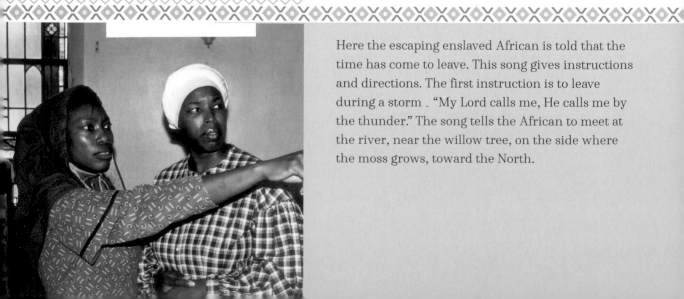

Here the escaping enslaved African is told that the
time has come to leave. This song gives instructions
and directions. The first instruction is to leave
during a storm – "My Lord calls me, He calls me by
the thunder." The song tells the African to meet at
the river, near the willow tree, on the side where
the moss grows, toward the North.

MEATS

—————◆————

I remember my father bringing home deer meat for my mother to prepare. By the time my mother was done with it, not only was it tender, but we had forgotten that we were eating deer meat.

During the enslavement period, the Africans were rarely given any meat to eat. If they were given meat, it was usually the undesirable parts of the hog. Yet they were able to create meals that are still part of our culture today.

The saying, "living high on the hog," indicated that you were eating the finer parts of the hog: ribs, pork chops, and ham. This term came to represent economic and social status.

Africans who were brought to this country tried to recreate the natural diet they maintained in their mother countries. In order to supplement the protein in their diet, they incorporated game meat, such as deer, squirrel, and rabbit, into their meals whenever possible.

—PHOEBE BAILEY

MEATS *Traditional*

FRIED CHICKEN

MAKES 12-15 SERVINGS

2 (3½-pound) frying chickens, each cut into
    8 pieces
salt to taste
fresh ground pepper to taste
2 cups flour
3 tablespoons paprika, divided
oil

1. Trim fat and skin from chicken. Sprinkle with salt and pepper.

2. Combine flour and 2 tablespoons paprika in shallow bowl. Dredge chicken in flour mixture until well coated. Shake off excess flour.

3. Pour 2" oil into skillet. Heat to 375°F.

4. Fry chicken in oil, making sure pieces do not touch each other. Turn chicken until golden brown on all sides and cooked through. Drain.

5. Sprinkle pieces with 1 tablespoon paprika before serving.

NOTE: To adapt a traditional recipe to a more modern convenience, pour ¼" oil into an electric frying pan and set it at 325°F. Legs and thighs will take about 30–40 minutes. Large breast pieces will take about 45 minutes.

—LINDA MAISON

FRIED CHICKEN

Wanda Davis
MAKES 6-8 SERVINGS

1 broiler chicken
1 teaspoon salt and more to taste
1½ cups flour
pepper to taste
paprika to taste
1½ cups shortening

1. Cut chicken into pieces.

2. Season flour with salt, pepper, and paprika.

3. Heat shortening in frying pan.

4. Dredge chicken in flour and place in hot oil. Cook until golden brown on both sides, about 30–40 minutes total.

5. Remove to plate covered with paper towels to drain.

FRIED CHICKEN

Betty Jean Joe
MAKES 3-4 SERVINGS

2–3 cups vegetable oil
½ teaspoon salt
3 teaspoons poultry seasoning
½ teaspoon garlic salt
½–¾ cup self-rising flour
6–7 pieces chicken

1. Heat oil in kettle.

2. Mix salt, poultry seasoning, garlic salt, and flour together in large bowl.

3. Dredge chicken, a piece at a time, in seasoned flour until well coated.

4. Place chicken in hot oil. Fry 10–20 minutes per side, depending on the size of the pieces.

OXTAILS

Marilyn Parks
MAKES 4-6 SERVINGS

1 cup flour
salt to taste
pepper to taste
4 oxtails, cut into 2" pieces
1 clove garlic, minced
oil
1 onion, chopped

1. Combine flour, salt, and pepper.

2. Trim fat from oxtails. Dredge in seasoned flour. Sprinkle with garlic.

3. Brown tails on all sides in hot oil. Drain off fat.

4. Add onion to tails and cover with water. Cook slowly until tender, about 2 hours.

5. Serve with rice, buttered lima beans, and salad.

{
We had talked long enough; we were now ready to move. If not now, we never would be, and if we do not intend to move now, we had as well fold our arms, sit down, and acknowledge ourselves fit only to be slaves.
—FREDERICK DOUGLASS
}

MEATS & Traditional

LIVER AND ONIONS

Brothers and Sisters Cafe
MAKES 4 SERVINGS

2 pounds liver, sliced
salt to taste
pepper to taste
½ cup flour
2 tablespoons oil
½–1 cup sliced onions

1. Season liver with salt and pepper. Roll in flour.
2. Fry in oil just until golden brown on both sides. Remove liver and keep warm.
3. Add onions to hot drippings. Cook for about 10 minutes, or until tender and brown.
4. Serve liver topped with onions.

PORK SAUSAGE AND GRAVY

MAKES 6-8 SERVINGS

1½ pounds country-style pork sausage links
2 tablespoons oil
⅓ cup flour
1 cup water
1 cup milk
1 cup heavy cream
salt to taste
pepper to taste

1. Fry sausage in oil for 15–20 minutes, turning often. Place sausage on serving plate and cover with foil. Place in warm oven.
2. Remove all but ⅓ cup of drippings in the skillet. Sprinkle flour over drippings. Stir quickly over medium heat.
3. Add water, a little at a time, stirring quickly to keep mixture from getting lumpy.
4. Stir in milk, cream, salt, and pepper. Bring to a boil and continue stirring until gravy is thick and bubbly.
5. Serve gravy in tureen with browned sausage.

{ A lot of times when we were hungry we'd go down to the ditches near our house out by the road. We would go down there and look in the water and see the crayfish crawling. We'd catch them. They have these little things on them that would pinch you if you didn't catch them across the back! Sometimes we'd take a little sack and drag it in the water and get the crayfish that way. We'd take them home and boil them in salt water for 15 minutes or so. We'd make Crayfish Dunk out of ketchup and horseradish and dunk the crayfish in that before we ate them.

—FRANCES MORANT,
Bothers & Sisters Cafe }

TALMADGE HAM
AND RED-EYE GRAVY

Rebecca Carter
MAKES 2 SERVINGS

ham slice, ⅛" thick
oil
½ cup hot water

1. Rinse ham. Pat dry.

2. Fry ham in oil in heavy skillet. Cut gashes in fat of ham to prevent curling. Fry over medium heat until fat is glazed, turning several times. Remove from skillet. Cover and keep warm.

3. Add ½ cup hot water to drippings in skillet. Cook, stirring, until gravy turns red.

PIG'S FEET

MAKES 6 SERVINGS

6 medium-sized pig's feet
1 cup apple cider vinegar
1 large onion, chopped
1 green pepper, sliced
1 clove garlic, minced
2 bay leaves
⅛ teaspoon cayenne pepper or 1 hot pepper
salt to taste
pepper to taste

1. Simmer pig's feet in water and vinegar for 2 hours.

2. Add onion, green pepper, garlic, bay leaves, cayenne pepper, salt, and pepper. Simmer for another 2 hours, or until meat is fork-tender.

3. Drain feet of liquid and serve with vegetables.

{ My mother told me that my crib was a wooden fish box with a burlap sheet over the box for shade. When I was an infant my mother would take me in the field with her while she picked cotton. She'd take a little time to nurse me, put me back in the box, and keep picking cotton. She said many times she'd break down and cry because she couldn't just sit and hold her child.

—ELIZABETH McGILL,
a member of Bethel AMEC,
Lancaster, PA }

CREGG'S PIGS FEET

Cregg Carter
MAKES 4-6 SERVINGS

5 pig's feet split
1 cup vinegar
2 teaspoons salt
1 teaspoon whole peppercorns
3 bay leaves, broken in pieces
2 medium potatoes
3 carrots
1 medium onion

1. Place enough water to cover pig's feet in stockpot. Bring water to a boil. Add pig's feet. Boil for 5 minutes. Discard cooking water and rinse feet in fresh hot water.

2. Again, place enough water to cover pig's feet in stockpot. Bring water to a boil. Add vinegar, salt, peppercorns, and bay leaves. Again, add pig's feet. Boil about 1 hour.

3. Cut potatoes into quarters. Add to stockpot.

4. Slice carrots. Add to stockpot.

5. Cut onion in quarters. Add to stockpot.

6. Simmer until meat and vegetables are well done, about 2 hours.

7. Lift meat and vegetables out of liquid and serve.

CHITLINS AND MAW

MAKES 6-8 SERVINGS

2 pounds pork maw (hog's throat or mouth)
2 tablespoons salt and more to taste
2 teaspoons crushed red pepper flakes
4 ribs celery, finely chopped
4 small onions, finely chopped
4 small green bell peppers, cored, seeded, and finely chopped
5 pounds precooked chitlins
pepper to taste

1. Place pork maw in large pot. Fill cooking pot with cold water 2 inches above the meat.

2. Add 2 tablespoons salt, red pepper flakes, and half the celery, onions, and green peppers.

3. Heat to boiling. Reduce to simmer. Cover and cook until tender, from 1½–3 hours. Remove maw to platter to cool. Reserve cooking broth.

4. Place chitlins in large pot. Add enough of the maw cooking liquid to cover by 2 inches. Add remaining celery, onions, and green peppers.

5. Heat to boiling. Reduce heat to simmering. Cover and cook until tender, about 1½ hours.

6. Meanwhile, when maw is cool enough to handle, cut into 1" pieces.

7. When chitlins are tender, stir in maw pieces. Simmer together for 15 minutes. Season with salt and pepper.

FRIED FISH

MAKES 6 SERVINGS

6 pieces fresh catfish fillet
1 cup white cornmeal
½ cup flour
1 teaspoon salt
½ teaspoon pepper
oil

1. Rinse fish in cold water. Gently dry with paper towels.

2. Combine cornmeal, flour, salt, and pepper in paper bag. Shake to mix ingredients.

3. Put piece of fish in paper bag. Shake to coat. Lay fish on waxed paper. Continue until all fillets are coated.

4. Pour ½" oil into skillet. Heat until hot. Gently fry fish for 3–4 minutes on each side. Drain fried fish on paper towels.

SEAFOOD BATTER DIP

Linda Maison
MAKES ENOUGH BATTER FOR 4-6 SERVINGS

½ cup self-rising flour
½ cup enriched cornmeal
1 teaspoon salt
¼ teaspoon pepper
1 cup cold water
1½ pounds fish fillets or shrimp
oil for frying

1. Combine flour, cornmeal, salt, and pepper.

2. Add water. Mix well.

3. Dip fish into batter. Drain off excess.

4. Fry in 375°F oil for 3–4 minutes. Drain on paper towels.

BASIC TEMPURA

Dianne Prince
MAKES 2 CUPS BATTER, ENOUGH TO SERVE 6

1 cup ice water
1 egg
1 cup all-purpose flour
1 teaspoon salt
¼–½ teaspoon black pepper, according to your preference
fresh vegetables
seafood
peanut oil

1. Combine water and egg. Mix well.

2. Add flour, salt, and black pepper. Do not beat, but stir only until blended. Batter should be lumpy.

3. Dip well-chilled vegetables and seafood into batter, a few pieces at a time.

4. Drop into 375°F oil and fry until golden brown. Drain on tempura rack or paper towels. Serve immediately.

When I was small my uncle had a pig farm and he used to butcher. Then we'd make cracklins out of the skin and my grandmother would make cracklin bread and we used to eat that all the time . . . delicious cracklin bread.

—MARY BOOTS,
a member of Bethel AMEC,
Lancaster, PA

MEATS *Other Favorites*

———◆———

BARBECUED CHICKEN

Betty Jean Joe
MAKES 3–4 SERVINGS

6–7 pieces of chicken
1 teaspoon salt, divided
½ teaspoon garlic salt
1 tablespoon poultry seasoning
1 cup tomato sauce
¼ cup prepared mustard
¼ cup mayonnaise
½ cup honey
⅓ cup vinegar
2 teaspoons brown sugar
¼ teaspoon black pepper

1. Place chicken in large pot. Cover with water. Add ½ teaspoon salt. Bring to a boil. Boil 3 minutes. Drain chicken.

2. Season chicken with garlic salt, poultry seasoning, and 1/2 teaspoon salt. Place in baking pan.

3. Bake at 250°F for 30 minutes. Turn chicken and bake another 30 minutes.

4. Combine remaining ingredients. Brush chicken with sauce.

5. Bake at 300°F for 10 minutes.

6. Heat remaining sauce and serve with chicken.

PARMESAN BAKED CHICKEN LEGS

Mrs. Margaret Bailey
MAKES 12 SERVINGS

2 cups fine bread crumbs
¾ cup Parmesan cheese
¼ cup chopped parsley
1 clove garlic, minced
2 teaspoons salt
½ teaspoon black pepper
24 chicken legs
1 cup (2 sticks) butter, melted

1. Combine bread crumbs, Parmesan cheese, parsley, garlic, salt, and pepper in mixing bowl.

2. Dip each chicken leg into melted butter and then into crumb mixture.

3. Lay pieces in shallow roasting pan. Pour remaining butter over chicken.

4. Bake at 350°F for 45–60 minutes, or until tender, basting frequently.

SESAME FRIED CHICKEN

Mrs. Margaret Bailey
MAKES 6 SERVINGS

1¼ cups flour
¼ cup sesame seeds
1½ teaspoons salt
1½ teaspoons poultry seasoning
½ teaspoon paprika
freshly ground black pepper
2 (2½–3-pound) frying chickens, quartered
⅔ cup evaporated milk
½ cup (1 stick) butter
½ cup oil

1. Combine flour, sesame seeds, salt, poultry seasoning, paprika, and pepper in mixing bowl.

2. Dip chicken in milk. Roll in sesame seed mixture.

3. In large skillet, sauté chicken in butter and oil for 30 minutes, or until golden brown and tender.

HONEY BUFFET CHICKEN

MAKES 10–12 SERVINGS

3 pounds chicken legs and thighs
2 tablespoons butter or margarine, melted
2 tablespoons soy sauce
2 tablespoons lemon juice
¼ cup honey
1 teaspoon salt
¼ teaspoon pepper

1. Arrange chicken in shallow baking pan.

2. Combine butter, soy sauce, lemon juice, honey, salt, and pepper. Mix well. Pour over chicken, turning pieces to coat.

3. Bake uncovered at 325°F for 1 hour, or until chicken is tender. Turn oven to 375°F and bake another 10 minutes to brown chicken.

4. Serve chicken and sauce with rice, pasta, or mashed potatoes.

{
Every year around Thanksgiving we'd have a goose. I hated that time of year because we had to take goose grease and sugar for a tonic. Then they'd rub us down with it. We had to take it for the croup.

—NELSON POLITE, SR.,
a member of Bethel AMEC,
Lancaster, PA
}

HONEY BAKED CHICKEN

Nancy Perkins
MAKES 6 SERVINGS

3-pound fryer, cut up
5⅔ tablespoons (⅓ cup) butter or margarine,
  melted
⅓ cup honey
2 tablespoons prepared mustard
1 teaspoon salt
1 teaspoon curry powder

1. Arrange chicken in shallow baking pan, skin-side up.

2. Combine butter, honey, mustard, salt, and curry powder. Pour over chicken.

3. Bake at 350°F for 75 minutes, until chicken is tender and browned.

4. Serve with rice.

LEMONY CHICKEN THIGHS

Dianne Prince
MAKES 2 SERVINGS

2 chicken thighs, deboned
salt to taste
pepper to taste
1 large carrot
1 large rib celery
2 tablespoons butter, melted
¼ cup lemon juice

1. Flatten each thigh and then sprinkle with salt and pepper.

2. Cut carrot and celery into strips, ¼" thick and 4–5" long. Drop vegetables into small amount of boiling water. Boil 2 minutes. Drain well.

3. Arrange strips in center of each boned thigh. Wrap chicken around strips and place, seam-side down, in greased shallow baking pan.

4. Combine butter and lemon juice. Brush over chicken.

5. Bake at 350°F for 30–45 minutes until chicken is done, basting occasionally.

ORANGE BAKED CHICKEN

Patricia Washington
MAKES 4–5 SERVINGS

⅓ cup flour
1 teaspoon salt
⅛ teaspoon pepper
1 chicken, cut up and skin removed
⅓ cup shortening
½ teaspoon celery seed
½ cup diced onion
¾ cup orange juice
1 unpeeled orange, cut into 8 wedges

1. Combine flour, salt, and pepper in small bag. Add chicken. Shake thoroughly.

2. Fry chicken in shortening. Sprinkle with celery seed and onion. Place in greased casserole.

3. Bake at 350°F until tender, about 45 minutes.

4. Pour orange juice over chicken. Top with orange wedges. Bake 30 more minutes.

ORANGE GINGER CHICKEN

MAKES 4 SERVINGS

2½–3-pound chicken, cut up
salt to taste
pepper to taste
¼ cup oil
½ cup barbecue sauce
2 tablespoons flour
1 cup orange juice
2 tablespoons packed brown sugar
1 tablespoon chopped candied, or crystallized, ginger
dash of Tabasco sauce
1 unpeeled orange, sliced

1. Season chicken with salt and pepper. Brown in oil. Drain. Place in slow cooker.

2. Combine barbecue sauce and flour. Mix well.

3. Stir in orange juice, brown sugar, ginger, and Tabasco sauce. Mix well. Pour over chicken. Cover.

4. Simmer for 30 minutes.

5. Add orange slices. Simmer uncovered for 10 minutes, or until chicken is tender.

6. Arrange chicken and orange slices on serving plate. Serve with sauce.

CHICKEN TERIYAKI

2 tablespoons butter or margarine
1 pound boneless chicken breast, cubed
½ red pepper, sliced thin
½ green pepper, sliced thin
¼ pound (1¾ cups) mushrooms, sliced
½ pound (2½ cups) broccoli florets
½ teaspoon salt

SAUCE:
¼ cup flour
5 tablespoons teriyaki sauce (see next recipe)
seasoned salt to taste
pepper to taste
1½ cups warm water

1. Melt butter in skillet. Add chicken and stir until brown. Stir in red pepper, green pepper, and mushrooms. Cook until vegetables are crisp-tender.

2. In separate saucepan steam broccoli in salted water. When crisp-tender, drain and set aside.

3. Combine flour, teriyaki sauce, seasoned salt, pepper, and warm water. Mix well.

4. Add all vegetables and sauce to chicken. Stir together gently. Simmer for 10–15 minutes, or until sauce thickens.

5. Serve over cooked rice.

TERIYAKI SAUCE

Rina Mckee
MAKES ABOUT 2 CUPS SAUCE

1 cup soy sauce
¾ cup sugar
3 tablespoons fresh ginger, grated
2 teaspoons garlic, minced

1. Combine ingredients in saucepan. Simmer for 30 minutes.

2. Strain. Cool.

3. Refrigerate in airtight container, or pour over chicken legs and thighs and bake, basting chicken with sauce every 20 minutes while baking.

———◆———

I remember when I was little we were blessed to have enough to eat, but for some reason I loved to eat grease sandwiches. I used to just lay my slice of bread down in the leftover grease in the frying pan, and then I'd get another slice of bread and make a sandwich, or just fold one slice in half.

—BARBARA McFADDEN ENTY,
a member of Bethel AMEC,
Lancaster, PA

CHICKEN IN WHITE WINE

Norine Dickter
MAKES 4–6 SERVINGS

2–2½ pounds chicken pieces
1 tablespoon oil
½ pound fresh mushrooms, sliced
½ pound pearl onions or 8 small white onions
1 cup dry white wine
1 cup water
1 chicken bouillon cube
1 garlic clove, chopped
¼ teaspoon pepper
½ pound fresh green beans, cut lengthwise into
  long strips
parsley, for garnish

1. Brown chicken in oil. Remove chicken from pan; reserve drippings.

2. Sauté mushrooms and onions in drippings until tender. Add more oil if needed.

3. Return chicken to pan. Stir in wine, water, bouillon cube, garlic, and pepper.

4. Heat to boiling. Reduce heat. Cover and simmer for 45 minutes.

5. Add beans. Return to boiling. Reduce heat. Cover and simmer until beans are done, 15–20 minutes. Cover and refrigerate for 24 hours.

6. Twenty minutes before serving, spoon off fat. Heat chicken and vegetables to boiling. Reduce heat. Cover and simmer for 10 minutes.

7. Garnish with parsley and serve.

CHICKEN MARSALA

Willie Jean Murray
MAKES 8 SERVINGS

3½-pound chicken, cut into 8 pieces
3 tablespoons margarine or butter
12 small white onions, peeled
3 white turnips, pared and quartered
3 carrots, peeled and cut in 1½" pieces
2 ribs celery, cut in 1½" pieces
1 cup chicken stock or canned chicken broth
½ cup dry marsala wine
2 tablespoons tomato paste
1 bay leaf
¼ cup chopped fresh parsley
¼ teaspoon tarragon
salt to taste
pepper to taste

1. Melt margarine in large saucepan over medium heat. Brown chicken on all sides. Remove meat.

2. Drain all but 2 tablespoons drippings from pan. Return chicken to saucepan. Add remaining ingredients. Stir to combine well.

3. Bring to a boil. Cover pan and simmer gently until chicken and vegetables are tender, about 30–35 minutes.

4. Serve over couscous or rice, or with hearty bread.

ROSY GLAZED CHICKEN

MAKES 4–6 SERVINGS

2½–3-pound broiler-fryer chicken, cut up
salt to taste
pepper to taste
8-ounce can tomato sauce
1 tablespoon oil
7-ounce can whole cranberry sauce
2 tablespoons brown sugar
1 tablespoon lemon juice
¼ teaspoon salt
29-ounce can yams, drained

1. Sprinkle chicken with salt and pepper. Place in 9" x 13" baking dish.

2. Bake at 375°F for 30 minutes.

3. Combine remaining ingredients, except yams, in saucepan. Heat and stir until smooth.

4. Add yams to chicken. Pour sauce over all. Continue baking until chicken is tender, about 30 minutes, basting occasionally.

CHICKEN PICCATA

Germaine W. Pickney
MAKES 4 SERVINGS

2 whole chicken breasts, each flattened to ¼" thick
⅛ teaspoon salt
⅛ teaspoon pepper
¼ cup flour
3 tablespoons butter
1 tablespoon olive oil
2 garlic cloves, peeled and minced
½ pound mushrooms, thinly sliced
2 teaspoons lemon juice
½ cup dry white wine
2 teaspoons capers, drained, optional
3 tablespoons minced parsley, optional
half a lemon, thinly sliced, optional

1. Sprinkle chicken with salt and pepper. Dredge in flour. Shake off excess.

2. Melt butter and olive oil in large skillet. Add garlic and sauté briefly. Add chicken and sauté until lightly browned. Remove chicken.

3. Sauté mushrooms for 1 minute.

4. Return chicken to pan. Stir in lemon juice and wine. Simmer, covered, for 10 minutes, or until chicken is tender.

5. Stir in capers. Heat well.

6. Place chicken on platter. Spoon on juices and mushrooms. Garnish with parsley and lemon slices.

SMOKED
ALMOND-CRUSTED CHICKEN

MAKES 4 SERVINGS

2 eggs, lightly beaten
¾ cup milk
1½ cups flour
salt to taste
pepper to taste
1½ cups smoked almonds
3 tablespoons olive oil
4 6-ounce boneless, skinless chicken breasts
barbecue sauce, warmed slightly

1. Combine eggs and milk.

2. Season flour with salt and pepper.

3. Puree almonds in food processor or blender.

4. Heat oil over medium flame.

5. Dip chicken in seasoned flour, then in egg mixture, and finally in almonds.

6. Place chicken in oil. Cook until browned on both sides, about 5–7 minutes.

7. Serve with warm barbecue sauce for dipping.

LEMON
BARBECUED CHICKEN

Carletha Akins
MAKES 4 SERVINGS

1½ pounds skinless, boneless chicken breasts
dash of paprika
dash of cayenne pepper
3 tablespoons lemon juice
1 tablespoon honey
1 tablespoon toasted sesame seeds

1. Season chicken with paprika and pepper.

2. Combine lemon juice and honey. Set 2 tablespoons aside.

3. Place chicken on broiler rack or charcoal grill. Broil 4–5" from heat for 15 minutes, basting occasionally with lemon honey mixture.

4. Turn chicken over. Baste with honey mixture and broil 15 additional minutes.

5. Combine sesame seeds and reserved lemon-honey mixture. Spoon over chicken just before serving.

{ I resolved that, however long I might remain a slave in form, the day had passed forever when I could be a slave in fact.
—FREDERICK DOUGLASS }

MEATS & Other Favorites

CHICKEN LEMONAISE

Willie Jean Murray
MAKES 6 SERVINGS

3 whole chicken breasts, halved, skinned, and boned
¼ cup mayonnaise
½ cup fine dry bread crumbs
3 tablespoons margarine
½ cup chopped onion
3 tablespoons flour
1½ cups water
3 chicken-flavored bouillon cubes
¼ cup chopped parsley
3 tablespoons lemon juice
½ cup mayonnaise

1. Brush chicken with ¼ cup mayonnaise. Coat with bread crumbs.

2. Melt margarine in skillet. Cook chicken, 3 pieces at a time, for 15 minutes, or until tender. Keep warm.

3. Sauté onion in pan drippings. Add more margarine if needed. Stir in flour until well blended. Gradually stir in water.

4. Add bouillon cubes, parsley, and lemon juice. Cook and stir until mixture boils.

5. Blend in mayonnaise. Cook until hot. Spoon sauce over chicken to serve.

CHICKEN PARMESAN

MAKES 4 SERVINGS

⅓ cup seasoned dried bread crumbs
¼ teaspoon pepper
2 tablespoons milk
1 large egg
4 large skinless, boneless chicken breast halves
2 tablespoons oil
14–16-ounce jar marinara sauce
8 ounces mozzarella cheese, shredded

1. Combine bread crumbs and pepper on waxed paper.

2. Slightly beat milk and egg together in pie plate.

3. Dip chicken breasts in milk mixture and then in bread crumb mixture, coating well.

4. Cook each chicken breast in hot oil for 3–4 minutes on each side, until golden brown.

5. Pour half of marinara sauce in 12" x 8" baking dish. Top with chicken breasts. Spoon remaining sauce over chicken. Sprinkle with cheese.

6. Bake at 350°F for 20–30 minutes, until cheese melts and mixture is hot and bubbly.

MEXICAN CHICKEN

MAKES 6 SERVINGS

6 medium-sized skinless, boneless chicken breast
  halves
½ pound pepper Jack cheese
1 cup flour
1¼ teaspoon salt
1 large egg
¼ cup milk
¾ cup cornmeal
3 tablespoons salad oil
12-ounce jar thick and chunky hot salsa
8-ounce jar hot or mild taco sauce
⅓ cup water

1. Make 2½" horizontal cut in the meatier part of
   each chicken breast to make a deep pocket.

2. Cut half of cheese into 6 slices. Shred remaining
   cheese.

3. Place 1 slice of cheese in each pocket, cutting
   cheese to fit.

4. Combine flour and salt on waxed paper.

5. Combine egg and milk in bowl.

6. Pour cornmeal on another sheet of waxed paper.

7. Dredge each chicken breast in flour, then dip
   into egg mixture, then dredge in cornmeal.

8. Sauté each breast in skillet in hot oil for about
   5 minutes, until browned on both sides. Remove
   to plate.

9. When breasts are all browned, in same skillet add
   salsa, taco sauce, and water. Heat to boiling.

10. Arrange chicken in sauce. Reduce heat to low.
    Simmer, uncovered, for 15 minutes.

11. Sprinkle with shredded cheese. Cover and cook
    until cheese melts. Serve chicken in sauce.

CHAMPAGNE AND MUSHROOM CHICKEN

MAKES 4–6 SERVINGS

2 tablespoons flour
½ teaspoon garlic powder
¼ teaspoon white pepper
½ teaspoon salt
¼ teaspoon paprika
4 chicken breast halves, skinned and boned
1 tablespoon butter
1 tablespoon oil
¾ cup champagne or dry white wine
½ cup sliced fresh mushrooms
½ cup heavy cream
2 tablespoons chopped parsley

1. Combine flour, garlic powder, white pepper, salt,
   and paprika.

2. Lightly coat chicken in flour mixture.

3. Heat butter and oil in skillet over medium heat.
   Add chicken. Brown 4 minutes on each side.

4. Add champagne. Continue cooking over medium
   heat until chicken is tender, about 10 minutes.
   Place chicken on platter. Keep warm.

5. Add mushrooms and cream to skillet. Cook over
   low heat, stirring constantly until thickened.
   Return chicken to skillet. Spoon sauce over
   chicken and heat until warmed through.

6. Garnish with parsley just before serving.

MEATS & Other Favorites

SUNSHINE CHICKEN

MAKES 2 SERVINGS

1½ tablespoons butter
2 chicken breast halves, skinned and boned
1 package dry onion soup
2 teaspoons cornstarch
1 cup orange juice
2 teaspoons honey

1. Melt butter in small baking dish.

2. Add chicken to dish, turning to coat both sides.

3. Combine soup mix, cornstarch, orange juice, and honey. Pour over chicken. Cover with foil.

4. Bake at 350°F for 15 minutes. Flip chicken. Bake an additional 15 minutes.

5. Serve topped with sauce.

HAWAIIAN CHICKEN

MAKES 6-8 SERVINGS

6–8 chicken breast halves
21-ounce can pineapple chunks
1 package dry onion soup mix
½ cup (1 stick) butter or margarine
2 teaspoons lime juice
1 teaspoon cornstarch

1. Place chicken in ungreased baking dish.

2. Drain pineapple, reserving juice. Distribute pineapple chunks over chicken.

3. Sprinkle onion soup mix over chicken and fruit.

4. Melt butter in skillet. Stir in lime juice and reserved pineapple juice. Heat for 5 minutes. Stir in cornstarch to thicken sauce. Pour over chicken.

5. Bake at 350°F for 45 minutes.

PORTUGUESE CHICKEN

Nancy Perkins
MAKES 6 SERVINGS

3 whole boneless chicken breasts
2 tablespoons oil
½ cup water or chicken stock
1 cup chopped onions
1 clove garlic, minced
14½-ounce can diced tomatoes
2 tablespoons flour
1 tablespoon salt
½ teaspoon pepper

1. Cut chicken into small bite-sized pieces.

2. Brown chicken in oil.

3. Add water or stock, onions, and garlic to chicken. Cook until onions begin to soften.

4. Add tomatoes, flour, salt, and pepper. Mix well. Bring to a boil.

5. Serve over rice.

With 14 children, my mother was very creative with her cooking. She'd take whatever was left over from breakfast and make supper. She didn't waste anything. We didn't have a lot of cooking pots, so Mama just put it all together. White folks would call what she made a "casserole." Back then it was just a meal.

—**FRANCES MORANT**,
Brothers & Sisters Cafe

ASIAN FRIED CHICKEN

MAKES 6-8 SERVINGS

½ cup pancake/waffle mix
10¾-ounce can condensed chicken broth
1⅓ cups water, or more
½ teaspoon salt
dash of pepper
1 pound boneless chicken, cut into 1" pieces
oil
1 large green pepper, cut into 1" pieces
1 large onion, cut into 12 wedges
8-ounce can pineapple chucks
2 tablespoons cornstarch
½ cup maple syrup
¼ cup vinegar
1 tablespoon soy sauce
1 medium tomato, cut into wedges
hot cooked rice

1. Combine pancake mix with chicken broth, water, salt, and pepper. Mix well.

2. Add chicken. Mix until well coated.

3. In large skillet, heat 1" oil to 375°F. Fry 10–12 pieces of chicken at a time for 3–4 minutes, or until crisp and golden brown. Place on absorbent paper until well drained. Place chicken on rack in shallow baking pan. Keep warm in 250°F oven.

4. Drain all but 2 teaspoons drippings from skillet.

5. Sauté green pepper and onion in hot drippings. Remove vegetables from skillet.

6. Drain pineapple, reserving ¼ cup juice. Combine juice with cornstarch and mix until smooth.

7. Combine syrup, vinegar, and soy sauce. Pour into skillet. Bring to a boil, gradually stirring in pineapple juice-cornstarch mixture. Simmer for 1 minute, or until thick and clear.

8. Add pineapple chunks. Simmer for 1 minute.

9. Stir in chicken, green pepper, onion, and tomato.

10. Cook 1–2 minutes until thoroughly heated.

11. Serve over hot rice.

GRILLED CHINESE FIVE-SPICE SKEWERED CHICKEN

Rina Mckee
MAKES 3-4 SERVINGS

1 pound boneless, skinless chicken breast
½ cup soy sauce
¼ cup white wine
2 tablespoons rice wine vinegar
1½ teaspoons sugar
1 teaspoon five-spice powder

1. Cut chicken into long, thin strips.

2. Combine remaining ingredients. Pour over chicken. Toss well. Cover and refrigerate for 2 hours.

3. Weave chicken strips onto bamboo skewers. Brush with sauce; then grill 3–4 minutes. Brush with sauce and turn chicken over. Grill another 3–4 minutes.

SWEET AND SOUR CHICKEN

MAKES 4–6 SERVINGS

2 pounds boneless chicken, cut in cubes
2 tablespoons oil
1 clove garlic, minced
1 cup green pepper strips
1 cup carrot matchsticks
1½ cups chicken broth
¼ cup soy sauce
3 tablespoons vinegar
8 tablespoons brown sugar
½ teaspoon ground ginger
8-ounce can pineapple chunks with juice
⅓ cup teriyaki sauce
1½ cups minute rice

1. Brown chicken in oil.

2. Add garlic, green pepper, and carrots. Sauté briefly.

3. Add broth, soy sauce, vinegar, sugar, ginger, pineapple chunks with juice, and teriyaki sauce. Bring to full boil.

4. Stir in rice. Cover. Remove from heat and let stand a few minutes. Stir before serving.

I have seen hundreds of escaped slaves, but I never saw one who was willing to go back and be a slave. I think slavery is the next thing to hell.

—HARRIET TUBMAN

BUFFALO CHICKEN DRUMSTICKS

MAKES 6 SERVINGS

3 tablespoons flour
12 medium-sized drumsticks
2 tablespoons oil
1 medium onion, minced
¾ cups cayenne pepper sauce
1 teaspoon cornstarch
celery stalks
blue cheese salad dressing

1. Place flour in sturdy plastic bag. Toss drumsticks, a few at a time, in flour.

2. Heat oil in skillet over medium heat. Cook drumsticks until browned on all sides. Remove to plate.

3. In drippings, sauté onion until golden, about 5 minutes. Return chicken to skillet.

4. Combine cayenne pepper sauce and cornstarch. Pour over drumsticks. Heat to boiling. Reduce heat to low. Cover and simmer for 25 minutes, basting occasionally, until chicken is tender.

5. Arrange drumsticks on platter. Spoon pepper sauce over chicken. Serve with celery and blue cheese dressing.

BUFFALO WINGS

Tammy Lynn Oatis
MAKES 3-4 SERVINGS

2½ pounds chicken wings (12–15 wings)
¼ cup red hot sauce
½ cup (1 stick) butter or margarine, melted

1. Split wings at joint. Discard tips.

2. Deep-fry at 400°F for 12 minutes, or until completely cooked and crispy. Drain.

3. Combine hot sauce and butter. Dip wings in sauce until coated.

4. Serve with celery and blue cheese dressing.

NOTE: You can bake the wings in a 425°F oven for 35 minutes, instead of deep-frying them.

BARBECUED CHICKEN WINGS

Brenda Fowlerberry
MAKES 6 SERVINGS

¼ cup oil
3 medium onions, diced
3 cups tomato sauce
1½ cups packed brown sugar
¾ cup white vinegar
3 tablespoons Worcestershire sauce
4 tablespoons chili powder
2 tablespoons salt
¼ teaspoon dry mustard
2½ pounds chicken wings (about 24 wings)

1. Sauté onions in oil until tender, about 5 minutes.

2. Add tomato sauce, brown sugar, vinegar, Worcestershire sauce, chili powder, salt, and dry mustard. Heat to boiling, stirring constantly. Reduce heat and simmer for 30 minutes, stirring occasionally.

3. Split wings at joint. Discard tips. Place in baking pan. Cover with sauce.

4. Bake at 400°F for 60 minutes.

NOTE: This sauce also works well over chicken legs and thighs.

ITALIAN-STYLE FRIED CHICKEN WINGS

MAKES 3-4 SERVINGS

1 cup Italian-style bread crumbs
1 cup flour
1 tablespoon black pepper
1 tablespoon garlic powder
2 tablespoons seasoned salt
2 eggs
15 chicken wings
2 cups cooking oil

1. Combine bread crumbs, flour, pepper, garlic powder, and seasoned salt in large plastic bag.

2. Beat eggs.

3. Dip each chicken wing in eggs. Drop 3–4 wings into bag at a time and shake to coat.

4. Fry in hot oil until cooked.

NOTES:
1. Follow the same procedure through Step 3, then bake wings in oven at 400°F for 35–45 minutes, or until done.

2. Use chicken legs instead of wings and follow same procedure through Step 3, then bake legs in oven at 350°F for 45–60 minutes, or until done.

CHICKEN COBBLER

Elena Helmuth
MAKES 6 SERVINGS

¼ cup (½ stick) butter or margarine, melted
2 cups milk
1 cup cooked rice
2 cups diced, cooked chicken
1 cup flour
2 teaspoons baking powder
1 teaspoon salt
1 tablespoon sugar
1 cup milk

1. Pour butter into 1½-quart casserole.

2. Combine 2 cups milk, rice, and chicken. Spoon into casserole.

3. Sift together flour, baking powder, salt, and sugar. Add 1 cup milk. Mix well. Spread over chicken-rice mixture.

4. Bake at 350°F for 50 minutes. Let stand 5 minutes before serving.

TURKEY SCALLOPINI PICCATA

Willie Jean Murray
MAKES 6–8 SERVINGS

7-pound turkey breast, skinned
¾ –1 cup flour
2 teaspoons salt
1 teaspoon pepper
½ teaspoon dried thyme
½ teaspoon dried marjoram
½ cup (1 stick) margarine or butter
2 cloves garlic, minced
juice of 1 lemon
½ cup chicken broth
½ cup dry white wine
3 tablespoons chopped fresh parsley

1. Slice turkey meat off bone, as thinly as possible. Reserve carcass for making stock.

2. Place individual slices of turkey between sheets of waxed paper. Pound each slightly.

3. Season flour with salt, pepper, thyme, and marjoram.

4. Dredge turkey slices in flour mixture, one at a time.

5. Sauté turkey slices in batches, each in about 2 tablespoons margarine, for about 2 minutes per side. Remove from pan and keep warm. Reserve drippings.

6. When finished, sauté garlic in drippings. Add cooked turkey slices, lemon juice, broth, and wine. Simmer for 5 minutes.

7. Sprinkle with parsley and serve immediately.

WINGS TERIYAKI

Linda Maison
MAKES 4 SERVINGS

1 pound chicken wings
1 teaspoon ground ginger
1 clove garlic, minced
⅓ cup soy sauce
¼ cup sherry
1 teaspoon sugar

1. Cut wings into pieces at joints. Place in a single layer in a shallow roasting pan.

2. Roast uncovered at 375°F for 30 minutes, or until skin is crisp.

3. Combine remaining ingredients and pour over wings.

4. Cover pan tightly with foil and bake another 30 minutes, or until wings are browned and tender, but not dry.

—◆—

We never had hand lotion. We always had to use lard.
— **BARBARA MCFADDEN ENTY**,
a member of Bethel AMEC,
Lancaster, PA

HOT CHICKEN SALAD

MAKES 6–8 SERVINGS

7 chicken breast halves, cooked and chopped
1 cup chopped celery
4–5 hard-boiled eggs
¼ cup finely chopped onions
½ cup chopped red bell peppers
½ cup sweet relish
½ teaspoon garlic powder
½ teaspoon onion powder
⅛ teaspoon cayenne pepper
1½ to 1¾ cups salad dressing
10½-ounce can cream of chicken soup
¼ cup (½ stick) margarine
1 roll butter crackers, crushed

1. Combine chicken, celery, eggs, onions, red peppers, relish, garlic powder, onion powder, and cayenne pepper.

2. Stir in enough salad dressing for mixture to hold together.

3. Fold in chicken soup.

4. Spoon into greased casserole dish.

5. Melt margarine in 8" skillet. Add crackers. Stir to mix. Spread on top of chicken mixture.

6. Bake at 350°F for 20–25 minutes, or until lightly browned.

TURKEY WINGS AND GRAVY

MAKES 4 SERVINGS

6 turkey wings
2 ribs celery, sliced ½" thick
1 small onion, thinly sliced
1 medium green bell pepper, thinly sliced
1½ teaspoons poultry seasoning
2 teaspoons salt
¼ teaspoon fresh ground pepper
½ cup flour
½ cup water
2 teaspoons Gravy Master

1. Cut each wing into 3 pieces. Place wing pieces, celery, onion, and green pepper in large pot. Cover with cold water.

2. Add poultry seasoning, salt, and pepper. Heat to boiling. Reduce heat and simmer until wings are very tender, about 75 minutes. Adjust seasoning if needed.

3. Combine flour and water until smooth. Slowly stir flour mixture into simmering turkey liquid until it is smooth and thickened. Stir in Gravy Master.

4. Serve wings and gravy with mashed potatoes or rice.

BAKED TURKEY WINGS

ANN M. BEARDEN

one wing per person
salt to taste
pepper to taste
¼ cup (½ stick) margarine, melted
¼ cup water
onion halves, according to your preference
celery sticks, according to your preference
¼ cup water

1. Season wings with salt and pepper. Place in roasting pan.

2. Pour margarine over wings. Add a little water.

3. Bake at 350°F, turning and basting until browned, about 60 minutes.

4. Add onions, celery, and water to pan. Cover. Continue baking until tender.

The laws of this country do not protect us, and we are not bound to obey them. You whites have a country and may obey its laws, but we have no country.

—WILLIAM PARKER

TURKEY SUPREME

Marlene Clark
MAKES 6 SERVINGS

1 cup herb-seasoned stuffing mix
16-ounce package frozen string beans, cooked lightly
¼ cup slivered, blanched almonds
2 cups cooked turkey, cut in large pieces
10½-ounce can condensed cream of mushroom soup
½ cup milk

TOPPING:
1 cup herb-seasoned stuffing
2 tablespoons melted butter
¼ cup water

1. Layer stuffing mix, string beans, almonds, and turkey in greased baking dish.

2. Combine soup and milk. Pour over casserole.

3. Combine topping ingredients. Spread over casserole.

4. Bake at 400°F for 25–30 minutes until browned and bubbly.

TURKEY LOAF

Marlene Clark
MAKES 8-10 SERVINGS

2 eggs, slightly beaten
4 tablespoons (½ stick) butter, melted
1 package (4 cups) herb-seasoned stuffing mix
1½ cups turkey or chicken broth
2 cups cooked and cut-up turkey or chicken
2 tablespoons minced parsley
1 tablespoon minced onion
2 tablespoons minced green peppers

SAUCE:
10½-ounce can condensed cream of celery soup
¾ cup milk

1. Combine eggs, butter, stuffing mix, broth, turkey, parsley, onion, and green peppers. Spoon into greased 9" x 5" loaf pan.

2. Bake at 375°F for 30–40 minutes, or until firm.

3. Combine sauce ingredients in saucepan. Simmer for 2 minutes.

4. Slice loaf and pour sauce over slices just before serving.

William Whipper (1804–1876) and the Underground Railroad

William Whipper was born in Lancaster County's Southern End and was sent to Philadelphia to be educated. He married the half sister of Stephen Smith and ca. 1837 moved to Columbia to manage the Smith-Whipper office there. He and his partner were involved in the lumber industry and also real estate. Stephen Smith had become ordained in the A.M.E. Church and moved to the Philadelphia area. The railroad had come to Pennsylvania in the 1830s and the firm of Smith-Whipper owned thirteen cars with which they shipped their products to Philadelphia. Unbeknownst to the authorities, the railroad cars had a false compartment and into that space freedom seekers could be placed to continue their journey to Philadelphia and ultimately to William Still. According to William Whipper's own calculations, from about 1843 until 1861 he spent $1,000 of his own money to aid freedom seekers. When the railroad was taken over by the state in the late 1850s, Whipper bought a steamboat with which he transported lumber and freedom seekers on the Great Lakes. During almost two decades of transporting freedom seekers per railroad, not one person was apprehended by the authorities.

TURKEY CROQUETTES

Nanette Akins
MAKES 4 SERVINGS

1½ cups cooked turkey, finely chopped
10½-ounce can condensed cream of chicken
    soup
1 cup herb-seasoned stuffing mix
2 eggs, slightly beaten
1 tablespoon minced onion
flour
oil

SAUCE:

10½-ounce can condensed cream of mushroom
    soup
⅓–½ cup milk

1. Combine turkey, ⅔ can of soup, stuffing
   mix, eggs, and onion. Pour into shallow dish.
   Refrigerate for 2–3 hours until firm and chilled.

2. Divide mixture into 8 equal parts. Form into log
   shapes. Lightly dust with flour.

3. Deep-fry in oil until golden brown.

4. Combine sauce ingredients. Simmer in saucepan
   for 2 minutes. Serve over croquettes.

LEITHS ROAST DUCK

Doris Kelly
MAKES 8 SERVINGS

2 5-pound ducks
1 tablespoon vinegar
½ cup chicken stock
2 oranges, juiced, and zest grated
3 tablespoons brandy
2 small onions, finely chopped
2 celery ribs, finely chopped
1 teaspoon salt
1 teaspoon pepper
3 ounces sliced almonds
2 whole oranges, unpeeled and sliced in rounds
2 bunches watercress

1. Prick ducks all over with fork. Place in roaster,
   breast-side down.

2. Roast at 400°F for 30 minutes. Turn breast-
   side up and roast another 30 minutes. Test that
   ducks are tender; pierce to see if juice runs
   clear. If not, turn ducks over again and roast
   another 20 minutes. Test again. Continue baking,
   checking every 15 minutes, until they are done.

3. Remove ducks from roaster. Drain well. Remove
   skin and cut into pieces. Place in clean roaster.

4. Combine vinegar, chicken stock, orange juice,
   orange zest, and brandy. Pour over ducks.

5. Return to oven and heat, basting occasionally,
   for about 20 minutes more, until ducks are
   heated through. Remove meat to an ovenproof
   platter and keep warm.

6. Skim sauce to remove fat. Strain sauce into
   saucepan. Add onions and celery. Boil for
   5 minutes, or until vegetables just begin to soften.
   Add salt and pepper. Serve sauce separately.

7. Brown almonds over low heat, stirring
   constantly. Scatter over ducks.

8. Garnish with sliced oranges and watercress.

ROAST DUCK WITH ORANGE SAUCE

5–5½-pound duck
salt
8 ounces (1 cup) currant jelly
1 quart orange juice
1 pint concentrated orange juice mix
stock

1. Rub salt over duck. Place on wire rack in roasting pan.

2. Roast at 350°F for 2 hours.

3. Prepare orange sauce while duck is roasting. Boil jelly and 1 quart orange juice until reduced to half original amount. Add stock to make amount of gravy desired. Bring to a boil. Boil for a few minutes until slightly reduced. Stir in concentrated orange juice. Heat through.

4. Remove duck from oven. Drain off drippings. Pour orange sauce over duckling.

The workings of the human heart are the profoundest mystery of the universe. One moment they make us despair of our kind, and the next we see in them the reflection of the divine image.

—FREDERICK DOUGLASS

ROAST CORNISH HENS WITH MELON SAUCE

4 2-pound fresh Cornish hens, split
2 tablespoons margarine or butter, melted
salt to taste
pepper to taste
3 cups chicken stock or canned chicken broth
2 carrots, coarsely chopped
2 ribs celery, coarsely chopped
1 medium onion, coarsely chopped
2 cloves garlic, peeled
2 tablespoons dried tarragon
1 ripe cantaloupe

1. Place the hens, skin-side up, in a single layer in one or two baking pans. Brush with melted margarine. Season with salt and pepper.

2. Roast at 350°F for about an hour, or until juices run clear.

3. Meanwhile, combine chicken stock, carrots, celery, onion, garlic, and tarragon in saucepan.

4. Cut cantaloupe in half. Scoop out seeds into a piece of cheesecloth. Tie cheesecloth into bag with string. Add bag to saucepan.

5. Bring to a boil. Lower heat and simmer for 30 minutes. Remove and discard seed bag.

6. In food processor or blender, puree vegetables with half of stock. Return puree to saucepan.

7. Dice cantaloupe into ½" cubes. Add to sauce and heat slowly.

8. Transfer hens to heated serving platter. Spoon portion of sauce over hens. Serve with remaining sauce on the side.

CHUCK WAGON ROAST

MAKES 10 SERVINGS

5-pound chuck roast
½ cup vegetable oil
1 cup beer or ale
2 tablespoons lemon juice
2 cloves garlic, crushed
¾ teaspoon salt
2 bay leaves
½ teaspoon pepper
¾ teaspoon dry mustard
1 teaspoon dried basil
1 teaspoon dried oregano

1. Place meat in deep bowl.

2. Combine oil, beer, lemon juice, and seasonings. Pour over steak. Cover and refrigerate for several hours.

3. Place roast in roasting pan. Baste with marinade.

4. Bake at 425°F for 2½ hours. Slice and serve.

PEPPER STEAK

MAKES 5 SERVINGS

1½-pound round steak
3 green peppers, diced
1 large onion, chopped
14-ounce bottle ketchup
½ cup water
1 tablespoon Worcestershire sauce
salt to taste
pepper to taste

1. Place meat in skillet or greased baking dish.

2. Combine remaining ingredients. Pour over steak.

3. Cover and simmer on top of stove for 1½–2 hours, or bake covered at 350°F for 1½ hours. Uncover and continuing cooking or baking 30 minutes longer, or until tender.

MEXICAN-STYLE POT ROAST

MAKES 6 SERVINGS

2 tablespoons flour
1 teaspoon chili powder
2 teaspoons paprika
1 teaspoon salt
3½-pound chuck blade roast
2 tablespoons butter or margarine
2 medium onions
10 whole cloves
2 cinnamon sticks or ½ teaspoon ground cinnamon
½ cup water

1. Combine flour, chili powder, paprika, and salt.

2. Dredge meat in mixture.

3. Brown in butter in heavy kettle or Dutch oven.

4. Stud each onion with 5 cloves.

5. Add onions, cinnamon, and water to meat.

6. Bring to a boil. Cover and simmer for 2½ hours, or until meat is very tender, turning several times. Remove meat to hot platter and slice.

7. Discard onions and cinnamon sticks. Skim off fat.

8. Add more water if needed to make gravy of right consistency. Heat. Pour over meat and serve.

CHUCK ROAST WITH VEGETABLES

MAKES 8 SERVINGS

4-pound boneless chuck roast
salt to taste
pepper to taste
4 potatoes, quartered
4 carrots, sliced
5 small onions
1 package dry onion soup mix
10½-ounce can mushroom soup

1. Place large sheet of heavy-duty foil in baking pan.

2. Season roast with salt and pepper. Place in baking pan.

3. Place vegetables around meat.

4. Sprinkle with dry soup mix. Pour mushroom soup over top.

5. Seal foil tightly.

6. Bake at 350°F for 3–3½ hours, or until meat and vegetables are tender.

My kids every year had to line up and take castor oil to clean them out in the springtime.

—NELSON POLITE, SR.,
a member of Bethel AMEC,
Lancaster, PA

POT ROAST

Rev. Roger Bowman
MAKES 10–12 SERVINGS

1–2 garlic cloves
4–5-pound boneless chuck roast
1 tablespoon oil
1 package dry onion soup mix
pepper to taste
2–4 carrots, cut into chunks
2 bay leaves
1 cup water

1. Cut garlic cloves into slivers. With a sharp knife, cut slits on all sides of roast. Insert clove slivers into meat.

2. Brown roast in oil in Dutch oven.

3. Sprinkle with onion soup mix, pepper, carrots, and bay leaves.

4. Pour in water. Cover.

5. Bake at 300–325°F for 3–3½ hours, or until meat and vegetables are tender.

6. Skim off excess fat and remove bay leaves. Thicken pan juices for gravy.

OVEN-BAKED POT ROAST

MAKES 8 SERVINGS

3–4 pound chuck roast
1 envelope dry onion soup mix
3–4 medium potatoes, cut in quarters
1 large rib celery, cut into pieces
4 carrots, cut into chunks

1. Place roast in baking dish or casserole with lid.

2. Sprinkle soup mix over roast. Cover.

3. Bake at 350°F for 2–2½ hours.

4. Add vegetables. Continue baking for 60 more minutes.

5. Slice meat and serve surrounded with vegetables. Ladle broth over all.

———◆•✕•◆———

We used to live on a sharecropper's farm. At the end of the harvest season, when we'd gathered our last crop, the man that owned the farm would make a big pot of catfish and serve it over rice. There'd be music and we would be dancing and celebrating that it was the end of the season. Each year we looked forward to this big festivity.

The difference between slavery and sharecropping was that when you were a sharecropper, they didn't whip you and they paid you a little bit of money for working for them. But you were still depending on them for your food and the things you needed. But you could move off their farm if you wanted to. You didn't have to stay there, like when you were enslaved.

—**FRANCES MORANT**,
Brothers & Sisters Cafe

BEEF STROGANOFF

Doris Kelly
MAKES 4 SERVINGS

1 pound beef tenderloin or sirloin steak, cut ½"
thick
⅛ teaspoon pepper
½ pound fresh mushrooms, sliced
1 medium onion, sliced
1 tablespoon oil
2 tablespoons flour
2 bouillon cubes
2 cups water
¼ cup tomato paste
½–1 teaspoons dry mustard
½ teaspoon dried oregano
½ teaspoon dried dill
¼ cup sherry
1 cup yogurt

1. Cut meat into thin strips, about 2" long. Sprinkle with pepper.

2. Sauté mushrooms and onion in oil in heavy skillet. Remove with slotted spoon. Set vegetables aside.

3. Add flour to oil in skillet.

4. Dissolve bouillon cubes in boiling water. Gradually add to skillet and simmer, stirring constantly until thickened.

5. Add tomato paste, mustard, oregano, dill, and sherry. Mix until smooth.

6. Stir in beef, mushrooms, and onions. Cover. Simmer for 2–3 minutes, or until beef is cooked through.

7. Five minutes before serving, stir in yogurt. Heat, but do not boil.

8. Serve over cooked rice.

MEAT LOAF

Betty Jean Joe
MAKES 12–16 SERVINGS

3–4 pounds ground beef
2 cups seasoned bread crumbs
4 eggs
½ cup chopped onion
½ cup chopped green pepper
½ teaspoon pepper
1 cup tomato sauce
6-ounce can tomato paste
1 teaspoon salt

1. Combine all ingredients.

2. Form into loaf and place in baking pan.

3. Bake at 350°F for 90 minutes.

INDIAN MEAT LOAF

Nancy Perkins
MAKES 6–8 SERVINGS

1 pound ground beef
½ pound ground pork
1 egg
½ cup cornmeal
1 teaspoon salt
¼ teaspoon pepper
½ teaspoon dried sage
½ cup chopped onions
¼ cup chopped green pepper
½ cup cream-style corn
1¼ cups canned tomatoes

1. Combine all ingredients. Mix well.

2. Pack into 9" x 5" loaf pan.

3. Bake at 350°F for 75 minutes.

STATELY MEAT LOAF

Michelle Akins
MAKES 8 SERVINGS

2 pounds ground beef
½ teaspoon salt
1 teaspoon pepper
1 teaspoon chopped parsley
1 medium onion, minced
⅓ cup ketchup
2 egg whites, slightly beaten
¼ cup ice water
2 tablespoons prepared mustard
1 tablespoon ketchup
3 cups coarsely shredded carrots
8 medium-sized, fresh mushrooms, sliced

1. Combine beef, salt, pepper, parsley, and onion.

2. Gradually add ketchup, egg whites, and water, working all ingredients together thoroughly. Shape mixture into loaf. Place meat in baking dish large enough to accommodate the meat and its bed of carrots (to be added later).

3. Bake at 375°F for 30 minutes.

4. Combine mustard and ketchup. Spread over loaf.

5. Surround loaf with shredded carrots. Place mushrooms on top. Bake an additional 30 minutes.

ITALIAN MEAT LOAF

Nanette Akins
MAKES 6 SERVINGS

1 medium onion chopped
2 tablespoons butter or margarine
1 egg, slightly beaten
½ cup milk
½ cup herb-seasoned stuffing mix
1 pound ground beef
2 tablespoons chopped parsley
1 tablespoon salt
¼ teaspoon pepper
6 ounces tomato sauce
¼ teaspoon dried oregano

1. Sauté onion in butter over low heat until golden.

2. Mix together sautéed onion, egg, milk and stuffing mix. Let stand 5 minutes.

3. Add beef, parsley, salt, and pepper. Mix lightly but thoroughly.

4. Shape meat into loaf in shallow baking dish.

5. Bake at 375°F for 30 minutes.

6. Pour tomato sauce over meat. Sprinkle with oregano. Bake 30 minutes longer.

7. Remove from oven and let sit 5–10 minutes before slicing.

SWEET-AND-SOUR MEATBALLS

Susan Dyen
MAKES 8 SERVINGS

2–2½ pounds ground veal or beef
2 eggs, slightly beaten
2 cups unsalted crackers, crushed fine
minced garlic to taste
1 tablespoon Italian seasoning

SAUCE:
1 large jar homestyle marinara sauce
1 jar all-fruit black cherry jelly

1. Combine meat, eggs, crackers, garlic, and Italian seasoning. Form into meatballs.

2. Combine sauce and jelly in large baking dish. Add meatballs.

3. Bake at 350°F for 60–75 minutes, until cooked through and browned.

BRAISED VEAL IN CIDER

Doris Kelly
MAKES 6–8 SERVINGS

3 pounds boneless veal, cut in 2" cubes
1 tablespoon sweet Hungarian paprika
salt to taste
pepper to taste
2 tablespoons margarine or butter
2 tablespoons oil
2 onions, thinly sliced
2½ cups apple cider
½ cup chicken broth
1 bunch carrots, peeled and cut in
    1" pieces

1. Season veal with paprika, salt, and pepper.

2. Heat margarine and oil over medium heat in Dutch oven. Brown veal on all sides. Drain meat and return to Dutch oven.

3. Add onions, cider, and broth. Bring to a boil.

4. Cover and bake at 325°F for 45 minutes.

5. Add carrots. Continue to bake 20–25 minutes, until veal and carrots are tender.

NOTE: You may substitute pork cubes for the veal cubes.

CAJUN CHOPS

MAKES 4 SERVINGS

1 tablespoon paprika
1 teaspoon seasoned salt
1 teaspoon dried sage
½ teaspoon cayenne pepper
½ teaspoon black pepper
½ teaspoon garlic powder
4 pork chops, ½" thick
2 tablespoons butter or margarine

1. Combine paprika, seasoned salt, sage, cayenne pepper, black pepper, and garlic powder.

2. Coat chops on both sides with seasoning mixture.

3. Heat butter until it starts to brown.

4. Cook chops until done, 45–60 minutes.

——◆◆◆——

You have seen how a man was made a slave; you shall see how a slave was made a man.

—FREDERICK DOUGLASS

INDIVIDUAL BAKED PORK CHOP DINNER

Jim Johnson
MAKES 4 SERVINGS

4 pork chops or steaks
2 tablespoons oil
black pepper to taste
1 small onion, thinly sliced
2 medium potatoes, thinly sliced
4 fresh or frozen ears of corn on the cob
1 teaspoon dillweed
¼ cup (½ stick) margarine or butter
4 (16" x 12") rectangles heavy-duty
    aluminum foil

1. Brown pork chops in oil. Season with pepper.

2. Place one pork chop in center of each piece of foil.

3. Place one-fourth of onion and one-fourth of potato slices on top of each chop.

4. Place one ear of corn next to each pork chop.

5. Sprinkle each chop with 1/4 teaspoon dillweed. Dot each top with 1 tablespoon margarine.

6. Fold aluminum foil around pork chop and corn. Seal top and sides securely. Place on jellyroll pan.

7. Bake at 350°F for 60 minutes.

PORK CHOPS AND RICE

Lee Williams
MAKES 5-6 SERVINGS

5–6 center pork chops
¼ cup oil
1 onion chopped
1 cup regular rice
1 can beef bouillon
1 can water

1. Brown chops in oil. Remove chops and keep warm.

2. Sauté onion in meat drippings until tender.

3. Pour rice into 9" x 13" pan. Pour in and water. Add browned onion. Mix well. Lay pork chops on top. Cover with foil.

4. Bake at 350°F for 45 minutes. Remove foil and bake an additional 15 minutes, allowing meat and rice to brown slightly.

ORANGE BAKED PORK CHOPS

Sonya Gibson
MAKES 4 SERVINGS

4 pork chops, cut about ½" thick
seasoned salt to taste
¼ cup orange juice
½ teaspoon dried mustard
2 teaspoons brown sugar

1. Sprinkle chops with seasoned salt. Place on rack in baking pan.

2. Bake at 350°F for 20 minutes.

3. Combine remaining ingredients. Baste chops.

4. Continue baking for 15 more minutes. Turn chops. Bake another 10 minutes. Baste frequently throughout baking time.

CRANBERRY PORK CHOPS

MAKES 4 SERVINGS

4 1"-thick pork chops
1 teaspoon salt
pepper to taste
2 tablespoons oil
½ cup dry red wine
½ cup honey
1 cup fresh cranberries

1. Season pork chops with salt and pepper. Brown in hot oil, about 2 minutes on each side.

2. Combine wine and honey. Pour over chops. Cover and simmer for 50 minutes.

3. Add cranberries. Cook 10 minutes longer.

STUFFED PORK CHOPS

MAKES 6 SERVINGS

6 1½"-thick, loin-end pork chops
salt to taste
pepper to taste
1 cup herb-stuffing mix
½ cup chopped unpeeled apples
2 tablespoons raisins
2 tablespoons butter or margarine, melted
2 tablespoons orange juice
½ teaspoon salt
⅛ teaspoon ground cinnamon

1. Make a pocket along thickest side of each chop. Season inside and outside with salt and pepper.

2. Combine stuffing mix, apples, and raisins.

3. Combine butter, orange juice, ½ teaspoon salt, and cinnamon. Gently mix into stuffing and fruit mixture.

4. Stuff chops. Hold pockets shut with toothpicks. Place in shallow baking dish.

5. Bake at 350°F for 90 minutes. Cover during the last 30 minutes if chops become too brown or begin to dry out.

HERBED PORK ROAST

MAKES 8 SERVINGS

4-pound boneless top loin roast
1 clove garlic, cut into halves
1 teaspoon dried sage
½ teaspoon dried marjoram
½ teaspoon dried thyme leaves
salt to taste
pepper to taste

1. Rub roast with cut sides of garlic.

2. Combine remaining ingredients. Sprinkle over roast. Place roast, fat-side up, on rack in shallow roasting pan. Insert meat thermometer so that tip is in center of thickest part of pork.

3. Roast uncovered at 325°F until temperature reaches 170°F, about 2–2½ hours. Allow to sit 15–20 minutes before carving.

—◆✕◆—

I can remember when we needed a physic our mother would send us up to the drugstore to get a mix of castor oil and cherry soda. I can't drink cherry soda to this day because of that!

— **DORIS JOHNSON**,
a member of Bethel AMEC,
Lancaster, PA

BARBECUED SPARERIBS

Willie Jean Murray
MAKES 6–8 SERVINGS

1 teaspoon minced garlic
2 medium onions, chopped fine
¼ cup vegetable oil
6-ounce can tomato paste
½ cup white vinegar
1 teaspoon salt
1 teaspoon dried basil or thyme
½ cup honey
¼ cup Worcestershire sauce
1 teaspoon dry mustard
½ can beef stock
4 pounds ribs

1. In skillet, sauté garlic and onions 3–4 minutes in oil without letting onion brown.

2. Combine tomato paste and vinegar. Add to skillet.

3. Stir in salt, basil or thyme, honey, Worcestershire sauce, mustard, and beef stock. Mix well. Simmer over low heat, uncovered, for 10–15 minutes. Remove from heat.

4. Place ribs, fat-side up, on rack in shallow roasting pan. With pastry brush, cover ribs with sauce.

5. Bake at 400°F for 45–60 minutes. Baste frequently. When brown and crisp, cut into individual portions and serve.

SPARERIBS

6 pounds pork spareribs
1 teaspoon salt
1 teaspoon freshly ground black pepper
6-ounce can tomato juice
1 medium onion, finely chopped
½ cup cider vinegar
½ cup firmly packed dark brown sugar
¼ cup vegetable oil
1 tablespoon Worcestershire sauce
1 teaspoon dry mustard

1. Season ribs with salt and pepper. Place in a large, flat (17" x 12" is an ideal size) roasting pan.

2. Combine remaining ingredients. Mix well. Pour over ribs, coating well.

3. Cover with heavy-duty aluminum foil. Refrigerate for 3–8 hours.

4. Uncover and bake at 350°F for 60 minutes. Tent with foil near end of baking time if ribs begin to get too brown.

5. Cut ribs into 2–3 rib sections before serving. Serve with sauce from pan.

SPICY RIBS

8 pounds spareribs
2 tablespoons vinegar
3 8-ounce cans tomato sauce
½ cup chicken stock or broth
½ cup minced onion
3 tablespoons Worcestershire sauce
3 tablespoons packed brown sugar
2 tablespoons honey
1 tablespoon lemon juice
1 garlic clove, minced
2 teaspoons dry mustard
1½–3 teaspoons chili powder
1 teaspoon salt

1. Place spareribs in large stockpot. Cover with water, mixed with 2 tablespoons vinegar. Simmer for about 15 minutes. Set aside until sauce is ready.

2. Meanwhile, combine all other ingredients in saucepan. Bring to a boil. Reduce heat. Simmer uncovered for 30 minutes.

3. Brush ribs with sauce. Grill 45 minutes or until tender, basting and turning frequently.

4. Separate ribs into serving portions with scissors.

5. Serve with remaining basting sauce.

NOTE: Ribs may also be prepared in the oven. Place parboiled ribs on rack over baking sheet. Brush with sauce. Bake at 425°F for 45–60 minutes, basting and turning frequently.

BAKED HAM

Carletha Akins

MAKES 30 OR MORE SERVINGS

8-10-pound precooked ham
whole cloves
12 maraschino cherries
1-pound can sliced pineapple, drained
    (juice reserved)
1 cup light brown sugar
20-ounce bottle ginger ale

1. If ham has a skin, use a sharp knife to cut around edge of skin; then pull it off gently. Place meat in shallow roaster.

2. Score ham in diamond pattern. Insert whole clove at each juncture.

3. Cover ham with pineapple slices. Place one cherry in center of each slice. Secure each cherry with a toothpick.

4. In small saucepan, dissolve brown sugar in pineapple juice. Cook, stirring constantly, until smooth. Spoon half over ham.

5. Add half bottle of ginger ale. Cover meat with foil.

6. Bake at 300°F for 70 minutes, basting often with remaining juice and ginger ale.

7. Remove foil. Bake an additional 20 minutes, continuing to baste.

8. To serve, cut ham lengthwise and then cut each half in slices. Serve with basting broth.

GRILLED LAMB CHOPS

MAKES 6-8 SERVINGS

6-8 thickly cut lamb chops
1 teaspoon dried oregano
¼ cup olive oil
¼-½ teaspoon cayenne pepper
salt to taste
1 tablespoon dried mint
2 lemons, juiced
2 tablespoons white wine
1 teaspoon soy sauce

1. Trim fat from lamb chops. Place in deep dish.

2. Combine remaining ingredients. Pour over lamb chops, coating lamb on all sides. Cover and refrigerate for at least 1 hour.

3. Grill or broil lamb chops for 2-3 minutes on each side. Lamb should be tender, but not pink.

GRECIAN LAMB

Carletha Akins
MAKES 6 SERVINGS

1 teaspoon dried thyme
1 teaspoon salt
2 teaspoons dried oregano
2 tablespoons finely chopped fresh dillweed
2 bay leaves, crushed
1 small hot red pepper, crushed
3–4 cloves garlic, crushed
¼ cup finely chopped green pepper
1¼–1½ cups finely chopped onion
6-ounce can tomato paste
1 cup dry white wine
6 rib lamb chops

1. Combine all ingredients except chops. Mix well.

2. Place chops in shallow baking dish. Brush sauce over chops. Marinate 8–10 hours.

3. Bake at 375°F for 45–50 minutes.

MARINATED LAMB CHOPS

Clara Green
MAKES 4 SERVINGS

2 tablespoons French dressing
1 tablespoon Worcestershire sauce
¼ teaspoon garlic powder
¼ teaspoon black pepper
¼ teaspoon dried thyme
4 shoulder lamb chops

1. Combine all ingredients except lamb chops.

2. Brush on chops.

3. Cover and refrigerate for at least 8 hours.

4. Broil until done.

GARLIC HERB LAMB KABOBS

Rina Mckee
MAKES 4–6 SERVINGS

2-pound boneless leg of lamb, cut into 1" cubes
1 tablespoon minced garlic
2 teaspoons dried oregano
2 teaspoons dried rosemary
¼ cup olive oil
¼ cup lemon juice
¾ cup red wine
onions, peeled and quartered
mushrooms
bell peppers, cut into squares

1. Combine lamb, garlic, oregano, rosemary, olive oil, lemon juice, and red wine in large, heavy plastic bag. Close tightly and knead until well mixed. Refrigerate for 8 hours, turning often.

2. Remove meat from bag. Alternate meat and vegetables on skewers.

3. Broil or grill lamb and vegetables for 12–15 minutes, turning and basting often.

BROILED SHRIMP AU PORTO

Doris Kelly
MAKES 6–8 SERVINGS

2 pounds large shrimp
1½ cups white port wine
3 tablespoons olive oil
juice of 1 lemon
2 shallots, minced
1 clove garlic, minced
1 tablespoon Worcestershire sauce
½ teaspoon salt
¼ teaspoon dried oregano
pinch of dried thyme
pinch of cayenne pepper

1. Split shrimp down the back but do not peel. Remove and discard the black vein.

2. Combine remaining ingredients. Pour over shrimp. Marinate in refrigerator for 8 hours.

3. Place shrimp in single layer in broiler pan. Broil 2–3 minutes on each side, until they just turn pink. Serve shrimp in shells.

GARLIC SHRIMP

MAKES 3–4 MAIN-DISH SERVINGS

¾ pound large shrimp, peeled and deveined
3 tablespoons olive oil
1½ teaspoons garlic, minced
⅛ teaspoon crushed red pepper flakes
dash salt
chopped parsley

1. Cook shrimp in oil until just pink.

2. Add garlic, crushed pepper, and salt.

3. Remove skillet from flame and let sit for 4 minutes, allowing shrimp to absorb the flavor of the seasonings.

4. Return pan to medium-low burner. Reheat for 2 minutes.

5. Garnish with parsley.

{ Their routes were many and varied, they often traveled in disguise, through woods and farms, by wagon, boat and train, hiding in stables and attics and storerooms, and fleeing through secret passages, but the destination they sought was always freedom.

—CHARLES BLOCKSON,
Hippogreen Guide to the Underground Railroad }

SHRIMP BAKE

MAKES 4-6 SERVINGS

2½ pounds unpeeled large or jumbo shrimp
2 lemons, thinly sliced
2 onions, thinly sliced
⅔ cup (10⅔ tablespoons) butter or margarine, melted
⅓ cup lemon juice
½ cup Worcestershire sauce
2 teaspoons salt
½ teaspoon coarsely ground pepper
¾ teaspoon dried rosemary
pinch of ground red pepper
1-2 teaspoons hot sauce, according to your preference
3 garlic cloves, minced
fresh rosemary sprigs

1. Rinse shrimp with cold water. Drain well.

2. Layer shrimp, lemon slices, and onion slices in ungreased 9" x 13" baking dish.

3. Combine butter, lemon juice, Worcestershire sauce, salt, pepper, dried rosemary, red pepper, hot sauce, and garlic. Pour over shrimp.

4. Bake uncovered at 400°F for 20-25 minutes, or until shrimp turn pink, basting occasionally with juices.

5. Garnish with rosemary sprigs.

SWEET AND SOUR SHRIMP

MAKES 6-8 SERVINGS

21-ounce can cherry pie filling
3 tablespoons firmly packed brown sugar
3 tablespoons vinegar
1 teaspoon ground ginger
1 green pepper, sliced in thin strips
8-ounce can sliced water chestnuts, well drained
1 pound peeled and cooked medium shrimp
hot cooked rice

1. Combine pie filling, brown sugar, vinegar, and ginger. Mix well.

2. Add green pepper, water chestnuts, and shrimp. Mix just to combine.

3. Cover with waxed paper. Microwave 4-5 minutes on high, stirring 2-3 times.

4. Pour over rice in serving dish.

Frog legs! We used to catch frogs. Those legs are expensive now, but back then we were just eating!

—FRANCES MORANT,
Brothers & Sisters Cafe

SHRIMP AND MUSHROOMS WITH PAPRIKA SAUCE

Sonya Gibson
MAKES 4 SERVINGS

½ pound fresh mushrooms, sliced thin
3 tablespoons finely chopped shallots
salt to taste
pepper to taste
2 tablespoons butter
1 teaspoon paprika
¾ cup dry cooking sherry
1 cup heavy cream
¼ teaspoon dried hot red pepper flakes
24 large shrimp (about 1½ pounds), peeled and deveined
¼ cup sour cream
juice from half a lemon

1. Sauté mushrooms, shallots, salt, and pepper in butter. Sprinkle with paprika. Cook, stirring for 1 minute.

2. Add sherry. Cook over relatively high heat for 5 minutes, stirring constantly until sherry is almost evaporated.

3. Stir in cream. Cook for 1 minute.

4. Add pepper flakes and shrimp. Cook, stirring gently for 1 minute.

5. Stir in sour cream and lemon juice. Bring to a boil. Remove from heat and let stand 5 minutes before serving.

6. Serve over cooked pasta.

SHRIMP NEWBURG

Addison Lockett
MAKES 3–4 SERVINGS

2 tablespoons butter
2 tablespoons flour
½ cup milk
2 hard-boiled eggs
salt to taste
pepper to taste
¼ cup sherry
2 cups cooked shrimp

1. In saucepan, melt butter. Stir in flour until smooth. Over low heat, stir in milk until smooth, continuing to stir until mixture thickens.

2. Cut up egg whites finely. (Use yolks in another dish.) Add chopped whites to milk sauce.

3. Stir in salt, pepper, sherry, and shrimp.

4. Serve over hot rice.

CHAFING DISH À LA NEWBURG

Bernadette Dabney
MAKES 12–16 SERVINGS

6 tablespoons butter
6 tablespoons flour
3 egg yolks
3 cups milk
salt to taste
red pepper to taste
1 pound small shrimp, cooked
1 pound crabmeat, flaked
1 pound lobster meat, cut up and cooked

1. Melt butter in double boiler.

2. Add flour and eggs. Mix well.

3. Stir in milk and seasonings. Cook over medium heat until thickened.

4. Stir in seafood. Heat until warm.

5. Serve over melba toast, patty shells, or rice.

My train never ran off the track, and I never lost a passenger.

—**HARRIET TUBMAN**,
the woman called "Moses"

OVEN-FRIED FILLETS OF SOLE

Rev. Walter Price
MAKES 4 SERVINGS

1 pound fresh sole or other mild whitefish fillets
1 tablespoon vegetable oil
4 tablespoons Oven Frying Mix

1. Rinse fish. Pat dry. Lightly coat both sides with oil.

2. Sprinkle Oven Frying Mix on shallow platter. Coat oiled fish with crumbs. Arrange in single layer on shallow nonstick baking pan or greased cookie sheet.

3. Bake at 425°F for 8–10 minutes.

OVEN FRYING MIX:
1½ cups unseasoned bread crumbs
½ cup flour
½ teaspoon pepper
2 teaspoons celery salt
2 teaspoons onion salt
2 teaspoons paprika

1. Combine ingredients. Store in airtight container.

MUSHROOM-STUFFED FLOUNDER

MAKES 4 SERVINGS

2 pounds flounder
salt to taste
pepper to taste
¼ cup chopped onions or scallions
1 cup chopped mushrooms
1 teaspoon oil
⅛ teaspoon thyme
1 tablespoon chopped parsley
1 teaspoon lemon juice
½ teaspoon lemon zest
2 teaspoons oil

1. Sprinkle flounder on both sides with salt and pepper.

2. Sauté onions and mushrooms in 1 teaspoon oil for 5 minutes.

3. Stir in thyme. Spread mixture over flounder.

4. Roll fish up jelly-roll fashion. Fasten with toothpicks. Sprinkle with parsley, lemon juice, and zest, and 2 teaspoons oil.

5. Bake at 400°F for 15–20 minutes.

BAKED FLOUNDER FILLETS IN CHEESE SAUCE

MAKES 6 SERVINGS

10½-ounce can condensed cheddar cheese soup
1 soup can of milk
¼ cup chopped fresh parsley or 2 tablespoons dried parsley
1 tablespoon capers
1 tablespoon paprika
6 flounder fillets or any other whitefish
2 tablespoons butter

1. Combine soup, milk, parsley, capers, and paprika.

2. Pour into shallow baking dish. Top with flounder. Dot with butter.

3. Bake at 375°F for 25 minutes.

GRILLED SALMON WITH LEMON AND HERB BUTTER

Rina Mckee
MAKES 4 SERVINGS

3 tablespoons butter, softened
1 teaspoon lemon juice
½ teaspoon lemon zest
1 teaspoon chopped fresh chives
1 teaspoon chopped fresh parsley
2 12-ounce salmon fillets

1. Place butter, lemon juice, zest, and herbs in food processor. Pulse until well blended. Place in parchment paper or plastic wrap. Shape into log and roll up. Refrigerate for at least 30 minutes.

2. Cut each salmon fillet into two portions. Grill.

3. Cut butter "log" into 4 slices.

4. Divide salmon among 4 plates. Immediately top each with a butter circle and serve.

BAKED SALMON

14¾-ounce can red salmon
½ cup bread crumbs, divided
½ tablespoons grated or finely chopped onion
½ tablespoons grated or finely chopped celery
3 tablespoons butter
2 teaspoons flour
½ cup milk

1. Drain salmon of juice and remove skin and bones.

2. Crumble half the salmon into an 8"-square greased baking dish. Top with a layer of half the bread crumbs. Repeat those two layers.

3. Sprinkle onion and celery over the top.

4. Melt butter in small saucepan. Stir in flour. Add milk and heat until thickened. Pour over casserole.

5. Bake at 350°F until brown, about 20–30 minutes.

SALMON OR TUNA LOAF

1 tablespoon lemon juice
16-ounce can salmon
¾ cup medium white sauce (see below)
½ cup milk
½ teaspoon salt
1 egg, beaten
½ cup chopped celery
1 cup dry bread crumbs

1. Flake salmon with fork. Combine with lemon juice.

2. Mix together remaining ingredients. Add to salmon.

3. Form into loaf and place in greased loaf pan.

4. Bake at 350°F for 30 minutes, until browned.

MEDIUM WHITE SAUCE
1½ tablespoons butter or margarine
1½ tablespoons flour
scant ¼ teaspoon salt
¾ cup milk

1. Melt butter. Stir in flour and salt and mix together until smooth.

2. Cook until mixture bubbles.

3. Slowly whisk in milk, stirring constantly until smooth and thickened.

SALMON LOAF

Nancy Perkins
MAKES 6–8 SERVINGS

2 pounds canned salmon
2 cups soft bread crumbs
½ cup finely chopped celery
⅓ cup chopped parsley, plus more for garnish
2 eggs, slightly beaten
½ cup evaporated milk
⅓ cup fresh or bottled lemon juice
¼ cup melted butter
1 teaspoon salt
1 teaspoon Worcestershire sauce
hard-boiled eggs

1. Drain and flake fish.

2. Combine all ingredients except hard-boiled eggs.
   Pat into 9" x 5" loaf pan or 1½-quart casserole.

3. Bake at 375°F for 35–40 minutes, or until firm.

4. Garnish with parsley sprigs and sliced eggs.

CRAB CAKES

MAKES 4 SERVINGS

1 pound crabmeat
1 egg, slightly beaten
½ cup bread crumbs
1 tablespoon finely chopped green pepper
1 tablespoon chopped onion
¼ cup mayonnaise, or more if needed to hold
   ingredients together
1 tablespoon prepared mustard
1 tablespoon lemon juice
salt to taste
pepper to taste
butter or margarine

1. Slightly flake crabmeat.

2. Add remaining ingredients.

3. Form into cakes and brown on both sides in
   butter or margarine.

———◆❈◆———

Sing! I say they did sing. Sing about the cooking and
about the milking and sing in the field.

—HANNAH HANCOCK

We raise the wheat,
    they give us the corn;
We bake the bread,
    they give us the crust;
We sift the meal,
    they give us the skin;
And that's the way
    They take us in . . .

—SONG LYRIC

DEVILED CRAB

Minnie Wilson
MAKES 4–6 SERVINGS

4 tablespoons (½ stick) margarine or butter
2 tablespoons flour
1 tablespoon chopped parsley
2 teaspoons lemon juice
1 teaspoon prepared mustard
½ teaspoon horseradish
1 teaspoon salt
2 cups crabmeat
2 hard-boiled eggs, cut up fine
6 crab shells
½ cup buttered bread crumbs

1. Melt margarine in saucepan. Stir in flour until smooth. Add remaining ingredients except shells and bread crumbs. Mix well.

2. Divide mixture among crab shells. Sprinkle each with bread crumbs.

3. Bake at 400°F for 10 minutes.

BAKED OYSTERS ITALIAN STYLE

Nancy Perkins
MAKES 6 SERVINGS

½ cup olive oil or less
2 bunches green onions, tops and bottoms finely chopped
1¼ cups cracker crumbs
¾ cup grated Parmesan cheese
⅓ teaspoons salt
1 quart oysters, drained and patted dry

1. Coat bottom of baking dish with thin layer of olive oil.

2. Combine onions, cracker crumbs, cheese, and salt. Generously sprinkle a portion over bottom of pan.

3. Place layer of oysters over crackers. Sprinkle with crumb mixture. Repeat until oysters and crumbs are used up, ending with crumbs on top. Stream olive oil over entire top.

4. Bake at 375°F for 45 minutes, or until juices are thickened and casserole is golden brown.

HAM BARBECUE

Marian L. Mosser
MAKES 4 SANDWICHES

¼ cup vinegar
2 tablespoons water
2 tablespoons grape jelly
½ teaspoon paprika
2 tablespoons light brown sugar
dash of pepper
half a standard-sized bottle of ketchup
½ teaspoon dry mustard
1 pound chipped boiling ham

1. Combine all ingredients except ham. Cook for 2 minutes.

2. Stir in ham. Heat to boiling.

3. Serve on buns.

GRILLED MEAT STICKS

Nancy Perkins
MAKES 4–6 SERVINGS

12-ounce can luncheon meat
⅓ cup honey
½ cup vinegar
¼ cup salad oil
1 teaspoon dry mustard
½ teaspoon ground cloves

1. Cut luncheon meat into six finger-shaped sticks. Put in single layer in small dish.

2. Combine remaining ingredients. Mix well. Pour over meat. Refrigerate for at least 2 hours, turning meat several times.

3. Grill over hot coals until browned on all sides, basting frequently.

Run away from Joseph Coleman in the Great Valley in Chester County, a Negro Man, named Tom, aged about 30 years, of middle stature, HE SPEAKS VERY GOOD ENGLISH, having on a white Shirt, Stockings and Shoes, a great riding Coat tyed round him with blew Girdles.
—*The American Weekly Mercury* (Philadelphia), July 11, 1723

To be Sold, Three Very likely Negro Girls being about 16 years of age, and a Negro Boy about 14, SPEAKING GOOD ENGLISH, enquire of the Printer hereof.
—*The American Weekly Mercury* (Philadelphia), June 20, 1723.

A likely Negro Boy about 14 Years of Age, country born, CAN SPEAK DUTCH OR ENGLISH, to be sold: Enquire of Printer hereof.
—*The New York Gazette*, revived in the *Weekly Post-Boy*, Feb. 26, 1750

RAN - AWAY from Luykas Joh. Wyngaard, of the City of Albany, Merchant, a certain Negro Man named Simon, of a middle size, a slender spry Fellow, has a handsome smooth Face, and thick Legs; SPEAKS VERY GOOD ENGLISH: Had on when he went away a blue Cloth Great Coat.
—*The New York Gazette*, revived in the *Weekly Post-Boy*, Feb 25, 1750

SWING LOW

Swing low, sweet chariot,
Coming for to carry me home,
Swing low, sweet chariot,
Coming for to carry me home.

I looked over Jordan, and what did I see,
Coming for to carry me home?
A band of angels coming after me,
Coming for to carry me home.

If you get there before I do,
Coming for to carry me home,
Tell all my friends I'm coming too,
Coming for to carry me home.

I'm sometimes up, I'm sometimes down,
Coming for to carry me home;
But still my soul feels heavenly bound,
Coming for to carry me home.

This spiritual was a favorite of Harriet Tubman.
She reportedly sang this song on her deathbed.

VEGETABLES

＊━━◆━━＊

Gardening was my mother's favorite pastime, and ours, because we knew that soon the garden would be bursting with fresh tomatoes on the vine (my favorite—a tomato in one hand and a salt shaker in the other), cucumbers, carrots, turnips, string beans, melons, and strawberries, just to name a few. My mother loved a bountiful harvest, and she would often sing when she worked, not unlike the enslaved Africans who labored in the fields, stables, and the Big House.

Singing was medicine to get through the misery and the pain. It was also a way to pace oneself while working. Most importantly, singing allowed open communication from African to African, sharing stories, giving valuable information. "Swing low, sweet chariot . . . I ain't got long to stay here."

—**PHOEBE BAILEY**

VEGETABLES *Traditional*

BLACK-EYED PEAS

MAKES 6-8 SERVINGS

1 pound dried black-eyed peas
skin from a smoked ham or 2 ounces slab bacon, diced
¼ cup pork-ribs drippings, fried chicken drippings, or bacon drippings
¾–1 teaspoon salt
¼–½ teaspoon black pepper
½ teaspoon sugar

1. Pick over peas to remove stones and dirt. Rinse well. Soak in cold water for 20 minutes. Drain well.

2. Combine all ingredients in large pot. Add cold water to cover peas by 1".

3. Heat to simmering. Cover. Cook about 1½ hours, until peas are tender but still hold their shape. Add more water if needed.

4. Remove ham skin, if used, before serving.

HOPPIN JOHN

Carrie Alford
MAKES 4-6 SERVINGS

1 cup dried black-eyed peas
½ pound salt pork, cut into ½" cubes
½ onion, chopped
½ hot red pepper, seeded and coarsely chopped
1 cup uncooked long-grain rice
1 teaspoon salt
⅛ teaspoon pepper

1. Sort and wash peas. Place in Dutch oven. Cover with water 2 inches above peas. Let soak overnight. Drain peas and return to Dutch oven.

2. Add salt pork, onion, and red pepper to peas. Add enough water to cover ingredients. Cover cooking pot and bring to a boil. Reduce heat and simmer for 1 hour.

3. Stir in remaining ingredients. Bring to a boil. Reduce heat and simmer for 20 minutes.

4. Check if mixture is creamy in texture. If it is drier than that, add 2 cups water so rice has enough liquid to cook tender.

5. Continue cooking another 10 minutes. When rice and peas are both tender, remove from heat and serve with cornbread and collard greens.

HOMINY GRITS

MAKES 8 SERVINGS

4 cups water
1 cup quick grits
2 eggs, separated
½ cup heavy cream
1 teaspoon salt
¼ teaspoon pepper

1. Bring water to boil. Pour grits into boiling water. Cover. Cook over low heat for 5 minutes. Set aside to cool.

2. Pour 2 cups cooked and cooled grits into large bowl. Beat with wooden spoon until smooth.

3. Beat egg yolks with wooden spoon. (Reserve egg whites.) Stir into grits.

4. Add cream, salt, and pepper.

5. Whip eggwhites until they form stiff peaks, approximately 5 minutes. Gently fold into grits mixture until well blended. Spoon mixture into greased casserole dish.

6. Bake at 375ºF for 90 minutes, or until golden brown.

SOUTHERN COOKED GREEN PEAS

Carrie Alford
MAKES 6 SERVINGS

3 cups shelled, fresh green peas, cleaned (about 3 pounds unshelled)
1 cup water
¼ pound salt pork
½ teaspoon salt
2 tablespoons butter, optional

1. Combine green peas, water, salt pork, and salt in a small saucepan. Bring to a boil.

2. Reduce heat. Cover and simmer for 25 minutes, or until peas are tender. Drain.

3. Add butter, if desired, and toss lightly.

———◆———

For racism to die, a totally different America must be born.

—**KWAME TURE**
(Stokely Carmichael)

PEAS AND OKRA

Brothers and Sisters Cafe
MAKES 8-10 SERVINGS

4 cups field peas
4–5 cups water
1 tablespoon salt
¼ teaspoon black pepper
¼ pound salt pork
1 teaspoon sugar, optional
8–10 small, tender, fresh okra, each about
  2"–4" long

1. Combine all ingredients, except okra, in large stockpot. Bring to a boil. Reduce heat to simmer. Cook 15 minutes.

2. Add okra. Cook 15 minutes longer.

———◆✕◆———

As a people, our most cherished and valuable achievements are the achievements of spirit.
—MOLEFIKETE ASANTE

FRIED OKRA

1 pound okra, tender and each about
  2"–4" long
4 tablespoons vegetable oil, divided
2 teaspoons salt, or to taste
2 teaspoons black pepper, freshly ground

1. Wash okra in cold water and drain. Remove stems and cut okra into ½" chunks.

2. Heat 2 tablespoons oil in large heavy skillet over medium heat. Add half the okra and spread evenly over the bottom of the skillet with a spatula. Sprinkle with salt and pepper. Fry, turning the okra with a metal spatula to cook evenly, until tender, crispy, and well browned, about 10 minutes.

3. Remove okra and drain on paper towels, keeping warm until ready to serve.

4. Repeat with remaining oil and okra. Serve hot.

Robert Boston (1814–1888)

Robert Boston was probably born in Lancaster. His parents, John and Sarah Boston, are buried in the cemetery of Lancaster's Bethel A.M.E. Church. A barber by trade, Boston operated a hairdressing salon near Central Square of Lancaster in the 1840s. In the 1880s, when the housekeeper of Thaddeus Stevens, Lydia Hamilton Smith, was interviewed by a local editor, the question of Congressman Stevens's involvement in the Underground Railroad was mentioned. Elwood Griest, the editor of Lancaster's *Intelligencer*, issued a call for information about Stevens' involvement. Edward Rauch, the editor of the *Democrat* in Mauch Chunk (today's Jim Thorpe) responded that he was Stevens's agent who spied on George Hughes, a sometime constable and agent for slave catchers in Maryland. Rauch stated that five men knew of his secret role as Stevens's agent. One of them was Robert Boston. Rauch also hinted at the important role which Boston played in protecting freedom seekers coming to Lancaster County. George Hughes had a spy, a free African who traveled about the county to identify newcomers or individuals who lived alone. They were all potential prey for the slavecatchers. Boston identified the spy and made him disappear. Boston's work for the Underground Railroad soon translated into service at Bethel A.M.E. Church, where he became a pastor in the 1860s and a political leader. He presided over the celebration of the ratification of the 15th Amendment in April 1870.

PAN-FRIED OKRA

Carrie Alford
MAKES 4-6 SERVINGS

1 pound okra, tender and each 2"–4" long,
  cleaned
¾ cup cornmeal
½ teaspoon salt
vegetable oil

1. Cut okra crosswise into ½" slices; set aside.
2. Combine cornmeal and salt.
3. Dredge sliced okra in cornmeal mixture.
4. Cook in ½" oil over high heat until lightly
   browned, stirring occasionally.
5. Drain. Serve immediately.

BATTER-FRIED OKRA

Carrie Alford
MAKES 4-6 SERVINGS

1 pound small fresh okra, cleaned with stems
  removed
1 teaspoon salt
¼ teaspoon pepper
4 eggs, beaten
2½ cups fine, dry bread crumbs
vegetable oil

1. Cut okra into 2"-chunks and place in
   medium saucepan. Cover with water. Bring
   to a boil. Reduce heat, cover, and simmer for
   5 minutes. Drain well.
2. Sprinkle okra with salt and pepper.
3. Dip in eggs. Roll in bread crumbs.
4. Deep-fry in hot oil until golden rown. Drain well
   on paper towels.

SOUTHERN COOKED BUTTER BEANS

Carrie Alford
MAKES 2-3 SERVINGS

2 cups shelled fresh butter beans
2 cups water
2 tablespoons butter or margarine
1 tablespoon bacon drippings
½ teaspoon salt

1. Combine all ingredients in saucepan. Cover.
2. Cook over medium heat for 45 minutes, or until
   tender, but with beans still holding their shape.

DRY LIMA BEANS

Edna Hardrick
MAKES 6-8 SERVINGS

16-ounce package dry lima beans
3 pig knuckles
1 medium onion, chopped
¼ teaspoon dill
salt to taste
pepper to taste

1. Soak beans as directed on package.
2. Cover pig knuckles with water and cook in large
   stockpot for 45 minutes.
3. Drain beans of their soaking water and add
   beans, onion, and dill to knuckles and broth.
   Cook until beans are soft, adding water as
   needed.
4. Season with salt and pepper.
5. Serve with cornbread.

FRIED NEW POTATOES

Carrie Alford
MAKES 4 SERVINGS

4 slices bacon
1 pound new potatoes, scrubbed, peeled, and
   cooked until just tender
½ teaspoon salt
dash of pepper

1. Cook bacon in a large skillet until crisp. Remove
   bacon from skillet, reserving drippings. Drain
   bacon on paper towels, then crumble and set
   aside.

2. Cook potatoes in bacon drippings for
   10 minutes, or until browned, turning frequently.
   Drain.

3. Place potatoes in serving dish. Sprinkle with salt,
   pepper, and crumbled bacon.

FRIED CABBAGE AND BACON

MAKES 8-10 SERVINGS

½ pound sliced bacon
3-pound cabbage head
½ cup water
1 tablespoon sugar
1½ teaspoons salt
¼ teaspoon freshly ground black pepper

1. In 4-quart stockpot, cook bacon over medium
   heat until crisp. Remove bacon and drain, but
   reserve drippings.

2. Cut cabbage into 1"-thick wedges. Add to bacon
   drippings. Cook for about 3 minutes, stirring
   constantly, until cabbage begins to brown.

3. Add water, sugar, salt, and pepper. Cover and
   cook about 10 minutes, until cabbage is tender.

4. Crumble bacon onto cabbage. Serve warm.

NOTE: Reduce the amount of bacon to
3–4 slices. You'll benefit from the bacon
flavoring, but with fewer calories.

SOUTHERN COOKED DRIED LIMA BEANS

Carrie Alford
MAKES 6 SERVINGS

2 cups dried lima beans (soaked and drained)
4½ cups water
¼ pound salt pork, sliced
1 teaspoon salt
½ teaspoon pepper

1. Combine all ingredients in large saucepan. Bring to a boil.

2. Reduce heat. Cover and simmer for 2½ hours, or until beans are tender.

FRIED SWEET POTATOES

Carrie Alford
MAKES 6 SERVINGS

4 medium-sized sweet potatoes, cleaned and peeled
water
½ teaspoon salt
⅓ cup bacon dripping
2 tablespoons sugar

1. Slice potatoes into slices ¼" thick. Place in bowl, cover with water, and stir ½ teaspoon salt into water. Let soak for 30 minutes, then drain.

2. Heat bacon drippings in large skillet. Add potato slices. Cook until tender and golden brown, turning once. Drain on paper towels.

3. Sprinkle with sugar.

CANDIED YAMS

MAKES 10 SERVINGS

2 pounds fresh yams, peeled and sliced ¼" thick
1 cup water
1 teaspoon vanilla extract
4 tablespoons (½ stick) unsalted butter, softened
½ cup granulated sugar, or more to taste
½ cup brown sugar, or more to taste
½ teaspoon ground cinnamon
½ teaspoon allspice
1 cup raisins
2 cups pineapple chunks, drained

1. Place the yams in a greased 12" x 12" baking pan.

2. Combine water and vanilla. Pour over yams.

3. Combine butter, sugars, cinnamon, and allspice. Sprinkle over yams.

4. Cover tightly. Bake at 400°F for 45 minutes.

5. Sprinkle raisins and pineapple chunks over yams. Baste with the juices in the pan. Cover.

6. Continue baking about 20 minutes, or until yams are tender and juices are bubbling. Serve hot.

FRIED GREEN TOMATOES

MAKES 4 SERVINGS

2 large green tomatoes, unpeeled
1 egg, beaten with 1 tablespoon water
¾ cup dry bread crumbs, lightly salted
3 tablespoons bacon fat or vegetable oil

1. Cut tomatoes into slices that are a little over ¼" thick.

2. Dip tomato slices in egg-water mixture. Coat with bread crumbs.

3. Fry in hot oil over medium heat until golden brown on both sides and tender throughout.

4. Drain on paper towels.

PAN-FRIED GREEN TOMATOES

Carrie Alford
MAKES 4 SERVINGS

½ cup flour
½ teaspoon salt
¼ teaspoon pepper
2 large green tomatoes, cut into ½"-thick slices
¼ cup (½ stick) butter or margarine
2 tablespoons plus 2 teaspoons brown sugar, divided

1. Combine flour, salt, and pepper.

2. Dredge tomato slices in flour mixture.

3. Melt butter in large skillet. Fry tomato slices on one side until browned. Remove from skillet, and place in 9" x 13" x 2" baking dish, browned-side down.

4. Top each tomato slice with 1 teaspoon brown sugar. Broil 3 inches from heat for 5 minutes, or until browned and bubbly.

{ If the white people can give festivals to raise funds for the relief of suffering soldiers, why should not the well-to-do colored people go to work to do something for the benefit of the suffering blacks? I made a suggestion in the colored church, that a society of colored people be formed to labor for the benefit of the unfortunate freedmen . . . and in two weeks "the Contraband Relief Association" was organized with forty working members. }

—ELIZABETH KECKLEY

SOUTHERN COOKED RUTABAGAS

Carrie Alford
MAKES 4–6 SERVINGS

2-pound rutabaga, peeled and cubed
3 cups water
¼ pound salt pork, rinsed and sliced
1 teaspoon sugar
½ teaspoon salt
⅛ teaspoon pepper, plus additional pepper
   to taste

1. Combine rutabaga, water, salt pork, sugar, and salt in large saucepan. Bring to a boil. Reduce heat. Simmer, uncovered, for 35 minutes, or until rutabaga is tender.

2. Drain. Remove and discard salt pork.

3. Add ⅛ teaspoon pepper to rutabaga and mash to desired consistency. Sprinkle with additional pepper.

GLAZED HONEY CARROTS

Nanette Akins
MAKES 6–8 SERVINGS

¾ teaspoon salt
1½ cups water
5–6 cups sliced carrots
½ cup honey
3 tablespoons butter
1½ teaspoons lemon juice

1. Add salt to water and bring to a boil.

2. Add carrots. Return to boil.

3. Add remaining ingredients. Reduce heat and cook until carrots are tender.

HARVARD BEETS

Carrie Alford
MAKES 2–4 SERVINGS

1 pound fresh beets
3 tablespoons sugar
1 tablespoon cornstarch
½ cup water
¼ cup vinegar
1 tablespoon butter or margarine
½ teaspoon salt
fresh parsley sprigs

1. Trim beets and cut into chunks if large. Simmer over medium heat in a small amount of water until soft. Dice.

2. Combine sugar and cornstarch in medium saucepan. Mix well. Gradually add water, or liquid from cooking beets, stirring until smooth.

3. Add vinegar and butter. Constantly stir over medium heat until butter melts and sauce is thickened.

4. Stir in beets and salt. Cook for 5 minutes until thoroughly heated.

5. Garnish with parsley sprigs.

VEGETABLES *Other Favorites*

CORN PUDDING

MAKES 6–8 SERVINGS

3 eggs, well beaten
2 cups corn, fresh or frozen
2 tablespoons butter, melted
1 cup milk
1 cup cream
¼ cup flour
½ teaspoon salt
¼ teaspoon pepper

1. Fill 9" x 13" baking pan with an inch of water. Set in oven. Preheat oven to 325°F.

2. Combine all ingredients. Pour into greased casserole dish. Place in baking pan of water in oven.

3. Bake uncovered for 75 minutes, or until knife inserted in center of casserole comes out clean.

NOTE: Substitute fat-free half-and-half for cream if you like.

SUCCOTASH

MAKES 4–6 SERVINGS

10-ounce package frozen baby lima beans
10-ounce package frozen whole-kernel corn
16-ounce can tomatoes
½ cup chopped onions
2 tablespoons margarine
salt to taste
pepper to taste
10-ounce package frozen cut okra

1. Combine lima beans, corn, tomatoes, onions, margarine, salt, and pepper in 2-quart saucepan. Bring to a boil. Reduce heat and simmer for 20 minutes.

2. Add okra and cook for 10 minutes more.

My grandmother would can all week in the Mason jars. Tomatoes, green beans, peaches, and when she'd get them done she'd line them along the cellar way. You could smell it all outside when she'd be cooking.

—SANDRA POLITE SIMMS,
a member of Bethel AMEC,
Lancaster, PA

COLLARD GREENS SAUTÉED

3–4 pounds collard greens
2 tablespoons bacon drippings
large onion, chopped
half a firm ripe tomato, diced
salt to taste
pepper to taste
pinch of nutmeg

1. Trim stems off collards and discard. Wash leaves thoroughly. Slice into ¼" strips. Blanch in boiling water for 30 minutes. Drain well.

2. In large skillet or saucepan, sauté onion in drippings until tender.

3. Stir in tomato and cook until just tender.

4. Add collard greens. Stir until well coated. Cook until tender.

5. Season with salt and pepper. Stir in pinch of nutmeg.

CHEESE GARLIC GRITS

MAKES 6-8 SERVINGS

3 cups water
1 cup quick grits
1 teaspoon salt (or less)
3 tablespoons butter
1½ cup shredded sharp cheddar cheese, divided
2 large cloves garlic, pressed
2 eggs, beaten
¼ cup milk

1. Bring water to boil in saucepan.

2. Add grits and salt. Reduce heat to simmer. Cook and stir for 4–5 minutes until thickened.

3. Stir in butter, 1 cup cheese, and garlic. Remove from heat.

4. Stir until butter and cheese are melted.

5. Stir in eggs and milk.

6. Pour into 1-quart greased casserole. Sprinkle with remaining ½ cup cheese.

7. Bake at 350°F for 45 minutes, or until set.

MASHED SWEET POTATOES

MAKES 4-6 SERVINGS

2 pounds sweet potatoes
2 tablespoons butter, softened
8-ounce carton pineapple yogurt, pineapple orange yogurt, or mandarin orange yogurt, at room temperature
2 tablespoons honey, optional
½ teaspoon salt
dash of white pepper

1. Boil sweet potatoes in their skins until tender, about 45 minutes. Peel while potatoes are still hot.

2. Cut into chunks. Add butter. Mash until smooth.

3. Stir in yogurt, honey, salt, and pepper.

4. Serve.

SWEET POTATO PANCAKES

Mrs. Margaret Bailey
MAKES 3 SERVINGS OR ABOUT 12 PANCAKES

1 cup sifted flour
1 teaspoon baking powder
2 tablespoons sugar
dash of cinnamon
dash of ground cloves
⅔ cup cooked, mashed sweet potatoes
1 tablespoon margarine or butter, softened
1 egg, beaten
1–1¼ cups skim milk

1. Sift together flour, baking powder, sugar, cinnamon, and cloves.

2. In separate bowl combine sweet potatoes, margarine, egg, and milk until smooth and thoroughly blended. Add to dry ingredients. Mix until just blended.

3. For each pancake drop about 2 tablespoons batter onto greased griddle. Cook until undersides are browned. Turn and brown on other side.

4. Serve with maple syrup or applesauce.

HORSERADISH MASHED POTATOES

Rina Mckee
MAKES 6 SERVINGS

4 large potatoes
4 tablespoons (½ stick) butter, softened
¾ cup (or more) milk
salt to taste
white pepper to taste
1¼ tablespoons prepared horseradish

1. Peel potatoes. Cut into pieces. Place in large saucepan and cover with water. Cook until soft. Drain and place in electric mixer bowl.

2. Add butter and half the milk. Whip on low. Gradually add remaining milk. Increase mixer speed and beat until smooth.

3. Season with salt and pepper. Add horseradish. Mix well.

POTATOES PIZZIOLA

Nancy Perkins
MAKES 6 SERVINGS

1" boiling water
1 teaspoon salt
2 pounds medium-sized potatoes, peeled
2 tablespoons olive oil
2 tablespoons tomato paste
2½ cups chopped tomatoes
1 teaspoon salt
1 teaspoon dried basil
1 teaspoon dried oregano
½ teaspoon ground black pepper
¼ teaspoon garlic powder

1. Combine water and salt in saucepan. Bring to boil.

2. Add potatoes. Parboil for 15 minutes. Drain and cut into ⅛" slices. Set aside.

3. Heat olive oil. Stir in tomato paste, tomatoes, and seasonings. Cook 5 minutes.

4. Add potatoes. Cook 8–10 minutes, or until potatoes are tender.

5. Serve hot.

OAK HILL POTATOES

Rina Mckee
MAKES 4 SERVINGS

1½ pounds (4–5 medium-sized) potatoes
1½ teaspoon salt, divided
2 hard-boiled eggs, peeled and sliced
small onion, diced
¼–½ teaspoon pepper
2 tablespoons butter or margarine
4 tablespoons flour
2 cups milk
1 tablespoon butter or margarine
3 tablespoons dried bread crumbs

1. Peel and dice potatoes. Place in large saucepan and cover with cold water. Add 1/2 teaspoon salt. Bring to a boil. Reduce heat to low and cook 20–25 minutes, or until potatoes are tender. Drain.

2. Combine potatoes, eggs, onion, salt, and pepper in lightly greased 1½-quart casserole.

3. Melt 2 tablespoons butter in medium saucepan. Add flour and milk. Mix well. Cook, stirring constantly, until thickened. Add to ingredients in casserole. Blend lightly.

4. Melt remaining tablespoon of butter. Add bread crumbs. Mix well. Sprinkle over casserole.

5. Bake at 350°F for 30 minutes, uncovered.

SCALLOPED POTATOES

Marlene Clark
4–6 SERVINGS

4 medium-sized potatoes
grated nutmeg
salt to taste
pepper to taste
flour
milk
grated cheese

1. Peel and thinly slice potatoes. Place a thin layer in buttered casserole dish.

2. Sprinkle with nutmeg, salt, pepper, and flour. Repeat until casserole is three-quarters full.

3. Pour enough milk down side of dish to just cover potatoes (pouring it directly in the center will make the flour float to the top).

4. Bake at 350°F for 1 hour, or until potatoes are soft. Sprinkle with grated cheese. Return to oven for 15 minutes, uncovered.

Our grandfathers had to run, run, run. My generation's out of breath. We ain't running no more.

—**KWAME TURE**
(Stokely Carmichael)

POTATO PANCAKES

MAKES 4–6 SERVINGS

2 pounds raw potatoes, peeled and grated
1 onion, grated
1 cup boiling water
2 eggs
1 teaspoon salt
½ teaspoon freshly ground pepper
¼ cup flour, matzo meal, or
   cracker crumbs
½ cup oil
2 tablespoons butter

1. Place potatoes and onion in strainer over bowl. Pour boiling water over them. Mix briefly to press out some moisture. (The boiling water will keep the potatoes from discoloring.)

2. Drain water from bowl, but leave starch from potatoes in bottom of bowl.

3. Beat eggs in separate bowl. Add potatoes, starchy sediment, salt, pepper, and flour.

4. Place oil and butter in skillet. When hot, drop in potato mixture by heaping tablespoonfuls. Keep temperature of skillet low enough that pancakes cook through, but high enough that they get brown and crispy. When brown on one side, flip and brown other side.

5. Keep potatoes hot in 300°F oven until all batter is used. Serve with applesauce as a side dish.

FLAVORFUL COOKED BROWN RICE

Mrs. Margaret Bailey
MAKES 4–6 SERVINGS

1 cup brown rice
1 cup chicken broth
1 cup water

1. Combine ingredients. Bring to a boil, stirring occasionally.

2. Reduce heat to simmer. Cover tightly and simmer for 45–50 minutes, until liquid is absorbed. Fluff with fork before serving.

EASY PILAF

Mrs. Margaret Bailey
MAKES 6 SERVINGS

4-ounce can portabella mushrooms, undrained
1 small carrot, shredded
3 tablespoons minced onion
1 tablespoon raisins
pinch of curry powder
pinch of cumin seeds
2 cups Flavorful Cooked Brown Rice (above),
   or any cooked rice

1. Combine all ingredients except rice. Cover and simmer for 3–4 minutes.

2. Add rice. Cover and place over low heat until heated through. Stir frequently to prevent rice from sticking to bottom of pan.

BOMBAY RICE DRESSING

Mrs. Margaret Bailey
MAKES 8 SERVINGS

3 cups Flavorful Cooked Brown Rice (page 126),
   or any other cooked rice
1 unpared apple, shredded
½ cup chopped onions
½ cup finely minced celery
3 tablespoons chopped parsley or cilantro
2 teaspoons cumin seeds
1 teaspoon curry powder
pinch of ground cinnamon
pinch of ground ginger
pinch of allspice
¼ cup apple juice

1. Combine all ingredients except apple juice. Mix lightly.

2. Place in casserole. Pour apple juice over mixture and then cover.

3. Bake at 375°F for 25 minutes.

NOTE: This can be used as a side dish, or as stuffing for roasted chicken.

GLAZED CARROTS AND TURNIPS

MAKES 6 SERVINGS

3 tablespoons butter
1 pound white turnips
2 medium-sized carrots
1 cup chicken broth
½ teaspoon salt, optional
¼ teaspoon white pepper
2 tablespoons sugar
2 tablespoons chopped parsley

1. Melt butter in large skillet.

2. Peel turnips and carrots. Slice both into julienne strips. Add to butter. Stir until coated.

3. Pour in broth. Cover and cook over medium heat 6 minutes.

4. Season with salt and pepper.

5. Increase heat to high. Cook uncovered 10 minutes, or until vegetables are tender and liquid is reduced and syrupy.

6. Sprinkle sugar over vegetables. Reduce heat to medium.

7. Stir the vegetables gently to distribute the sugar. Cover and cook for another minute. Remove from heat. Vegetables should be glazed and shiny.

8. Garnish with parsley.

> Now I realize that my mother kept the family going with her prayer, much prayer. She used to have the three of us around her feet while she told stories about the Old Times. She'd read to us from a Little Red Riding Hood book and from the Bible. Of course, we didn't understand the "thee" and "thou," but we surely got the difference in living right or living wrong.
>
> —ELIZABETH McGILL,
> a member of Bethel AMEC, Lancaster, PA

VEGETABLES & Other Favorites

BROCCOLI CASSEROLE

Jean Townsend
MAKES 6–8 SERVINGS

2 (10-ounce) packages frozen broccoli, either spears or chopped
¼ pound (1 stick) butter, melted
1 pound cottage cheese
2 eggs, beaten
5 tablespoons flour
½ cup grated Swiss cheese
½ teaspoon salt
pepper to taste

1. Steam broccoli until just tender. Place in 9" x 9" baking dish.
2. Combine butter, cottage cheese, eggs, flour, Swiss cheese, salt, and pepper. Pour over broccoli.
3. Bake at 350°F for 45–60 minutes, or until edges are brown.

BROCCOLI CASSEROLE

Lisa Bowman
MAKES 8 SERVINGS

2 (10-ounce) packages frozen chopped broccoli
2 eggs, well beaten
1 cup mayonnaise
1 medium-sized onion, chopped
dash of salt
dash of pepper
10¾-ounce can cream of mushroom soup
8-ounce can sliced water chestnuts
1 cup grated cheddar cheese
4 tablespoons (½ stick) butter or margarine, melted
⅔ cup seasoned bread crumbs or stuffing cubes

1. Cook and drain broccoli. Set aside.
2. Combine eggs, mayonnaise, onion, salt, pepper, soup, and water chestnuts. Add broccoli and mix well. Pour into long greased baking dish.
3. Sprinkle with cheese.
4. Combine butter and crumbs. Spread over ingredients in pan.
5. Bake at 350°F for 40–45 minutes.

BROCCOLI AND RICE CASSEROLE

Mattie Mae Roche
MAKES 4–6 SERVINGS

10-ounce package frozen chopped broccoli
¾ cup chopped onions
¾ cup chopped celery
4 tablespoons (½ stick) butter or margarine
1½ cups cooked rice
10¾-ounce can mushroom soup
8-ounce jar cheese spread

1. Cook broccoli until just tender. Drain.
2. Sauté onions and celery in butter until clear.
3. Combine all ingredients. Pour into greased casserole dish.
4. Bake at 350°F for 30 minutes.

———————

I remember we ate sour grass. It had little leaves on it. And we used to eat white carrots. I don't know if they were really called carrots but they looked like carrots.

—JANET GANTZ

CREAMED SPINACH CASSEROLE

Dianne Prince
MAKES 4–6 SERVINGS

2 (10-ounce) packages frozen chopped spinach
10¾-ounce can cream of mushroom soup
4 tablespoons (½ stick) butter
2 teaspoons garlic salt
bread crumbs or cracker crumbs

1. Cook spinach according to package directions. Drain thoroughly.

2. Combine soup, butter, and salt in skillet. Cook for 3 minutes.

3. Add spinach. Mix well. Pour into greased casserole.

4. Top with bread or cracker crumbs.

5. Bake at 375°F for 20–30 minutes, until heated through and lightly browned.

STIR-FRY CABBAGE

Nanette Akins
MAKES 4–6 SERVINGS

2 strips bacon, cut into squares
½ cup chopped onions
½ cup chopped green peppers
1 firm head white cabbage
½ teaspoon garlic powder
¼–½ teaspoon black pepper, according to your taste preference
¼–½ teaspoon five-spice powder, according to your taste preference
⅔ cup water
2 tablespoons soy sauce

1. Cook bacon in Dutch oven until soft.

2. Stir in onions and green peppers. Sauté until clear.

3. Cut up cabbage coarsely. Rinse and drain. Add to Dutch oven. Mix well.

4. Sprinkle with garlic powder, pepper, and five-spice powder. Mix well.

5. Increase heat to high. Add water and soy sauce. Cover and steam quickly until cabbage is wilted. Serve immediately.

ITALIAN GREEN BEANS WITH MUSHROOMS

MAKES 6 SERVINGS

2 slices bacon, cut in half
2 cups sliced fresh mushrooms
½ cup chopped onions
1 small garlic clove, minced
½–1 teaspoon dried basil, according to your taste preference
10¾-ounce can condensed tomato soup, 8-ounce can pureed tomatoes, or 1 cup fresh tomatoes, chopped
¼ cup water
1-pound package frozen Italian green beans, cooked and drained
½ cup grated cheddar cheese

1. Fry bacon until crisp. Remove bacon, but reserve drippings.

2. In drippings, sauté mushrooms, onions, garlic, and basil until mushrooms are brown and onions are tender.

3. Combine tomatoes and water. Add to pan. Stir in cooked beans. Heat, stirring often, until heated through.

4. Just before serving, garnish with cheese and top with crumbled bacon.

ZUCCHINI PROVENCAL

Nancy Perkins
MAKES 2–3 SERVINGS

1 tablespoon olive oil
2 cups sliced zucchini
½ teaspoon minced garlic
½ cup sliced onions
1 tablespoon chopped fresh basil

1. Heat oil in heavy skillet. Add zucchini, garlic, and onions. Cook until just soft.

2. Stir in basil. Cook for one minute; then serve.

STUFFED ZUCCHINI

MAKES 4 SERVINGS

4 large zucchini
½ pound fresh mushrooms, sliced
¼ cup (½ stick) butter
¼ cup sour cream
salt to taste
pepper to taste
4 tablespoons chopped parsley
4 tablespoons firm dry bread crumbs
2 tablespoons melted butter
Parmesan cheese

1. Cut zucchini into 2"–3" pieces. Cut each of those pieces in half lengthwise. Steam for 5 minutes. Scoop out centers, leaving each piece with a ¼"-thick shell. Set aside.

2. Sauté mushrooms in ¼ cup butter. Stir in sour cream. Season with salt and pepper. Spoon into centers of squash pieces.

3. Combine parsley, bread crumbs, and 2 tablespoons butter. Sprinkle over squash.

4. Bake at 350°F for 20 minutes.

5. Sprinkle with Parmesan cheese.

YELLOW SQUASH AND ONIONS

MAKES 4 SERVINGS

3–4 medium yellow squash
salt to taste
pepper to taste
1–2 medium onions, sliced thin
2–3 tablespoons bacon drippings or butter

1. Cut squash into slices ¼" thick. Sprinkle with salt and pepper.

2. Place ¼" of water in heavy skillet. Bring to a boil.

3. Add squash. Lay onion slices on top. Cover and steam over medium heat until water has evaporated, being careful not to burn the squash.

4. Add bacon drippings, stirring so that squash is well coated.

5. Cook, uncovered, over low heat for 30 minutes, or until tender, stirring occasionally.

ASPARAGUS FRITTATA

MAKES 4 SERVINGS

12 asparagus spears, cooked
8 eggs
2 tablespoons grated onion
salt to taste
pepper to taste
½ teaspoon Tabasco sauce
1 cup shredded Swiss cheese, divided
3 tablespoons butter

1. Cut asparagus into 1½" pieces.

2. Beat together eggs, onion, salt, pepper, and Tabasco until well blended.

3. Stir in asparagus and 3 tablespoons shredded cheese.

4. Melt butter over medium heat in 10" skillet. Pour in asparagus-egg mixture. Cook gently until eggs start to set, about 5 minutes.

5. Sprinkle with remaining cheese. Place under preheated medium broiler, about 6" from the flame, for about 1½ minutes, until eggs are set and top is lightly browned.

6. Loosen edges of frittata with spatula. Slide onto plate.

The person who strays away from the source is unrooted and is like dust blown about by the wind.
—**MOLEFIKETE ASANTE**

STIR-FRIED ASPARAGUS WITH SNOW PEAS

Rev. Walter Price
MAKES 4–5 SERVINGS

1 tablespoon peanut oil
1 pound fresh asparagus, cut diagonally in 1"-long pieces
½ pound snow peas, ends and strings removed
3 tablespoons rich chicken broth
1 tablespoon soy sauce
2 tablespoons lemon juice
1 teaspoon sesame oil

1. Heat peanut oil in pan over high heat. Drop in asparagus and snow peas and stir-fry for several minutes, just until vegetables are well coated and shiny.

2. Combine broth, soy sauce, and lemon juice. Pour over vegetables in pan. Cover.

3. Cook on high, stirring occasionally for 4 minutes, or until liquid is gone.

4. Put vegetables in serving dish. Sprinkle with sesame oil. Serve hot.

ASPARAGUS WITH PARMESAN CHEESE

Rev. Walter Price
MAKES 6 SERVINGS

2 pounds fresh asparagus
⅔ cup Parmesan cheese
5 tablespoons butter, melted

1. Cook asparagus in salted water for 1–2 minutes. Plunge in cold water until chilled. Spread in bottom of cake pan.

2. Top with cheese and butter.

3. Bake at 350°F for 10 minutes.

CREAMED ASPARAGUS

Willie Jean Murray
MAKES 6–8 SERVINGS

2 pounds fresh asparagus, trimmed and cooked until crisp-tender
4 tablespoons (½ stick) butter
4 tablespoons flour
1 teaspoon salt
2 cups milk
1 cup grated cheese
1 ounce chopped pimento
4 slices buttered bread, cut into cubes

1. Place asparagus in baking dish.

2. Melt butter in saucepan. Add flour and salt and blend until smooth. Gradually stir in cold milk. Cook, stirring constantly, until sauce boils and becomes thick and smooth. Add cheese and pimiento. When fully blended, pour over asparagus.

3. Top with buttered bread cubes. Bake at 350°F until golden brown, about 15 minutes.

ASPARAGUS CASSEROLE

Rebecca Carter
MAKES 6 SERVINGS

1 pound fresh asparagus
10¾-ounce can cream of mushroom soup
¼–½ pound butter crackers
1 tablespoon onion, grated
½ cup grated cheese
½ cup cracker crumbs

1. Cut asparagus into 2" lengths and cook until just tender. Reserve cooking liquid. Set asparagus aside.

2. Place soup in saucepan. Drain liquid from asparagus into soup. Heat slowly.

3. Place layer of crackers in buttered 2-quart baking dish. Add one-third of asparagus. Sprinkle with one-third grated onion. Repeat process for 2 more layers.

4. Pour soup over ingredients in casserole.

5. Spread cheese and cracker crumbs over top.

6. Bake at 375°F for 15 minutes, or until soup bubbles and top turns slightly brown.

CREAMED VEGETABLE DISH

Willie Jean Murray
MAKES 8–10 SERVINGS

2 carrots, sliced
2 stalks celery, sliced
3 small onions, cut in bite-sized pieces
½ head of cabbage, cut in bite-sized pieces
½ teaspoon salt
¼ teaspoon pepper
½ cup chopped ham
2 tablespoons butter
2 tablespoons flour
½ teaspoon salt
1 cup milk
fresh parsley

1. Place carrots, celery, and onions in a small amount of boiling water. Simmer until almost done.

2. Add cabbage. Continue to cook until all vegetables are soft. Drain. Place in serving dish and keep warm.

3. Sprinkle with salt, pepper, and ham, and stir through.

4. While vegetables are cooking, melt butter in saucepan. Add flour and salt and blend until smooth. Gradually stir in cold milk. Cook, stirring constantly, until sauce boils and becomes thick and smooth. Pour over vegetables.

5. Garnish with fresh parsley.

VEGETABLES AU GRATIN

Christel Wayne
MAKES 6–8 SERVINGS

2 tablespoons butter
2 tablespoons flour
½ teaspoon salt
1 cup milk
1 cup shredded cheddar cheese
4 cups lightly cooked vegetables of your choice, drained
½ cup fine, soft bread crumbs
1 tablespoon butter, melted

1. Melt 2 tablespoons butter in saucepan. Add flour and salt and blend until smooth. Gradually stir in cold milk. Cook, stirring constantly, until sauce boils and becomes thick and smooth.

2. Stir in cheese until smooth. Add vegetables. Pour into greased 1½-quart casserole dish.

3. Toss crumbs with 1 tablespoon butter. Sprinkle over top of casserole.

4. Bake at 350°F for 20–25 minutes, or until browned.

———————❖———————

There is time enough, but none to spare.

—FREDERICK DOUGLASS

CAULIFLOWER CHEESE CASSEROLE

Rebecca Carter
MAKES 4 SERVINGS

medium-sized head of cauliflower
¼ cup (½ stick) butter or margarine
½ cup flour
½ teaspoon dill
½ teaspoon salt
⅛ teaspoon pepper
2 cups milk
1 cup grated cheddar cheese
1 tablespoon butter
½ cup bread cubes
fresh dill
black pepper

1. Trim leaves and stalk from cauliflower and separate into florets. Cook in boiling, salted water until just tender (about 10 minutes). Drain and place pieces in a greased 2-quart baking dish.

2. Melt ¼ cup butter in saucepan. Stir in flour, ½ teaspoon dill, salt, and pepper. Gradually blend in milk. Cook, stirring constantly, until sauce thickens.

3. Add grated cheese and stir until melted. Pour over cauliflower.

4. Melt remaining 1 tablespoon butter. Blend with bread cubes. Scatter buttered bread crumbs over top of casserole.

5. Bake at 350°F for 30 minutes.

6. Garnish with a few sprigs of fresh dill and freshly ground pepper just before serving.

BROWNED BRUSSELS SPROUTS

MAKES 4 SERVINGS

2 pints fresh brussels sprouts
3 tablespoons butter or margarine
2 tablespoons lemon juice or the juice from 1 lemon
2 teaspoons caraway seeds
salt to taste
pepper to taste

1. Cook brussels sprouts in a bit of water until just tender, about 15 minutes for fresh sprouts. Drain.

2. Heat butter until lightly browned. Add sprouts, lemon juice, caraway seeds, and seasonings. Heat for 2 minutes, stirring sprouts to coat.

TOMATO BAKE

Cregg Carter
MAKES 8–10 SERVINGS

2 (28-ounce) cans whole or stewed tomatoes
salt to taste
8 whole cloves
8 whole peppercorns
1 bay leaf
half a yellow onion, chopped
¾ cup brown sugar
3–4 slices bread, torn into dime-sized pieces
2 tablespoons butter or margarine

1. Pour tomatoes into saucepan. Season with salt.

2. Place cloves, peppercorns, and bay leaf into cheesecloth bag. Add to pan.

3. Cook over medium heat for 30 minutes, stirring occasionally. Remove spice bag.

4. Add onion, sugar, bread, and butter or margarine. Pour into greased baking dish.

5. Bake at 400°F for 60 minutes.

I had it often impressed upon my mind that I should one day enjoy my freedom; for slavery is a bitter pill . . .

—REV. RICHARD ALLEN

BEETS WITH ONIONS AND TOMATOES

MAKES 4–6 SERVINGS

2 (15-ounce) cans whole beets
2 to 4 tablespoons vegetable oil
1 teaspoon whole cumin seeds
1 clove garlic, minced
1 large onion, coarsely chopped
1 tablespoon flour
¼–½ teaspoon cayenne pepper, according to your preference
2–4 whole tomatoes, chopped
½ teaspoon salt, or to taste
1 cup beet liquid

1. Drain beets, reserving liquid. Cut beets into quarters.

2. Sizzle cumin seeds in hot oil for 5 seconds. Add garlic and stir-fry until golden brown.

3. Add onion and stir-fry 2 minutes.

4. Stir in flour and cayenne pepper. Stir-fry 1 minute.

5. Add remaining ingredients. Cook, uncovered, for 5 minutes, or until sauce is slightly thickened.

GO DOWN, MOSES

When Israel was in Egypt's land;
Let my people go;
Oppressed so hard they could not stand;
Let my people go.

Go down Moses, 'Way down in Egypt's land.
Tell old Pharaoh, Let my people go!

Thus saith the Lord, bold Moses said,
Let my people go;
If not, I'll smite your firstborn dead,
Let my people go.

Go down Moses, 'Way down in Egypt's land.
Tell old Pharaoh, Let my people go!

No more shall they in bondage toil;
Let my people go;
Let them come out with Egypt's spoil,
Let my people go.

Go down Moses, 'Way down in Egypt's land.
Tell old Pharaoh, Let my people go!

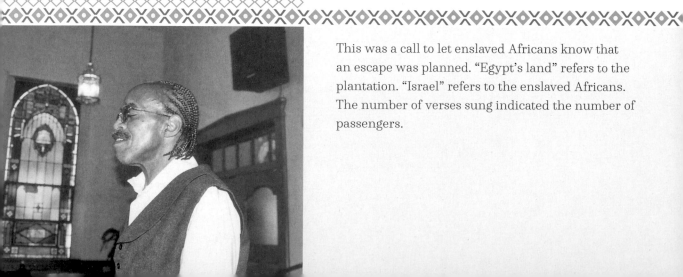

This was a call to let enslaved Africans know that an escape was planned. "Egypt's land" refers to the plantation. "Israel" refers to the enslaved Africans. The number of verses sung indicated the number of passengers.

SALADS

❖

Most enslaved Africans did not have the opportunity to eat fresh vegetables, even though they were agricultural giants, using their knowledge to grow and cultivate the finest farms on the plantations where they were confined. The orchards grew the sweetest and plumpest of fruits. But if an African was caught eating a piece of fruit from the Massa's orchards, he or she was whipped.

Avocado salad was a summer favorite in our home. I loved shrimp and scallops, and my mother would make a seafood salad for me.

I never knew how she could afford it, nor did I ever question her. Somehow God always made a way for her to treat her children special.

— **PHOEBE BAILEY**

SALADS *Traditional*

— ◆ —

POTATO SALAD

Anna Gantt
MAKES 8-10 SERVINGS

6 medium-sized potatoes, cooked, peeled, cubed
2 large ribs celery, diced
1 medium-sized onion, diced
3 hard-boiled eggs, diced
½ teaspoon salt
1 cup mayonnaise or salad dressing

1. Combine potatoes, celery, onions, and eggs.

2. Sprinkle with salt.

3. Stir in mayonnaise.

4. Chill and serve.

— ◆ —

NOTE: For additional flavor, add 1 teaspoon dry mustard and a scant ¼ teaspoon black pepper to Step 2. Add a dusting of paprika in Step 4, just before serving.

POTATO SALAD

Ann Beardan and Dana Beardan Frierson
MAKES 8 SERVINGS

1½ cups light mayonnaise or salad dressing
1 tablespoon vinegar
1–2 tablespoons sugar, according to your preference
1 tablespoon prepared mustard
1 teaspoon salt
¼ teaspoon pepper
2 pounds potatoes, cooked, peeled, cubed
2 medium ribs celery, chopped
¼ cup chopped onions
⅓ cup pickle relish
3 hard boiled-eggs, chopped

1. Combine mayonnaise, vinegar, sugar, mustard, salt, and pepper.

2. In large separate bowl, gently stir together potatoes, celery, onions, and pickle relish. Fold in dressing.

3. Add eggs. Chill.

— ◆ —

NOTE: Add half a green pepper, seeded and chopped, to Step 2, if you wish.

POTATO SALAD FOR A CROWD

Brothers and Sisters Cafe
MAKES 30 SERVINGS

10 pounds potatoes, cooked, peeled, cubed
1 cup chopped onions
12 hard-boiled eggs, cut up
1 cup celery
1 quart mayonnaise
1 cup sweet relish
¼ cup prepared mustard
¼ cup sugar
paprika to taste
soul food seasoning to taste
salt to taste

1. Gently combine first 4 ingredients in large bowl.

2. Combine next 7 ingredients in a separate bowl. When thoroughly mixed, fold into potato mixture.

3. Refrigerate, and serve when well chilled.

Then the fire must be kindled in the cabin, the corn ground in the small hand-mill, and supper and dinner for the next day in the field prepared. All that is allowed them is corn and bacon, which is given out at the corncrib and smokehouse every Sunday morning.

Each one receives, as his weekly allowance, three and a half pounds of bacon, and corn enough to make a peck of meal. That is all—no tea, coffee, sugar, and, with the exception of a very scanty sprinkling now and then, no salt.

When the corn is ground and the fire is made, the bacon is taken down from the nail on which it hangs, a slice cut off and thrown upon the coals to broil. The majority of the slaves have no knife, much less a fork. They cut their bacon with the axe at the woodpile. The cornmeal is mixed with a little water, placed in the fire, and baked. When it is "done brown," the ashes are scraped off and, being placed upon a chip which answers for a table, the tenant of the slave house is ready to sit down upon the ground to supper. By this time it is usually midnight.

—**SOLOMON NORTHUP**,
Twelve Years a Slave.
Buffalo: Miller, Orton & Mulligan, 1854.

SALADS *Other Favorites*

DILL POTATO SALAD

MAKES 8-10 SERVINGS

12 new, Red Bliss potatoes, cooked
3 scallions, chopped fine
½ bunch fresh dill, chopped fine, or 3
    tablespoons dried dill
1½ teaspoon salt
¼ cup wine vinegar
½ teaspoon black pepper
½ cup olive oil or salad oil

1. Peel and dice potatoes.

2. Add scallions and dill. Mix well.

3. Add remaining ingredients. Mix well.
   Refrigerate, chilling well before serving.

DIJON POTATO SALAD

MAKES 4-5 SERVINGS

1 cup mayonnaise
2 tablespoons Dijon mustard
2 tablespoons chopped fresh dill, or 1½ teaspoon
    dried dill
1 teaspoon salt
¼ teaspoon pepper
1½ pounds small red potatoes, cooked and
    quartered
1 cup sliced radishes
½ cup chopped green onions

1. Combine mayonnaise, mustard, dill, salt, and
   pepper.

2. In separate bowl, mix together remaining
   ingredients.

3. Pour dressing over vegetables and fold together.
   Chill.

{ My mother used to make potato salad. We had used all the salad dressing for sandwiches, so she had to use vinegar in the jar and cook the potatoes almost like mashed potatoes and use that. But it was still delicious.

—REUTILLA SMITH,
a member of Bethel AMEC,
Lancaster, PA }

RED-SKIN POTATO SALAD

MAKES 8 SERVINGS

2–3 pounds red potatoes, unpeeled
1 large onion, chopped
⅔ cup sweet relish or chopped sweet mixed
    pickles
3 hard-boiled eggs
1 tablespoon sugar
1 dash dry mustard
1½ cups diced celery
    or 1½ teaspoon celery seed
1–2 cups mayonnaise or salad dressing
chopped parsley

1. Cook potatoes until tender. Do not peel. Cube
   to desired size.

2. Lightly combine all ingredients except parsley.
   Pour into serving dish.

3. Garnish with parsley just before serving.

4. Use with lettuce or other fresh greens for a
   salad.

SOUTHWESTERN POTATO SALAD

MAKES 6 SERVINGS

2 pounds new potatoes, quartered
1 cup chopped peeled jicama
½ cup sliced pitted ripe olives
¼ cup sliced green onions
18 cherry tomatoes, halved
1 large avocado, chopped
8-ounce bottle ranch salad dressing
2 small fresh jalapeño peppers, finely chopped
    and seeds removed
2 tablespoons chopped cilantro or parsley
1 teaspoon lime zest
¼ teaspoon salt
¼ teaspoon pepper
lime juice

1. Cook potatoes in lightly salted boiling water for
   10–15 minutes, until just tender. Drain. Cool.

2. Add jicama, olives, onions, tomatoes, and
   avocado to potatoes. Toss lightly.

3. Stir together salad dressing, peppers, cilantro,
   lime zest, salt, and pepper. Pour over potato
   mixture and mix lightly. Refrigerate for at least
   8 hours before serving.

4. Squeeze lime juice over salad before serving to
   brighten flavors.

MACARONI SALAD

MAKES 5 SERVINGS

8-ounce package dry elbow macaroni
1 tablespoon salt
3 quarts water
½ cup chopped celery
¼ cup diced green pepper
2 tablespoons, or more, thinly sliced radishes
¾ cup mayonnaise or salad dressing
2 tablespoons prepared mustard
¼ teaspoon onion salt

1. Cook macaroni in 3 quarts salted boiling water for 11 minutes. Rinse with cold water. Drain.

2. Combine all ingredients. Toss lightly. Chill for several hours.

GREEN GODDESS SALAD DRESSING

Mary Alice Bailey
MAKES 8 SERVINGS

1 cup mayonnaise
⅔ cup sour cream
½ cup fresh parsley, chopped, or 3 tablespoons dried
2 tablespoons chives, chopped, or 2 teaspoons dried
1 tablespoon fresh tarragon or 1 teaspoon dried
2 teaspoon lemon juice
2 teaspoon anchovy paste
salt to taste
pepper to taste

1. Combine all ingredients in food processor. Pulse until well blended.

2. Pour over any fresh green salad.

LOW-FAT CHICKEN SALAD

MAKES 4 SERVINGS

3 cups diced, cooked chicken
1 cup chopped celery
1 small apple, chopped
2 tablespoons chopped onions
½ cup low-fat cottage cheese
1 teaspoon milk
pepper to taste
lettuce leaves, bread, or sandwich rolls

1. Combine chicken, celery, apple, and onions.

2. In blender, mix cottage cheese and milk. Whip for 2 minutes. Add to chicken mixture.

3. Season with pepper. Mix well.

4. Serve over lettuce leaves or as sandwich filling.

TURKEY SALAD

MAKES 12-14 SANDWICHES ON ROLLS

6 cups cooked turkey breast, cubed
1 small onion, chopped fine
1½ –2 cups coarsely chopped celery
8-ounce can crushed pineapple, undrained
1 tablespoon sugar
1 dash dry mustard
½ teaspoon celery seed
1 cup mayonnaise or salad dressing

1. Combine all ingredients except mayonnaise. Chill.

2. Add mayonnaise just before serving.

TUNA SALAD

MAKES 6-8 SERVINGS

6-ounce can tuna
1½ cups diced celery
3 hard-boiled eggs, diced
2 tablespoons minced onions
¼ teaspoon salt
¼ teaspoon pepper
½ cup mayonnaise, or salad dressing
lettuce leaves, bread or sandwich rolls

1. Combine all ingredients, except lettuce or bread, mixing lightly.

2. Chill. Serve as a salad, or as sandwich filling.

MACARONI AND TUNA PASTA SALAD

MAKES 9-12 SERVINGS

1 pound dry elbow macaronis, cooked
½ red pepper, diced
½ green pepper, diced
½ yellow pepper, diced
¾ cup chopped black olives
1 small red onion, diced
2 ribs celery, diced
4 hard-boiled eggs, chopped
3 6-ounce cans tuna
1 cup shredded carrots
1 tablespoon salt
¼–½ teaspoon black pepper, according to your preference
3 cups, or more, mayonnaise

1. Combine all ingredients except mayonnaise.

2. Stir in 3 cups mayonnaise. Add more if needed, so that salad coheres, but isn't runny.

GRAPEFRUIT TUNA SALAD

Nancy Perkins
MAKES 3-4 LUNCH-SIZE SERVINGS

1½ cups grapefruit sections, drained and cut up
7-ounce can tuna, drained and flaked
1 cup diced celery
2 tablespoons chopped pimento
lettuce
tart French dressing

1. Combine grapefruit, tuna, celery, and pimento. Chill about 30 minutes.

2. Serve on lettuce with dressing.

SHRIMP SALAD

MAKES 6 SERVINGS

2 cups cooked shrimp
1½ cups chopped green bell pepper
1½ cups chopped celery
¼ cup sliced pimentos
1 cup mayonnaise
1½ tablespoons lemon juice
1 teaspoon salt
¼ teaspoon lemon pepper or celery seed
lettuce leaves

1. Combine shrimp, green pepper, celery, and pimentos.

2. Combine remaining ingredients in separate bowl. Pour over shrimp mixture. Toss lightly. Chill.

3. Serve on lettuce.

———◆◆◆———

NOTE: To add more color to the salad, use a mixture of green, red, and yellow bell peppers, instead of just green.

SHRIMP AND RICE SALAD

MAKES 10–12 SERVINGS

1½ cups cooked rice
1½ cups cooked shrimp, cut into pieces
1 rib celery, chopped
1 carrot, shredded
3–4 tablespoons mayonnaise or salad dressing
1 tablespoon lemon juice
1 cup sliced radishes
½ cup chopped green onions
½ pound fresh, or 10-ounce package frozen, asparagus
pimento strips
tomato wedges
hard-boiled eggs, sliced

1. Combine rice, shrimp, celery, carrot, mayonnaise, lemon juice, radishes, and onions.

2. Cook asparagus until just tender. Cut into 2" lengths. Add to rice mixture and toss lightly. Chill.

3. Garnish with pimento, tomato, and hard-boiled eggs.

❖

We have a formidable history, replete with the voice of God, the ancestors, and the prophets.
— MOLEFIKETE ASANTE

SEAFOOD SALAD

MAKES 2 QUARTS SALAD

½ pound box dry elbow macaroni, cooked and drained
½ pound cooked shrimp, cut up
½ pound imitation crabmeat, cut up
1 cup mayonnaise
1 teaspoon prepared mustard
1 tablespoon ketchup
1 tablespoon sugar
½ cup celery, chopped fine
¼ cup green pepper, chopped fine
salt to taste
pepper to taste
seasoned salt to taste
garlic powder to taste
paprika

1. Combine all ingredients except paprika. Mix well. Pour into serving bowl.

2. Sprinkle with paprika. Chill.

CRAB SALAD

1 pint lump crabmeat
2 ribs celery, finely diced
5 tablespoons mayonnaise
1 tablespoon French dressing
1 teaspoon salt
ground red pepper to taste
lettuce
hard-boiled eggs, sliced

1. Combine all ingredients except lettuce and eggs. Chill salad ingredients.

2. Serve on lettuce. Garnish with eggs.

NOTE: If you're budget-conscious, substitute imitation crabmeat for the lump crabmeat.

COLD CRAB SALAD

1 cup freshly shredded cabbage
3 ounces cooked crabmeat
¼ apple, unpeeled and diced
half a small celery rib, finely chopped
salt to taste
pepper to taste
½ tablespoon melted margarine
lettuce or whole, cored tomato

1. Toss together cabbage, crabmeat, apple, celery, seasonings, and margarine. Chill.

2. Serve over lettuce or stuffed in tomato.

CRANBERRY SALAD

6-ounce package orange-flavored gelatin
1 cup boiling water
½ cup cold water
1 tablespoon lemon juice
14-ounce jar cranberry-orange relish
2 tablespoons crystallized ginger
5-ounce can water chestnuts, drained and chopped
½ teaspoon celery seed
lettuce leaves

1. Dissolve gelatin in boiling water. Add cold water and lemon juice. Chill until slightly thickened.

2. Fold in relish, ginger, water chestnuts, and celery seed.

3. Pour into mold. Chill until firm.

4. Unmold on lettuce-lined salad plates.

FRUITY GELATIN SALAD

Michael Flack
MAKES 12–15 SERVINGS

6-ounce package raspberry gelatin
1 cup hot water
16-ounce can whole cranberry sauce
20-ounce can crushed pineapple, undrained
2.25-ounce package chopped walnuts
lettuce leaves, optional

1. Dissolve gelatin in water.

2. When partially set, stir in remaining ingredients.

3. Pour into mold or serving bowl and chill until completely set.

4. To serve, unmold on lettuce-lined plate, or pass in serving bowl.

FRUIT SALAD

MAKES 4–6 SERVINGS

2½ cups pineapple chunks, drained
11-ounce can mandarin oranges
1 cup seedless grapes
1 cup small marshmallows
3½-ounce can flaked coconut
2 cups sour cream or frozen whipped topping, thawed

1. Combine pineapple, mandarin oranges, grapes, marshmallows, and coconut.

2. If using sour cream, whip until stiff peaks form. Fold into fruit mixture. Cool 8 hours before serving.

3. If using whipped topping, fold gently into fruit and serve immediately.

CRANBERRY JEWEL SALAD

MAKES 6 SERVINGS

3-ounce package raspberry-flavored gelatin
½ cup hot water
½ cup cold water
1-pound can jellied cranberry sauce
1 orange
lettuce leaves, optional

1. Dissolve gelatin in hot water. Add cold water. Chill until mixture begins to gel.

2. Beat cranberry sauce until saucy. Fold into gelatin. Chill until mixture is partially gelled.

3. Quarter orange. Remove seeds. Chop rind and pulp in food processor. Fold into gelatin.

4. Pour into mold or serving dish. Chill until firm.

5. Unmold on lettuce-lined salad plates, or pass in serving dish.

FROSTED FRUIT SALAD

2 (3-ounce) packages strawberry gelatin
2 cups hot water
24-ounce package frozen strawberries, thawed
2 large ripe bananas
20-ounce can crushed pineapple, undrained
8-ounce container sour cream
2.25-ounce package broken nuts
lettuce leaves

1. Dissolve gelatin in hot water.

2. Stir in thawed strawberries.

3. Mash bananas in separate bowl. Stir pineapple into bananas. Fold into gelatin mixture.

4. Pour into rectangular dish. Refrigerate for 8 hours.

5. Half an hour before serving, spread top of fruit salad with sour cream. Sprinkle with nuts. Cut into squares and serve on lettuce-lined salad plates.

PICKLED BEETS*

4 pounds fresh beets
1 clove garlic, sliced
a few thin slices of onion
1½–1¾ cups sugar, according to your preference
1 tablespoon pickling spices
¾ cup water
1¼ cups cider vinegar

1. Steam beets in small amount of water for 30–40 minutes, or until crispy tender. Do not overcook. Drain. Rinse with cold water. Peel and slice.

2. Place beets in four sterilized pint jars. Add garlic and onion slices.

3. Combine sugar, pickling spices, water, and vinegar in saucepan. Bring to a boil. Pour over beets, filling jars to within 1" of tops. Seal tightly.

*Refer to the USDA guidelines for safe canning methods: nchfp.uga.edu.

{
We had not been long upon our knees before I heard considerable scuffling and low talking. I raised my head up and saw one of the trustees (of the St. George church) having hold of the Rev. Absalom Jones, pulling him up off of his knees, and saying, "You must get up—must not kneel here."

Rev. Jones replied, "Wait until prayer is over, and I will get up and trouble you no more."

And we all went out of the church in a body, and they were no more plagued with us in the church.

—REV. RICHARD ALLEN
}

SALADS & Other Favorites

PICKLED EGGS AND BEETS

Dorothy Vancheri

MAKES 20–30 SERVINGS OF BEETS,
24 SERVINGS OF EGGS

2 cups water
2 cups white vinegar
1½ cups sugar
6 bay leaves
20 whole cloves
5 (16-ounce) cans sliced red beets, undrained
2 large onions, sliced into rings
2 dozen, hard-boiled eggs, peeled

1. Combine water, vinegar, and sugar in large kettle. Boil and stir until sugar is dissolved.

2. Stir in bay and cloves. Add beets. Chill for 8 hours.

3. Add onions and eggs. Refrigerate for 2–3 days before eating to allow spices to permeate eggs.

4. Serve beets and eggs together when chilled.

Thousands of my ancestors had waited, as I had done, for nightfall to cover their steps, had leaned on one true friend to help them, had felt, as I did, the very teeth of the dogs at the heels. It was simple. I had to be worthy of them.

—ANGELA DAVIS

GOLDEN EGGS

MAKES 8–10 SERVINGS

3 tablespoons prepared mustard
⅔ cup sugar
½ cup vinegar
1 cup water
⅛ teaspoon salt
8–10 hard-boiled eggs, quartered

1. In saucepan, combine mustard, sugar, vinegar, water, and salt. Bring to a boil. Allow to cool to room temperature.

2. Place eggs in container with lid. Cover with sauce. Refrigerate for 24 hours.

3. Serve cold or at room temperature.

GREEN TOMATO CHOW CHOW*

Inez B. William

MAKES 12 PINTS, APPROXIMATELY

2 gallons green tomatoes, ground
6 green peppers, ground
6 onions, ground
2 tablespoons cinnamon
5 cups vinegar
2 cups brown sugar
1 teaspoon salt
2 tablespoons cloves

1. Combine all ingredients in large kettle. Boil for 2 hours.

2. Transfer ingredients to glass jars. Seal while hot.

   *Refer to the USDA guidelines for safe canning methods: nchfp.uga.edu.

BREAD-AND-BUTTER PICKLES*

Emma Turney
MAKES 10-12 PINTS

4 quarts thinly sliced cucumbers
6 medium onions, thinly sliced
2 green peppers, chopped
3 cloves garlic, chopped
⅓ cup salt
2 bags ice
5 cups sugar
3 cups vinegar
1½ teaspoon turmeric
1½ teaspoon celery seed
2 tablespoons mustard seed
netting
large rubber band or sturdy string

1. Combine cucumbers, onions, green peppers, and garlic in very large bowl. Stir in salt.

2. Cover with ice. Place netting over bowl. Secure with large rubber band or string. Place another bag of ice on top of netting. Let stand 3 hours. Drain.

3. Place cucumber mixture in large kettle.

4. Add sugar, vinegar, turmeric, celery seed, and mustard seed. Bring to rolling boil. Cook until cucumbers turn green. Remove sliced cucumbers, but keep cooking syrup hot in kettle.

5. Spoon cucumbers and other vegetables into sterilized glass canning jars. Cover with boiling syrup, close with lids, and seal.

14-DAY SWEET PICKLES*

MAKES 8 PINTS

1 gallon sliced cucumbers
1 cup salt
1 tablespoon alum
4 cups boiling vinegar
4 cups sugar, divided
1 teaspoon celery seed
1 teaspoon ground cinnamon
1 tablespoon pickling spices
1 teaspoon whole allspice

1. Place cucumbers in large kettle. Add salt. Cover with boiling water. Let stand 6 days.

2. On Day 7, drain. Cover with fresh boiling water mixed with alum. Let stand 24 hours.

3. Drain. Cover with boiling water. Let stand 24 hours. Repeat and let stand for 24 hours.

4. Drain. Combine boiling vinegar, 1 cup sugar, celery seed, cinnamon, pickling spices, and allspice. Pour over cucumbers. Let stand 24 hours.

5. Each day for the next 3 days, drain liquid and reserve it. Bring to a boil. Add additional cup of sugar. Pour back over cucumbers.

6. On Day 14, drain syrup into a saucepan and bring to a boil. Spoon sliced pickles into sterilized jars. Cover with boiling syrup, close with lids, and seal.

*Refer to the USDA guidelines for safe canning methods: nchfp.uga.edu.

LET US BREAK BREAD TOGETHER

Let us break bread together on our knees,
Let us break bread together on our knees.
When I fall on my knees, With my face to the rising sun,
O Lord, have mercy on me.

Let us drink wine together on our knees,
Let us drink wine together on our knees.
When I fall on my knees, With my face to the rising sun,
O Lord, have mercy on me.

Let us praise God together on our knees,
Let us praise God together on our knees.
When I fall on my knees, With my face to the rising sun,
O Lord, have mercy on me.

This song gives location, time, and day. The breaking of the bread and drinking of wine refers to Holy Communion, which is taken at a church (location). Most people met for worship on Sundays (day of week). The time to meet— "with my face to the rising sun"—was sunrise.

BREADS

Till this day, I don't know anyone who makes yeast rolls like my mother. The holidays were always special because I knew there would be an abundance of freshly made yeast rolls on the table.

My mother's table was a work of art. Her finest china, sterling silverware, long-stemmed glasses, beautiful centerpieces . . . and serving dishes filled with the finest of "Mrs. Bailey's cuisine."

In Africa grain was an essential and pleasant staple in the diet. Here in America, the most common grain allowed was cornmeal, often served in the form of mush, given to the Africans to keep them healthy enough to work harder and longer. Frederick Douglass recalls that mush was placed in a trough, in the center of the room, and all of the enslaved children on the farm were to eat from it. Hopefully, you were big enough and strong enough to get your share.

— **PHOEBE BAILEY**

BREADS *Traditional*

- ❖ -

BUTTERMILK CORNBREAD

1 cup cornmeal
2 teaspoons baking powder
½ teaspoon salt
1 rounded teaspoons sugar
⅛ teaspoon baking soda
1 cup buttermilk
1 egg
2–4 tablespoons bacon drippings

1. Combine cornmeal, baking powder, salt, and sugar in mixing bowl.

2. In separate bowl stir baking soda into buttermilk. Add egg. Mix well. Add to dry ingredients.

3. Pour bacon drippings into iron skillet. Heat in 450°F oven.

4. Pour cornbread batter into skillet. Bake for 20 minutes.

- ❖ -

I sincerely regret the absence of statistics that would enable me to furnish you with many events, that would assist you in describing the operations of the Underground Railroad. I never kept record of those persons passing through my hands, nor did I ever anticipate that the history of that perilous period would ever be written.

—WILLIAM WHIPPER

OLD-FASHIONED CORNBREAD

MAKES 9–12 SERVINGS

3 tablespoons shortening
¾ cup sifted flour
1 tablespoon baking powder
1 teaspoon salt
3 tablespoons sugar
¾ cup cornmeal
2 eggs
½ cup evaporated milk
¼ cup water

1. Melt shortening in 8" square baking pan in 400°F oven.

2. Meanwhile, sift together flour, baking powder, salt, and sugar. Stir in cornmeal.

3. In separate bowl, slightly beat eggs. Stir in evaporated milk and water.

4. Remove baking pan from oven. Tilt pan in order to coat inside of pan with shortening, including the sides. Pour excess shortening into egg mixture and stir.

5. Add egg mixture to cornmeal mixture. Stir until dry ingredients are moistened. Pour into pan.

6. Bake for 15 minutes, until lightly browned.

CRACKLIN CORNBREAD

1 cup cornmeal
½ cup flour
¼ cup sugar
2 teaspoons baking powder
¼–½ teaspoon salt
¾ cup milk
1 egg
½ cup cracklins
¼ cup shortening, melted

1. Combine cornmeal, flour, sugar, baking powder, and salt.

2. Stir in milk and egg. Gradually stir in cracklins and shortening.

3. Pour batter into greased 8" square baking pan, cornstalk pan, or muffin tin.

4. Bake at 400°F for 25–30 minutes.

NOTE: Render sliced salt pork or bacon to make cracklins. To render, put salt pork in frying pan and cook until crisp. The cracklins are the crispy part that remains after the fat is cooked off.

BISCUITS

5 or more cups flour
½ cup sugar
4 teaspoons baking powder
2 teaspoons salt
1¼ cups milk
½ cup solid shortening
4 large eggs

1. Combine flour, sugar, baking powder, and salt until well blended.

2. Pour milk, shortening, and eggs into well in center of dry mixture. Mix with hands until eggs and milk are blended. (There will be some lumps of shortening.) Slowly work with fingertips until smooth. The finished dough should be soft but not sticky. Add additional flour if needed.

3. Turn dough onto lightly floured surface. Roll out to ½" thick. Cut into 3½" rounds. Place biscuits, slightly touching on greased 11" x 17" baking pan. Let stand in warm place 10–15 minutes.

4. Bake at 400°F for 20 minutes, until deep golden brown and light to touch when you pick them up. Break apart and serve.

BUTTERMILK BISCUITS

Mrs. Margaret Bailey
MAKES 2½–3 DOZEN BISCUITS

6 cups flour
2 teaspoons baking powder
1½ teaspoons baking soda
1¼ teaspoon salt
1½ cups shortening, at room temperature
2 cups buttermilk

1. Sift together flour, baking powder, baking soda, and salt.

2. Cut in shortening.

3. Make well in center. Add 2 cups buttermilk. Stir until just moist.

4. Knead 7–8 times.

5. Roll to ½" thick. Cut with floured biscuit cutter. Place biscuits on greased cookie sheet.

6. Bake at 450°F for 12–15 minutes, or until biscuits are lightly browned.

My mother made delicious potato rolls. As soon as they came out of the oven we were ready to eat them. They were made out of fresh potatoes.

—ANNA GANTT,
a member of Bethel AMEC,
Lancaster, PA

BUTTERMILK ROLLS

MAKES APPROXIMATELY 24 ROLLS

1¾ cups buttermilk
¼ cup sugar
2 teaspoons salt
¾ cup oil
½ teaspoon baking soda
1 package dry yeast
¾ cup lukewarm water
4½–5½ cups sifted flour
melted butter

1. Scald buttermilk. Stir in sugar, salt, oil, and baking soda. Cool to lukewarm.

2. Dissolve yeast in water. Add to buttermilk mixture.

3. Stir in enough flour to make soft dough. Knead until smooth.

4. Shape into rolls.

5. Place in greased pans or on baking sheet. Brush tops with melted butter. Cover.

6. Let rise in warm place until double in size.

7. Bake at 425°F for 15–20 minutes.

TASTY WHITE BREAD

Minnie Wilson
MAKES 2 LOAVES

2 eggs
4 tablespoons sugar
1 tablespoon salt
2 packages dry yeast
7 cups sifted flour
2 cups boiling water
4 tablespoons shortening, melted

1. Beat together eggs, sugar, salt, and yeast. Let stand for 10 minutes.

2. Stir in remaining ingredients. Set mixture in warm place and let rise until nearly double in size.

3. Shape into 2 loaves and place in greased bread pans.

4. Bake at 400°F for 12–15 minutes.

WHOLE WHEAT BREAD

Tamika Williams
MAKES 2 LOAVES

2 packages dry yeast
¼ cup molasses or honey
1 cup lukewarm water
1 tablespoon salt
¼ cup melted butter or oil
2 cups milk
6–8 cups whole wheat flour

1. In large mixing bowl, dissolve yeast and molasses in water. Allow to sit until bubbly.

2. Add remaining ingredients, saving approximately 1 cup flour to knead into bread.

3. Knead until dough stops sticking and looks smooth and shiny, about 15 minutes.

4. Place in greased bowl. Cover and let rise in warm place until double in size.

5. Punch down. Form into 2 loaves. Place in greased pans. Allow to rise until double in size.

6. Bake at 425°F for 10 minutes. Reduce heat to 375°F and bake for 30 minutes. Bread is done when a tap on the crust sounds hollow.

WHOLE WHEAT ROLLS OR BREAD

MAKES 9–12 SERVINGS

2 eggs, slightly beaten
1 cup milk
4 tablespoons shortening, melted
2 tablespoons brown sugar or honey
1 teaspoon salt
2½ teaspoons baking powder
1½ cups whole wheat flour

1. Mix together eggs, milk, shortening, and brown sugar.

2. In separate bowl combine salt, baking powder, and flour. Add to liquid mixture. Stir only enough to dampen dry ingredients. Let stand for a few minutes.

3. Drop mixture by spoonfuls into greased muffin tin, or pour into greased 8" x 8" baking pan.

4. Bake at 425°F for 20 minutes.

HOMEMADE ROLLS

MAKES ABOUT 40 ROLLS

2 packages dry yeast
½ cup lukewarm water
1 cup milk
7 tablespoons solid shortening
6 tablespoons sugar
¼ teaspoon salt
2 eggs
1 small cooked potato, mashed
5 cups flour

1. Dissolve yeast in water. Cover. Set aside.

2. Combine milk, shortening, sugar, and salt in saucepan. Scald. Cool to warm.

3. In large mixing bowl, beat together eggs, mashed potato, and yeast mixture. Stir in milk mixture. Mix well.

4. Stir in 1 cup flour. Continue adding flour until it can be turned onto floured board and kneaded. Place in large greased bowl. Cover. Allow to rise until double in size, about 60 minutes.

5. Form into small rolls. Let rise another 60 minutes.

6. Bake at 350°F for 10–15 minutes.

RAISIN BREAD

Hester Prince
MAKES 3 LOAVES

1 cup raisins
1½ cups boiling water
¾ cup butter (1½ sticks), at room temperature
¾ cup sugar
3 eggs
1 teaspoon cinnamon
4 cups flour
3 teaspoons baking powder
dash of salt
dash of nutmeg
1½ cups evaporated milk
1½ teaspoons lemon extract
grated rind from 1 orange or 1 lemon

1. Soak raisins in boiling water overnight. Drain.

2. Cream together butter, sugar, and eggs.

3. Sift together cinnamon, flour, baking powder, salt, and nutmeg. Add to creamed mixture.

4. Add remaining ingredients, including the raisins. Mix well.

5. Pour into 3 greased and floured loaf pans.

6. Bake at 350°F for 45–60 minutes.

HUSH PUPPIES

MAKES ABOUT 12 PIECES

cooking oil
2½ cups cornmeal
1 teaspoon salt
2 tablespoons baking powder
½ cup–1 cup chopped onions, according to your preference
1¼ cups milk, approximately
½ cup water, approximately

1. Pour cooking oil into deep skillet or deep fryer to a depth of ½" and heat to 360°F.

2. While oil is heating, combine cornmeal, salt, and baking powder.

3. Add onions. Mix well.

4. Blend in milk and water until dough is stiff enough to handle.

5. Shape dough into oblong, thumb-sized cakes. Drop into hot oil. Turn occasionally, until browned.

HUSH PUPPIES

Rina Mckee
MAKES ABOUT 16 PIECES

oil for frying
1 egg, slightly beaten
1 cup milk
2 tablespoons green onions, minced
1 cup white cornmeal
½ cup flour
¾ teaspoon baking powder
¼ teaspoon baking soda
¼ teaspoon salt

1. Heat oil to 375°F.

2. Combine egg, milk, and onions.

3. In separate bowl, combine cornmeal, flour, baking powder, baking soda, and salt. Stir into egg mixture.

4. Drop by 1½ tablespoons into hot oil. Cook for 3 minutes, or until brown. Drain on paper towels. Serve warm.

OLD SOUTH HUSH PUPPIES

MAKES APPROXIMATELY 3 DOZEN PIECES

½ pound onions, ground or finely chopped
¼ cup ketchup
1 cup canned tomatoes
1 small egg
½ cup buttermilk
1¼ cups yellow or white cornmeal
2 cups flour
3 teaspoons baking powder
1 teaspoon salt
½ teaspoon black pepper
oil
honey

1. Combine onions, ketchup, tomatoes, egg, and buttermilk.

2. In separate bowl, mix together cornmeal, flour, baking powder, salt, and pepper. Stir into liquid mixture.

3. Drop by tablepoonsful into deep oil. Fry until golden brown.

4. Serve with honey.

NOTE: These hush puppies are also good dipped in salsa, ranch dressing, or prepared mustard.

BREADS *Other Favorites*

CORNBREAD

MAKES 6-8 SERVINGS

1½ cups self-rising cornmeal
½ cup self-rising flour
1 teaspoon sugar
¼ cup shortening
¾ cup milk
1 egg

1. Combine cornmeal, flour, and sugar. Cut in shortening until mixture is crumbly.

2. In separate bowl, combine milk and egg. Pour wet ingredients into dry and stir until well mixed.

3. Pour into greased iron skillet or square baking pan.

4. Bake at 425°F for 25 minutes.

SOUTHERN-STYLE CORNBREAD

MAKES 5-6 SERVINGS

2 tablespoons bacon drippings
1¼ cups cornmeal
7½-ounce package corn muffin mix
2 teaspoons baking powder
1 teaspoon salt
1½ cups buttermilk
2 eggs, beaten

1. Pour bacon drippings into 8" square baking pan. Place in 400°F oven.

2. Combine dry ingredients. Stir in buttermilk and eggs. Mix until dry ingredients are just moistened.

3. Pour into hot pan.

4. Bake at 400°F for 25–30 minutes, or until golden brown.

William "Box" Brown (1816–1897)

A native of Virginia, William Brown decided in the 1840s that he should be free. With the help of a friend he devised an interesting scheme to secure his freedom. Prominent abolitionists in Philadelphia were contacted and with the help of a friend, Brown had himself put into a box which was then mailed to Philadelphia. After two days in transit, Brown arrived safe but fatigued in Philadelphia. He gained a reputation as an orator for abolition and often appeared with a box as a prop. He also performed as a magician. The last years of his life were spent in Toronto, Canada, not far from the expatriate communities created by freedom seekers who had found their way to Canada for decades before the Civil War.

BRAIDED EASTER BREAD

Mary Alice Bailey
MAKES 8-10 SERVINGS

2½ cups flour, divided
¼ cup white sugar
1 teaspoon salt
1 package dry yeast
⅔ cup milk
2 tablespoons butter
2 eggs
¼ cup raisins
5 hard-boiled eggs in their shells,
    dyed if desired
2 tablespoons butter, melted

GLAZE:
1 egg yolk
2 tablespoons milk

1. In large bowl, combine 1 cup flour, sugar, salt, and yeast. Mix well.

2. Combine milk and butter in small saucepan. Heat until milk is warm and butter is softened but not melted. Gradually add the milk and butter to the flour mixture, stirring constantly.

3. Add eggs and ½ cup more flour. Beat well.

4. Add remaining flour, ½ cup at a time, stirring well after each addition.

5. Turn bread onto lightly floured surface. Knead for 8 minutes, until smooth and elastic. Place in lightly oiled bowl. Turn to coat with oil. Cover with damp cloth and let rise in warm place until double in size, about 1 hour.

6. Punch down dough. Knead in raisins. Turn onto lightly floured surface. Divide dough in half. Cover and let rest for 10 minutes.

7. Roll each round into a long roll, about 36" x 1½". Twisting the two rolls of dough together, form a loosely braided ring. Seal the ends of the ring together and use your fingers to slide the eggs between the braided strands of dough.

8. Place loaf on buttered baking sheet and cover loosely with a damp towel. Place in warm place. Let rise until double in size, about 45 minutes.

9. Combine glaze ingredients and brush over risen ring.

10. Bake at 325°F for 50-55 minutes, or until golden brown.

MOTHER'S BREAD

MAKES 4 LOAVES

2 cups dry oatmeal
¼ cup brown sugar
½ cup molasses
2 tablespoons margarine, melted
2 tablespoons oil
1½ teaspoons salt
1 cup wheat germ
5 cups boiling water
2 packages yeast
1 teaspoon sugar
¼ cup warm water
4 cups whole wheat flour
5½-6 cups flour

1. Combine oatmeal, brown sugar, molasses, margarine, oil, salt, and wheat germ. Stir in boiling water and allow to soften for 15-20 minutes.

2. Dissolve yeast and sugar in warm water. Add to oatmeal mixture.

3. Stir in whole wheat flour. Mix well.

4. Stir in flour. Mix well. Knead 5-7 minutes.

5. Place in covered bowl. Let rise until double in size.

6. Knead and shape into 4 loaves. Place in greased loaf pans. Let rise again until double in size.

7. Bake at 375°F for 45 minutes. (If bread begins to brown too much, reduce heat to 350°F.) Remove from pans and grease tops with butter. Allow to cool before slicing.

COUNTRY CINNAMON ROLLS

Minnie Wilson
MAKES 1 DOZEN ROLLS

1 package dry yeast
½ cup warm water (105°F–115°F)
1 egg, slightly beaten
2 tablespoons milk
1 tablespoon sugar
3 cups buttermilk baking mix
2 tablespoons butter or margarine, softened
1 tablespoon sugar
1 teaspoon cinnamon
½ cup raisins

ICING
1 cup powdered sugar
1½ tablespoons water
¾ teaspoon almond extract

1. Dissolve yeast in warm water in large mixing bowl.

2. Stir in egg, milk, sugar, and baking mix. Beat well.

3. Turn onto well-floured board. Knead about 50 times.

4. Roll dough into 12" x 10" rectangle. Spread with butter.

5. Combine sugar and cinnamon. Sprinkle over rectangle.

6. Sprinkle on raisins.

7. Roll up tightly, beginning at 12" side. Seal by pinching edges of dough into roll.

8. Cut into 1" slices. Place slices, cut sides down, in well-greased muffin cups.

9. Cover. Let rise for 30 minutes.

10. Bake at 375°F for 12–15 minutes. Immediately remove from pan. Let stand 5 minutes.

11. Combine powdered sugar, water, and almond extract. Spread over rolls. Serve warm.

SUNDAY BRUNCH CHERRY NUT ROLLS

Minnie Wilson
MAKES 12 MUFFINS

⅓ cup butter or margarine, softened
½ cup brown sugar, packed
¼ cup chopped almonds
12 candied cherries
1 package dry yeast
⅔ cup warm water (105°F–115°F)
2½ cups buttermilk baking mix
2 tablespoons butter or margarine, softened
1/4 cup brown sugar, packed
¼ cup cut-up candied cherries

1. Combine ⅓ cup butter, ½ cup brown sugar, and almonds. Place about 1 tablespoon mixture in each of 12 medium muffin cups. Place cherry in each muffin cup.

2. Dissolve yeast in warm water.

3. Stir in baking mix. Beat well. Form into ball. Knead on floured surface until smooth, about 20 times.

4. Roll dough into 16" x 9" rectangle. Spread with butter. Sprinkle with ¼ cup brown sugar and ¼ cup cut-up cherries.

5. Roll up, beginning at 16" side. Pinch edges to seal. Cut into 12 1¼" slices. Place slices, cut sides up, in muffin cups.

6. Cover. Let rise in warm place until double, about 60 minutes.

7. Bake at 400°F for 15 minutes. Immediately invert onto baking sheet. Leave pan over rolls for a minute. Serve warm.

YANKEE DOUGHNUTS

Minnie Wilson
MAKES ABOUT 16 DOUGHNUTS

oil
2 cups buttermilk baking mix
2 tablespoons sugar
1 teaspoon vanilla
1 egg
¼ cup milk
¼ teaspoon cinnamon
¼ teaspoon nutmeg

CHOCOLATE GLAZE:
2 ounces semisweet chocolate
3 tablespoons butter or margarine
1 cup powdered sugar
¾ teaspoon vanilla
1–3 teaspoons hot water

1. Heat 3–4" oil in deep fryer or in kettle to 375°F.

2. Combine baking mix, sugar, vanilla, egg, milk, cinnamon, and nutmeg until smooth. Form into ball. Knead 8–10 times on floured board.

3. Roll dough ¼" thick. Cut with floured doughnut cutter. Drop rings into hot oil. Fry about 30 seconds on each side, or until golden brown. Drain.

4. Melt chocolate and butter over low heat. Remove from heat. Stir in sugar and vanilla. Add hot water, 1 teaspoon at a time, until glaze is of spreading consistency. Spread over doughnuts.

PARTY CRESCENTS

Minnie Wilson
MAKES 16 BISCUITS

2 cups buttermilk baking mix
½ cup cold water
butter or margarine, melted
celery seeds or sesame seeds

1. Combine baking mix and water. Form into ball. Knead 5 times on floured surface.

2. Roll dough into 12" circle. Brush with butter.

3. Cut into 16 wedges. Roll up each wedge, beginning at rounded edge. Place biscuits with points underneath on ungreased baking sheet. Curve ends of each biscuit to form crescents.

4. Brush tops with butter. Sprinkle with seeds.

5. Bake at 425°F for 10–12 minutes.

———◆———

April 1825—On my return I stopped at Lancaster; the Church (Bethel African Methodist Episcopal Church) was opened, and I preached to large congregations, and with powerful success; the dead were brought to life by the preaching of the cross of Christ. From there I left for Philadelphia.

—JARENA LEE,
first woman AME preacher

JAM DANDIES

Minnie Wilson
MAKES 8 SERVINGS

2 cups buttermilk baking mix
2 tablespoons sugar
½ cup cold water
½ cup jam or jelly
¼ cup finely chopped walnuts
2 tablespoons sugar

1. Combine baking mix, 2 tablespoons sugar, and water to make soft dough. Form dough into ball. Knead 5 times on floured surface. Divide in half. Pat or roll each half into 8" circle.

2. Place one circle in ungreased round layer pan. Spread with jam. Top with remaining circle.

3. Combine walnuts and 2 tablespoons sugar. Sprinkle over top of dough.

4. Bake at 400°F for 15–18 minutes. If the top begins to brown too much before the Dandies are done in the middle, tent with tinfoil.

5. Allow to cool for 10 minutes, then cut into 8 wedges and serve.

HERBY BISCUITS

Mrs. Margaret Bailey
MAKES 3–4 DOZEN BISCUITS

6½ cups flour
4 teaspoons baking powder
2 teaspoons salt
1½ cups (3 sticks) butter, cold
1½ cups milk
3 eggs
2–3 tablespoons dried herbs—basil, thyme, oregano, parsley, etc.

1. In large mixing bowl sift together flour, baking powder, and salt.

2. Cut in butter. Form well in center.

3. In separate bowl combine milk, eggs, and herbs. Pour into well in dry ingredients. Mix together.

4. Drop biscuits onto a greased sheet by tablespoonfuls. Bake at 450°F for 12–15 minutes, until biscuits are lightly browned.

YOGURT AND ONION BISCUIT SQUARES

Minnie Wilson
MAKES 9–12 SQUARES

2 cups sliced onions
½ teaspoon salt
dash of pepper
2 tablespoons shortening
2 cups buttermilk baking mix
½ cup cold water
1 egg
½ cup plain yogurt
¼ teaspoon salt

1. In skillet, sauté onions, ½ teaspoon salt, and pepper in shortening until onions are tender and golden. Set aside.

2. Combine baking mix and water. Form into ball.

3. Gently roll dough into 11" square. Pat firmly in bottom and up sides of greased 9" x 9" pan.

4. Spread onions over top.

5. Combine egg, yogurt, and ¼ teaspoon salt. Spread evenly over onions.

6. Bake at 425°F for 20 minutes, or until light brown. Cut into squares. Serve warm.

YOGURT AND CHIVES BISCUITS

Minnie Wilson
MAKES 10-12 BISCUITS

2 cups buttermilk baking mix
⅓ cup cold water
⅓ cup plain yogurt
1 tablespoon snipped chives or
    1½ teaspoons dried chives

1. Combine all ingredients. Form into ball.

2. Gently press dough out onto board into ½"–¾" thick circle. Cut with floured 2" round cutter. Place biscuits in greased round cake pan.

3. Bake at 425°F for 8–11 minutes, depending on the biscuits' thickness.

BLUEBERRY MUFFINS

MAKES 1 DOZEN MUFFINS

2 cups flour
⅓ cup sugar
2 teaspoons baking powder
½ teaspoon salt
1 egg, slightly beaten
¾ cup milk
½ cup (1 stick) butter or margarine, melted
1 cup blueberries

1. Combine dry ingredients.

2. Combine egg, milk, and butter. Add to dry ingredients. Mix until just moistened.

3. Fold in blueberries.

4. Spoon into greased and floured medium-sized muffin tin, filling each cup ⅔ full.

5. Bake at 400°F for 15–20 minutes, or until golden brown.

{ Lord, I remember when I worked from "can't see in the mornin'" to "can't see at night"—I remember the pain in my back from bending over so long. But, through it all, Lord, you kept me.

—*LIVING THE EXPERIENCE* }

WHOLE WHEAT MUFFINS

MAKES 1 DOZEN MUFFINS

1 cup whole wheat flour
¾ cup flour
1 tablespoon baking powder
1 cup sugar
1 teaspoon salt
¾ cup milk
¼ cup honey
3 tablespoons oil
1 egg

1. Combine all dry ingredients.

2. In separate bowl mix together milk, honey, oil, and egg. Stir into dry ingredients until they are just moistened.

3. Spoon into greased and floured medium-sized muffin tin, filling each cup ⅔ full.

4. Bake at 325°F for 20–25 minutes.

YUMMY HEALTHY MUFFINS

Minnie Wilson
MAKES 12 MUFFINS

2 cups buttermilk baking mix
1 cup whole-bran cereal
3 tablespoons wheat germ
2 tablespoons sugar
1 egg
⅔ cup milk
2 tablespoons molasses

1. Combine all ingredients. Mix well.

2. Grease bottoms of 12 muffin cups. Fill each cup ⅔ full.

3. Bake at 400°F for 15–17 minutes. Serve warm.

GRANOLA MUFFINS

Minnie Wilson
MAKES 1 DOZEN MUFFINS

2 cups buttermilk baking mix
1 cup granola
2 tablespoons honey
1 egg
⅔ cup milk
⅓ cup raisins

1. Combine all ingredients until well mixed.

2. Grease bottom of 12 muffin cups. Fill each cup ⅔ full.

3. Bake at 400°F for 15 minutes. Serve warm with butter and honey.

CHEESY MUFFINS

Minnie Wilson
MAKES 12 MUFFINS

2 cups buttermilk baking mix
2 tablespoons sugar
1 cup shredded cheddar cheese
1 egg
⅔ cup water or milk

1. Combine all ingredients. Mix well.

2. Grease bottoms of 12 muffin cups. Fill each cup ⅔ full.

3. Bake at 400°F for 15 minutes. Serve warm.

GIFT MUFFINS

Minnie Wilson
MAKES 1½ DOZEN MUFFINS

2 cups buttermilk baking mix
2 tablespoons sugar
1 egg
⅓ cup orange juice
½ cup orange marmalade
½ cup chopped pecans

TOPPING:
¼ cup sugar
1 tablespoon flour
½ teaspoon cinnamon
¼ teaspoon nutmeg
1 tablespoon butter or margarine, softened

1. Combine baking mix, 2 tablespoons sugar, egg, orange juice, marmalade, and pecans. Mix well.

2. Grease bottoms of 18 muffin cups. Fill each half-full.

3. Combine topping ingredients. Sprinkle over batter.

4. Bake at 350°F for 15–20 minutes. Serve warm.

SUPERMUFFINS

Minnie Wilson
MAKES 12 MUFFINS

2 cups buttermilk baking mix
2 tablespoons sugar
1 egg
⅔ cup water or milk
1½ cups Total cereal

1. Combine all ingredients except cereal. Mix well.

2. Fold in cereal.

3. Grease 12 muffin cups thoroughly. Fill each cup ⅔ full.

4. Bake at 400°F for 15 minutes. Serve warm.

HAM, CHEESE, AND RAISIN STICKS

Minnie Wilson
MAKES 2 DOZEN BREAD STICKS

½ cup (1 stick) butter or margarine
2 cups buttermilk baking mix
½–1 teaspoon dry mustard
⅔ cup raisins
½ cup finely chopped cooked ham
½ cup shredded cheddar cheese
½ cup cold water

1. Melt butter in 9" x 13" baking pan.

2. Combine remaining ingredients. Form into ball. Knead 5 times on floured board.

3. Roll dough into 10" x 6" rectangle. Cut in half lengthwise. Cut each half into 12 sticks, each about 3/4" wide. Roll each stick in butter in pan.

4. Grease a second baking pan. After all the sticks have been buttered, divide the sticks between the two baking pans and bake at 425°F for 15 minutes. Serve hot.

HOBO BREAD

MAKES 3 LOAVES

4 teaspoons baking soda
2 cups dark raisins
2 cups boiling water
2 cups sugar
4 tablespoons oil
½ teaspoon salt
4 cups flour

1. Combine baking soda, raisins, and boiling water in large bowl. Let sit overnight.

2. Add sugar, oil, salt, and flour to raisin mixture.

3. Divide dough between 3 greased and floured 1-pound coffee cans (paper labels removed).

4. Bake at 350°F for 30 minutes. Reduce heat to 325°F and bake an additional 30 minutes.

5. Remove from oven. Place cans on their sides for 10 minutes. Roll can to other side. Bread should slide out easily.

I remember when I was little and at home, my grandfather got the name "Coffee Bread," cause if he would drink coffee, he would dip his bread in his coffee. That was a favorite thing he would do. Dip his bread in the coffee.

—**SANDRA POLITE SIMMS**,
a member of Bethel AMEC,
Lancaster, PA

PUMPKIN NUT BREAD

MAKES 2 LOAVES

1 cup (2 sticks) butter or margarine, at room temperature
3 cups sugar
3 eggs
1 teaspoon vanilla
16-ounce can solid packed pumpkin
3 cups sifted flour
1½ teaspoons salt
1 teaspoon baking soda
1 teaspoon baking powder
1½ teaspoons cinnamon
1 teaspoon cloves
½ teaspoon nutmeg
1 cup chopped walnuts
1 cup dark or golden raisins

1. Cream together butter and sugar.

2. Beat in eggs and vanilla. Add pumpkin. Mix well.

3. Sift together flour, salt, baking soda, baking powder, cinnamon, cloves, and nutmeg. Blend into pumpkin mixture.

4. Stir in nuts and raisins.

5. Pour into 2 greased and floured 9" x 5" x 3" loaf pans.

6. Bake at 350°F for 60–65 minutes. Let stand 10 minutes. Remove from pan. Cool on rack before slicing.

NUTTY PUMPKIN BREAD

Hester Prince
MAKES 3 LOAVES

6 eggs
3¾ cups sugar
1½ cups oil
¾ cup water
3 cups cooked pumpkin
3½ cups flour plus 2 tablespoons flour
¾ teaspoon baking powder
3 teaspoons baking soda
1½ teaspoons salt
2 teaspoons cinnamon
1½ teaspoons ground cloves
2 cups chopped nuts
1 cup raisins

1. Combine eggs and sugar until thoroughly blended. Stir in oil and water and mix well. Stir in pumpkin until smooth.

2. In separate bowl, mix together flour, baking powder, baking soda, salt, cinnamon, and cloves. Stir into pumpkin mixture until well combined.

3. Stir in nuts and raisins.

4. Pour into 3 greased and floured 9" x 5" x 3" loaf pans.

5. Bake at 350°F for 45–60 minutes.

BAKE SALE PINEAPPLE BREAD

Minnie Wilson
MAKES 1 LOAF

2½ cups buttermilk baking mix
⅓ cup sugar
¼ cup (½ stick) butter or margarine, softened
2 eggs
8¾-ounce can crushed pineapple, well drained (reserve 3 tablespoons syrup and mix into batter)
½ cup chopped nuts

1. Combine all ingredients in bowl of stand mixer. Beat 2 minutes at medium speed.

2. Pour into greased and floured 9" x 5" x 3" loaf pan.

3. Bake at 350°F for 55 minutes. Cool 10 minutes. Remove from pan. Cool thoroughly before slicing.

William Still (1821–1902)

William Still was born in New Jersey but relocated to Philadelphia in 1847 where he worked for the PA Abolition Society. When the Fugitive Slave Law of 1850 was passed, he assumed the leadership of the Vigilance Committee of the Abolition Society. In that capacity he helped hundreds of freedom seekers who came to Philadelphia. He kept a record of every new arrival and published it as *The Underground Railroad* in 1872. In its pages, one finds some of the notable stories about the clandestine activity.

BANANA BREAD

Sharee Denson
MAKES 1 LOAF

2½ cups flour
½ cup sugar
½ cup brown sugar
1 teaspoon salt
3½ teaspoons baking powder
3 tablespoons vegetable oil
2 eggs
¾ cup milk
1 cup mashed ripe bananas
1 teaspoon vanilla extract

1. Combine dry ingredients in electric mixer bowl. In separate bowl mix together oil, eggs, and milk.

2. Mix wet ingredients into dry. Fold in bananas and vanilla.

3. Beat at medium speed for 3 minutes.

4. Pour into 9" x 5" x 3" greased and floured loaf pan.

5. Bake at 350°F for 55–65 minutes. Remove from pan. Cool before slicing.

Surely, God had put his curse not alone upon the slave, but upon the stealer of men! . . . The weed had been cut down, but its root remained, deeply imbedded in the soil, to spring up and trouble a new generation.

— FREDERICK DOUGLASS

SUNSHINE LOAF

Minnie Wilson
MAKES 1 LOAF

3 cups buttermilk baking mix
½ cup sugar
3 eggs
1 tablespoon grated orange peel
½ cup orange juice
1 package pitted dates, cut up
2 large bananas, mashed

1. Combine first 5 ingredients in large electric mixer bowl.

2. Stir in dates and bananas. Mix at medium speed for 2 minutes.

3. Pour into greased and floured 9" x 5" x 3" loaf pan.

4. Bake at 350°F for 60–70 minutes. Cool 10 minutes. Remove from pan. Cool thoroughly before slicing.

CARROT BREAD

Mrs. Margaret Bailey
MAKES 2 LOAVES

3 eggs, beaten
½ cup oil
⅔ cup honey
8-ounce can crushed pineapple, undrained
2 cups shredded carrots
½ cup chopped pecans, optional
1½ cups whole wheat flour
1 cup flour
1 teaspoon baking powder
1 teaspoon baking soda
1½ teaspoons ground cinnamon
¼ teaspoon salt

1. In large mixing bowl beat eggs with whisk. Add oil and honey. Whisk well.

2. Add pineapple, carrots, and pecans.

3. In a separate bowl stir together flours, baking powder, baking soda, cinnamon, and salt. Stir into wet ingredients. Mix well.

4. Pour batter into 2 greased 8½" x 4½" loaf pans. Smooth and level tops.

5. Bake at 350°F for 45 minutes. Remove from pan. Cool. Store a day before slicing.

NOTE: This bread is good spread with cream cheese.

APPLESAUCE BREAD

Minnie Wilson
MAKES 1 LOAF

2½ cups buttermilk baking mix
⅓ cup sugar
¼ cup (½ stick) butter or margarine, softened
2 eggs
1 cup applesauce
1 teaspoon cinnamon
½ teaspoon ground nutmeg
¼ teaspoon ground cloves
1 cup raisins

1. Combine all ingredients except raisins in large electric mixer bowl. Mix on low for 30 seconds. Beat at medium speed for 2 minutes.

2. Fold in raisins.

3. Pour batter into greased and floured 9" x 5" x 3" loaf pan.

4. Bake at 350°F for 55 minutes. Remove from pan and cool before slicing.

ZUCCHINI NUT BREAD

MAKES 2 LOAVES

3 eggs
1 cup cooking oil
2 cups sugar
1 teaspoon vanilla
2 cups raw, peeled and grated zucchini, drained
1 teaspoon baking soda
½ teaspoon baking powder
3 cups flour
1 teaspoon salt
3½ teaspoons cinnamon
1 cup chopped nuts

1. Beat eggs until foamy. Add oil, sugar, and vanilla. Mix well.

2. Stir in zucchini.

3. Sift together dry ingredients. Add to egg mixture. Mix well.

4. Fold in nuts.

5. Pour mixture into two 9" x 5" greased bread pans.

6. Bake at 350°F for 55 minutes.

HOBBY-BAKERS COFFEE-BREAKERS

Minnie Wilson
MAKES 12 ROLLS

¼ cup (½ stick) + 2 tablespoons butter or
   margarine, divided
⅓ cup brown sugar, packed
1 teaspoon light corn syrup
⅓ cup chopped pecans
1 package dry yeast
⅔ cup warm water (105°–115°F)
2½ cups buttermilk baking mix
¼ cup brown sugar
1 teaspoon cinnamon

1. Melt ¼ cup butter in small saucepan. Stir in
   brown sugar and corn syrup. Heat to boiling.
   Spread immediately in 15½" x 10½" jelly-roll
   pan. Sprinkle with pecans.

2. Dissolve yeast in warm water. Stir in baking mix.
   Beat well.

3. Form into ball. Knead 10 times on floured board.

4. Roll dough into 12" square. Brush with
   2 tablespoons butter.

5. Combine sugar and cinnamon. Sprinkle half of
   the mixture down center of dough.

6. Fold a third of dough over sugar/cinnamon
   mixture. Sprinkle with remaining sugar/cinnamon
   mixture. Fold over the remaining third of dough.

7. Cut into 4" x 1" strips. Twist two ends of each
   strip in opposite directions. Seal ends securely.

8. Place 1½" apart in jelly-roll pan. Cover. Let rise
   in warm place for 60 minutes.

9. Bake at 400°F for 15 minutes. Immediately
   invert onto heatproof tray. Leave pan over rolls
   for 1 minute. Serve warm.

FRONTIER NUT BREAD

Minnie Wilson
MAKES 1 LOAF

3 cups buttermilk baking mix
½ cup sugar
3 eggs
¾ cup milk
¾ teaspoon anise extract
¾ cup coarsely chopped walnuts or pecans
½ cup mixed candied fruit

1. Combine baking mix, sugar, eggs, and milk
   in large electric mixer bowl. Mix on low for
   30 seconds. Beat for 3 minutes at medium
   speed.

2. Stir in remaining ingredients.

3. Pour into greased and floured 9" x 5" x 3" loaf
   pan.

4. Bake at 350°F for 50–60 minutes. Cool for
   10 minutes. Remove from pan. Cool before
   slicing.

MONKEY BREAD

Carletha Akins
MAKES 10 SERVINGS

¾ cup granulated sugar
1 teaspoon ground cinnamon
1 cup chopped walnuts or pecans
3 cans refrigerated biscuits (8–10 in each can)

TOPPING:
¼ pound (1 stick) butter
1 cup brown sugar
1 teaspoon vanilla

1. Pour sugar, cinnamon, and nuts in paper or plastic bag. Shake to mix.

2. Cut each biscuit into quarters. Add a few biscuit pieces to bag. Shake until dough is well coated. Repeat until all biscuits are coated.

3. Pour coated biscuit quarters into a buttered tube, or Bundt pan. Arrange neatly.

4. Melt butter in saucepan. Stir sugar and vanilla into melted butter. Crumble over top of dough mixture.

5. Bake at 350°F for 25–35 minutes.

FRENCH TOAST

Rina McKee
MAKES 3 SERVINGS OF 2 SLICES EACH

2 eggs, lightly beaten
1¼ cups milk
1 tablespoon sugar
½ teaspoons vanilla
4 tablespoons (½ stick) butter
6 pieces bread, thickly sliced
warm syrup
powdered sugar

1. Whisk together eggs, milk, sugar, and vanilla.

2. Melt half the butter in heavy skillet.

3. Dip bread, a slice at a time, in egg mixture. Brown both sides of each slice in skillet, adding butter when needed.

4. Serve topped with warm syrup and powdered sugar.

{ You made mush by putting meal in water, stirring it up, and cooking it awhile. Then you put it in your bowl and poured milk over it. Some people knew how to make it good! When you were poor, you just used meal, salt, and water.

When my oldest brothers, Lawrence and Moses, went to school, the kids would say, "What did you have for breakfast?" They stretched it a little and said, "We had chicken and rice and all sorts of stuff!" Then the kids asked my sisters Mary and Martha what they had for breakfast and they said, "We had mush and milk."

Lawrence and Moses just went overboard! Now who eats all that for breakfast?!

—**FRANCES MORANT,**
Bothers & Sisters Cafe }

FOLLOW THE DRINKING GOURD

When the sun come back,
When the firs' quail call,
Then the time is come,
Follow the drinking gourd.

Chorus:
Follow the drinking gourd,
Follow the drinking gourd,
For the ole man say,
"Follow the drinking gourd."

The rivers bank am a very good road,
The dead trees show the way,
Left foot, peg foot going on,
Follow the drinking gourd.

The river ends between two hills,
Follow the drinking gourd.
Another River on the other side
Follows the drinking gourd.

Wait the Little River
Meet the great big one,
The old man waits—
Follow the drinking gourd.

This traditional spiritual was a map for escaping Africans, telling them to follow the Big Dipper and the North Star.

SOUPS

Daddy made the greatest soups. The memory of a bowl of Daddy's chicken and vegetable soup still warms my spirit.

In the slave quarters, where enslaved Africans lived in overcrowded conditions, too hot in the summer and freezing in the winter, the kettle pot sat in or over a small fire. In it was every piece of edible vegetable, and sometimes meat scraps, cooking. The pot was put on early in the morning, providing a source of nourishment, and sometimes comfort, for those who ate from it.

— PHOEBE BAILEY

SOUPS *Traditional*

HOMEMADE TOMATO SOUP

Mrs. Margaret Bailey
MAKES 4–6 SERVINGS

1 large onion, chopped
1 clove garlic, crushed
2 tablespoons oil
28-ounce can crushed tomatoes
2 cups chicken broth
2 potatoes, peeled and grated
salt to taste
pepper to taste
1 cup shredded cheese for garnish

1. Sauté onion and garlic in oil for 5 minutes.

2. Stir in tomatoes, chicken broth, potatoes, salt, and pepper. Cook 20 minutes or until potatoes are tender.

3. Ladle into bowls. Sprinkle with cheese just before serving.

TURKEY SOUP

MAKES 6–8 SERVINGS

3 cups cut-up turkey
1 cup water
2 cups diced turnips, optional
2 cups chopped celery
1 cup chopped onions
2 cups stewed tomatoes
2 cups diced potatoes
1 teaspoon salt
1 teaspoon pepper

1. Combine all ingredients in large kettle.

2. Cover and simmer for 1½–2 hours, or until vegetables are tender. Add more water as soup simmers if it seems too dry.

I don't know how we got ahold of it but we had an old abandoned refrigerator in our house, and it was full of Cheerios. We never ran out of cereal. We had Cheerios galore.

—BARBARA MCFADDEN ENTY,
a member of Bethel AMEC,
Lancaster, PA

CHICKEN AND RICE SOUP

MAKES 4-5 SERVINGS

2–2½-pound chicken
salt to taste
pepper to taste
5 cups water
1 cup uncooked rice

1. Cut chicken into small pieces. Season with salt and pepper. Put in large kettle. Add water. Cover. Cook on medium heat until chicken is tender, about an hour.

2. Remove chicken from broth. Debone and skim excess fat from top.

3. Add chicken and rice to broth. Season to taste. Cover. Simmer for approximately 20 minutes, or until rice is tender.

NOTE: Add 1 cup chopped celery when stirring in uncooked rice for additional flavoring.

PIG'S FEET SOUP

MAKES 4-6 SERVINGS

water to cover pig's feet
1 tablespoon vinegar
1½ pounds pig's feet
2 teaspoons salt
¼ teaspoon crushed red pepper
2 tomatoes, chopped
1 cup cooked lima beans
1 cup cooked corn

1. Combine water, vinegar, pig's feet, salt, and pepper in large stockpot. Cover, bring to a boil, and simmer for 1½ hours, until meat is tender.

2. Stir in tomatoes, lima beans, and corn. Bring to a boil. Remove pig's feet and debone.

3. Reduce heat. Stir meat back into soup. Cover and simmer for 15 minutes.

SOUPS *Other Favorites*

WASHINGTON CHOWDER

MAKES 8-10 SERVINGS

4 strips bacon, diced
1 medium onion, diced
2 ribs celery, diced
1 tablespoon flour
4 cups chicken broth
2 medium-sized potatoes, diced
2½ cups corn
⅛ teaspoon savory
¼ teaspoon dried thyme
1½ cups diced tomatoes
2 cups milk
salt to taste
pepper to taste

1. Brown bacon in heavy soup pot. Remove bacon and reserve drippings.

2. Add onion and celery. Cook until soft in drippings.

3. Sprinkle in flour. Cook, stirring for 3 minutes.

4. Whisk in broth. Slowly bring to a boil.

5. Add potatoes, corn, savory, thyme, and tomatoes. Simmer until potatoes are soft, about 25 minutes.

6. Stir in milk. Season with salt and pepper. Simmer for 20 minutes.

TOMATO AND RICE SOUP

MAKES 4 SERVINGS

1 pound beef stewing cubes
1 tablespoon shortening
2 cups water
2 cups stewed tomatoes
1½ teaspoons pepper
½ teaspoon salt
1 pound cut-up okra
¾ cup uncooked rice

1. Brown beef in shortening. Drain off drippings.

2. Add water, tomatoes, pepper, and salt. Bring to brisk boil.

3. Add okra and rice. Bring back to boil.

4. Cover and reduce heat. Simmer for 40 minutes.

We were so poor, Mother cut up her dresses to make dresses for my sister and me. Mother said that when she married she had 12 dresses with shoes and hats to match. After we children came, that was the end of her getting more fine clothing.

—ELIZABETH McGILL,
a member of Bethel AMEC,
Lancaster, PA

BEEF BARLEY MINESTRONE

Mrs. Margaret Bailey
MAKES 4 SERVINGS

- 1–2 meaty soup bones
- 6 cups water
- 2 onions, chopped
- 1 carrot, sliced
- 1 rib celery plus leaves, chopped
- 6-ounce can tomato paste
- 3 tablespoons regular barley, uncooked
- garlic salt to taste
- pepper to taste
- dried oregano to taste
- dried basil to taste
- 2 cups shredded cabbage

1. In stockpot, simmer bones in water for an hour. Remove from heat and chill until melted fat hardens on surface and can be lifted off. Discard fat. Trim meat off bones and reserve.

2. Combine all ingredients in stockpot except cabbage and reserved meat. Heat to boiling. Mix well. Cover and simmer for 40 minutes.

3. Add cabbage and meat. Simmer for 15–20 minutes more.

MINESTRONE SOUP

MAKES 6–8 SERVINGS

- 1½ pounds round steak, cut in 1" cubes
- 2 tablespoons oil
- 6 cups water
- 15-ounce can herby tomato sauce
- 1 onion, chopped
- 1 clove garlic, chopped
- 1 cup chopped celery
- 2 tablespoons chopped parsley
- 1 tablespoon salt
- ½ teaspoon dried oregano
- ¼ teaspoon pepper
- 1 cup broken, uncooked spaghetti
- 1½ cups sliced zucchini
- 10-ounce package frozen peas, partially thawed
- Parmesan cheese

1. Brown beef in oil in heavy kettle.

2. Add water, tomato sauce, onion, garlic, celery, parsley, and seasonings. Cover and simmer for 2 hours.

3. Add spaghetti. Simmer for 15 minutes.

4. Add vegetables. Simmer for 5 minutes.

5. Ladle into individual soup bowls and sprinkle each with cheese.

MINESTRONE WITH TORTELLINI

Carol Grassie
MAKES 10–12 SERVINGS

1 large yellow onion, cut into thin rings
⅓ cup olive oil
4 large carrots, peeled and thickly sliced
2 large potatoes, peeled and diced
1 green bell pepper, cored, seeded, and cut into
    ½" squares
3 medium-sized zucchini, diced
1½ cups green beans, sliced diagonally
5 cups (or 3 14½-ounce cans) beef stock
5 cups water
28-ounce can Italian plum tomatoes
2 tablespoons dried oregano
1 tablespoon dried basil
salt to taste
freshly ground pepper to taste
outer rind of a 2" chunk of Parmesan or Romano
    cheese
19-ounce can white kidney (or cannellini) beans,
    drained
1 pound uncooked cheese tortellini
grated Parmesan or Romano cheese

1. Sauté onion in oil for 10–15 minutes.

2. Stir in carrots. Sauté 2–3 minutes, tossing occasionally.

3. One by one, add potatoes, green pepper, zucchini, and green beans, sautéing each vegetable 2–3 minutes before adding the next.

4. Add stock, water, tomatoes with juice, oregano, basil, salt, and pepper.

5. Bury cheese rind in the middle of the soup. Heat to boiling. Reduce heat. Cover and simmer for 2½–3 hours. The soup will be very thick.

6. Fifteen minutes before serving, stir in cannellini beans and tortellini. Increase heat to cook tortellini, stirring occasionally to keep pasta and vegetables from sticking to bottom of pot.

7. Remove cheese rind. Ladle soup into individual bowls. Top with grated Parmesan or Romano cheese.

THREE-BEAN SOUP

Mrs. Margaret Bailey
MAKES 6 SERVINGS

1 large onion, diced
2 garlic cloves, minced
2 tablespoons olive oil
2 (14-ounce) cans beef bouillon
¼ cup dry rice
15-ounce can chickpeas, drained
15-ounce can red kidney beans, drained
15-ounce can white kidney (cannellini) beans,
    drained
2 tablespoons red wine vinegar
salt to taste
freshly ground black pepper to taste

1. In stockpot, sauté onion and garlic over medium-high heat in oil for 5 minutes.

2. Stir in bouillon, rice, chickpeas, and beans. Simmer for 20 minutes, or until rice is tender.

3. Remove half of soup and puree in blender. Return to pot.

4. Stir in vinegar. Season with salt and pepper.

———◆◈◆———

Race prejudice is the devil unchained.
—**CHARLES W. CHESNUTT**

BEAN SOUP

Wanda Davis
5½ QUARTS SOUP

½ cup dry great northern beans
½ cup dry kidney beans
½ cup dry navy beans
½ cup dry lima beans
½ cup dry butter beans
½ cup dry pinto beans
½ cup dry lentils
ham hock or beef soup bone
2 chicken bouillon cubes
28-ounce can diced tomatoes and juice
1 very large onion, chopped
4 ribs celery, chopped
2 garlic cloves, minced
3 bay leaves
2 tablespoons parsley
1 teaspoon dry thyme
1 teaspoon ground mustard
½ teaspoon cayenne pepper, optional
2 carrots, grated

1. Pour beans (but not lentils) into large stockpot and cover with water. Bring water to boil and allow to boil for 2 minutes. Cover, remove pot from heat, and soak 60 minutes.

2. While beans are soaking, place soup bones in another kettle and cover with water. Simmer meat for 30 minutes.

3. Add meat and its broth, and all remaining ingredients except carrots, to beans in large stockpot. Add more water if needed so that water is 2" above ingredients. Cook on low for 2–3 hours or until beans are tender.

4. Discard meat bone and bay leaves. Add carrots and additional water if needed. Cook for 15 minutes.

MUSHROOM SOUP

Mrs. Margaret Bailey
MAKES 4 TO 6 SERVINGS

1½ pounds fresh mushrooms
6 tablespoons butter, divided
1 medium onion, chopped
⅓ cup flour
4 cups chicken stock
1 teaspoon salt
¼ teaspoon ground nutmeg
white pepper to taste
1 cup heavy cream
whipped cream, lightly salted, for garnish

1. Wash mushrooms. Finely chop half of mushroom caps and all of the stems. Slice remaining mushroom caps.

2. Sauté onion in 5 tablespoons butter until translucent.

3. Add chopped (not sliced) mushroom caps and stems. Sauté for 3 minutes.

4. Stir in flour. Add chicken stock. Bring to a boil, stirring constantly. Lower heat and simmer for 15 minutes.

5. In a separate saucepan sauté sliced mushrooms in 1 tablespoon butter until they have given up their moisture but are not yet browned. Add to soup.

6. Season to taste with salt, nutmeg, and white pepper.

7. Stir in heavy cream. Heat.

8. Serve with a teaspoon of salted whipped cream floated on top of each bowlful.

BROCCOLI SOUP

Carol Grassie
MAKES 6 SERVINGS

4 tablespoons (½ stick) butter
1 small onion, finely chopped
1 rib celery, finely chopped
2 cups chicken stock
salt to taste
pepper to taste
1 small potato, finely chopped
3–4 cups finely chopped broccoli
1–2 cups half-and-half
salt, if needed
pepper, if needed

1. Sauté onion and celery in butter until tender.

2. Stir in chicken stock, salt and pepper to taste, potato, and broccoli. Cook until vegetables are tender.

3. Remove a few pieces of broccoli. Pour remaining cooked vegetables and ½ cup broth into blender or food processor. Puree. Return to saucepan.

4. Stir in half-and-half. Add reserved broccoli. Heat well, but do not boil.

5. Season with salt and pepper if needed.

ZUCCHINI SOUP

Mrs. Margaret Bailey
MAKES 4 SERVINGS

1 onion, chopped
10 ounces condensed chicken broth
2 cups boiling water
4 fresh zucchini, sliced
1 clove garlic, minced
4 tablespoons chopped fresh parsley
1 tablespoon chopped fresh basil or
    1 teaspoon dried
4 teaspoons grated Parmesan cheese
1 cup grated sharp cheddar cheese

1. Simmer onion in chicken broth for 5 minutes.

2. Stir in remaining ingredients, except cheeses. Simmer uncovered for 3–4 minutes.

3. Spoon into soup bowls. Sprinkle with Parmesan and cheddar cheeses.

VARIATION: For Creamy Zucchini Soup follow the recipe above, but reduce water to 1 cup. Simmer ingredients an extra 5 minutes until zucchini is very tender. Pour hot soup mixture into blender or food processor. Add ½ cup ricotta cheese to soup mixture and puree until smooth. Serve immediately.

VEGETABLE BROTH

Rina Mckee

1 gallon water
2 ribs celery, coarsely chopped
2 large onions, coarsely chopped
3 carrots, coarsely chopped
1 cup diced tomatoes
½ cup chopped cabbage
1 teaspoon minced garlic
8 stems parsley
1 turnip, coarsely chopped
salt to taste
pepper to taste

1. Combine all ingredients in large kettle. Slowly bring to a boil.

2. Reduce heat and simmer for 2½ hours.

3. Strain through colander, or puree in blender. Use as soup base.

———————◆———————

We used Arm & Hammer for toothpaste.

—**HATTIE MCFADDEN**,
a member of Bethel AMEC,
Lancaster, PA

CHICKEN SOUP

MAKES 4–6 SERVINGS

2 chicken legs
6 cups water
1 scallion, sliced
1 small piece ginger, peeled
1 tablespoon sherry
6 shiitake mushrooms
½ cup warm water
1 small bamboo shoot, sliced, or 1 (8-ounce) can bamboo shoots, drained
1½ teaspoons salt
½ teaspoon monosodium glutamate, optional

1. Boil chicken in water until tender. Debone and return meat to broth. Add scallion, ginger, and sherry. Bring water to boil, skimming off foam.

2. Meanwhile, soak mushrooms in mixing bowl in warm water for 10 minutes. Remove stems. Slice mushrooms.

3. Add mushroom and bamboo shoot slices to soup. Reduce heat. Simmer for 30 minutes. Remove ginger.

4. Season with salt and monosodium glutamate, if desired, and serve.

William Baker (1818–1892)

Born in Harford County, Maryland, William Baker's family had been enslaved for several generations. In 1845, he married a free African woman, Harriet Cole. When his owner decided to sell him, Baker and his wife fled to Columbia. In 1851, Baker was captured and sent to Philadelphia to be returned to his master in Maryland. Free African residents in Columbia raised $750 to buy his freedom. His wife Harriet mortgaged their house as collateral for the money raised by their friends. Baker was eventually able to pay his creditors and lived in Columbia into the 1880s. His wife Harriet was ordained in the A.M.E. Church and created at least two chapels, one most notably in Allentown.

STRACCIATELLA

Mrs. Margaret Bailey
MAKES 4 SERVINGS

4 cups chicken stock
2 eggs
¼ cup grated Parmesan cheese
2 tablespoons chopped fresh Italian parsley

1. In stockpot, bring chicken stock to full boil.
2. Beat together eggs, cheese, and parsley. Stirring constantly, pour the egg mixture slowly into the boiling stock. Cook 60 seconds or until the egg mixture is set.

CRAB SOUP

MAKES 12 SERVINGS

1 pound crabmeat
1 tablespoon prepared mustard
salt to taste
2 tablespoons Old Bay Seasoning
28-ounce can diced tomatoes
6 potatoes, diced
2 cups whole-kernel corn
2 carrots diced
1 cup lima beans
1 cup green beans
2 ribs celery, diced
½ cup chopped parsley

1. Cover crabmeat with water.
2. Combine mustard, salt, and seasoning. Add to crabmeat. Simmer for 30 minutes.
3. Stir in remaining ingredients. Simmer until vegetables are tender. Add additional Old Bay Seasoning if desired.

SHRIMP AND VEGETABLE GUMBO

Mrs. Margaret Bailey
MAKES 8-10 SERVINGS

1 cup chopped onions
1 cup chopped green peppers
½ cup chopped celery
1 clove garlic, pressed
2 tablespoons oil
1 bay leaf
½ teaspoon salt
¼ teaspoon pepper
28-ounce can tomatoes, undrained
13¾-ounce can chicken broth
10-ounce package frozen okra, thawed
½–1 pound large shrimp in shells
3–4 cups fluffy cooked rice
chopped parsley

1. Sauté onions, green peppers, celery, and garlic in oil in 6-quart Dutch oven. Stir over medium heat until celery is tender.
2. Add bay leaf, salt, pepper, tomatoes, and chicken broth. Mash tomatoes with fork. Bring to a boil, stirring frequently. Cover and simmer for 30 minutes.
3. Add okra to tomato mixture. Cover and simmer for 15 minutes.
4. Shell and devein shrimp. Cut in half lengthwise. Add to tomato mixture. Cover and cook for 3 minutes or until tender.
5. Spoon gumbo over ¼ cup cooked rice in each warm serving bowl. Sprinkle with parsley.

SHRIMP GUMBO WITH RICE

Rina Mckee
MAKES 4–6 SERVINGS

4 tablespoons (½ stick) butter
¼ cup flour
4 cups chicken broth
1 medium onion, diced
half a red bell pepper, diced
half a yellow bell pepper, diced
2 teaspoons garlic, minced
6 ounces okra, sliced
1 pound raw shrimp, peeled and deveined
dash Tabasco sauce

1. Melt butter in heavy stockpot. Whisk in flour. Cook over medium heat, stirring frequently until well mixed.

2. Add chicken broth. Bring to a simmer, whisking until broth is smooth and thickened.

3. Stir in vegetables. Simmer for 45–60 minutes or until vegetables are just soft.

4. Add shrimp and Tabasco. Simmer for 10 more minutes.

5. Serve over rice.

— ✦ —

I loved ketchup sandwiches.
—**BARBARA McFADDEN ENTY**,
a member of Bethel AMEC,
Lancaster, PA

SEAFOOD BISQUE

MAKES 12–15 SERVINGS

2 onions, diced
4 ribs celery, diced
2 tablespoons oil
12 shrimp, peeled and deveined
6 ounces fresh halibut
6 ounces fresh cod
6 ounces fresh red snapper
6 ounces fresh perch
2 quarts water
14½-ounce can tomato sauce
2 14½-ounce cans tomatoes
2 cans shrimp bisque
Old Bay Seasoning to taste
1 quart whole milk

1. In large kettle, sauté onions and celery in oil.

2. Add seafood and water. Bring to a boil.

3. Add tomato sauce, tomatoes, bisque, and seasoning. Simmer for 20 minutes.

4. Stir in milk. Bring soup to a simmer but do not boil. Serve immediately.

— ✦ —

NOTE: If you're budget-conscious, you may substitute any whitefish for the halibut, cod, and perch.

SEAFOOD SOUP

MAKES 8-10 SERVINGS

3 (10½-ounce) cans beef broth
14½-ounce can whole tomatoes
6 cups water
¼ cup chopped onions
2–2½ tablespoons Old Bay Seasoning
5 cups diced potatoes
2 10-ounce boxes frozen mixed vegetables
10–16 ounces fresh fish, crab, or shrimp

1. Combine broth, tomatoes, water, and onion in large pot. Bring to a boil.

2. Add seasoning, potatoes, and vegetables. Simmer for 1½–2 hours.

3. Stir in meat. Simmer for 15–20 minutes.

———◆✦◆———

Sins, like chickens, come home to roost.
— Charles W. Chesnutt

SALMON CORN CHOWDER

Mrs. Margaret Bailey
MAKES 6 SERVINGS

15-ounce can salmon
1 large onion, chopped
1 cup chopped celery
2 tablespoons butter
2 cups milk
2 cups chicken broth
10-ounce package frozen chopped spinach, defrosted and squeezed dry
17-ounce can creamed corn
1 teaspoon dried thyme

1. Drain salmon. Remove skin and bones. Flake. Set aside.

2. In stockpot, sauté onion and celery in butter for 5 minutes.

3. Stir in milk, chicken broth, spinach, corn, and thyme. Simmer for 15 minutes.

4. Stir in salmon. Bring back to simmer and continue cooking until heated through.

HARVEST SALMON CHOWDER

Mrs. Margaret Bailey
MAKES 4 TO 6 SERVINGS

7¾-ounce can salmon
1 clove garlic, minced
½ cup chopped onion
½ cup chopped celery
2 tablespoons margarine
1 cup diced potatoes
1 cup diced carrots
2 cups chicken broth
1 teaspoon salt
¼ teaspoon pepper
¼ teaspoon dried thyme
½ cup chopped broccoli
17-ounce can creamed corn
8½-ounce can evaporated milk
minced parsley

1. Drain and flake salmon, reserving liquid. Set salmon aside.

2. Sauté garlic, onion, and celery in margarine.

3. Add potatoes, carrots, liquid from salmon, chicken broth, and seasonings. Cover and simmer for 20 minutes, or until vegetables are nearly tender.

4. Add broccoli. Cook for 5 minutes.

5. Add salmon, corn, and evaporated milk. Heat well.

6. Sprinkle with parsley.

1825—I took stage and went on to Lancaster; but prospect not so good there; they had a new Church (Bethel African Methodist Church) but not paid for; the proprietor took the key in possession and deprived them of worshipping God in it. But I spoke in a dwelling house, and I felt a great zeal for the cause of God to soften that man's heart, or kill him out of the way; one had better die than many. Brother Israel Williams, a few days, called to converse with him on the subject, and he gave him the key; he was then on his deathbed, and died in a short time afterwards, and we must leave him in the hands of God, for he can open and no man can shut.

—JARENA LEE,
first woman AME preacher

BETHEL AME'S ANNUAL COOKOUT

Historic Bethel African Methodist Episcopal Church in Lancaster, Pennsylvania, holds an annual cookout, and it always includes food, fellowship, and fun—the primary ingredients for a great summer get-together! On a warm Sunday afternoon, after a spiritually uplifting combined service, we venture out to the churchyard, paying respect to the gravesites of the members of the past, those who served as pastors, those who served as conductors on the Underground Railroad, and those who served in the Civil War to fight for the Africans' freedom. We rally around for a word of prayer and thanksgiving, before we start competing for the first place in line for some of the pastor's famous ribs!

MENU:

Rev. Bailey's Famous Ribs
Fried Turkey
Fried Chicken
Hot Dogs
Hamburgers
Garden Salad
Potato Salad
Three-Bean Salad
Macaroni Salad with
   Hard-Boiled Eggs

Pasta Salad with Seafood
Pickled Red Beet Eggs
Baked Bean Casserole
Cakes
Watermelon
Fruit Salad
Plenty to Drink

Bethel AME Church's Vision—
To serve as Christ-centered, African-centered leadership for holistic community-building within ChurchTowne of the Seventh Ward, Lancaster, Pennsylvania.

SWEETS

————◆————

When my twin brothers went away to college in Connecticut, it was the first time they had been away from our mother. Every month Mama sent them a care package of her homemade cookies: chocolate chip, oatmeal, butter, and what she called her Fun Cookies, made with extra love.

My job was to protect the twins' cookies from everyone else in the family before Mama got them packed off. Naturally, I was rewarded for my hard work, in cookies, of course. My brothers turned out to be very enterprising. They started a "Mama's Cookies" business.

The women before my mother, who worked in the Big House, prepared the finest desserts and pastries for the plantation owner's family and guests. African women expressed their creativity on trays of sweet cakes, butter cakes, pies, and shortbreads. The sweetest thing the enslaved African desired, of course, was freedom!

— **PHOEBE BAILEY**

SWEETS *Traditional*

SWEET POTATO PUDDING

Carrie Alford
MAKES 10 SERVINGS

5 eggs, beaten
1 cup sugar
2 tablespoons butter or margarine, melted
3 cups grated raw sweet potatoes
2 cups milk
½ cup dark molasses
½ teaspoon salt
½ teaspoon ground cinnamon
½ teaspoon ground allspice
½ teaspoon ground nutmeg

1. Combine eggs, sugar, and butter. Mix well.

2. Stir in remaining ingredients.

3. Pour into 10" cast-iron skillet.

4. Bake uncovered at 375°F for 35 minutes, or until top is browned. Stir top crust under.

5. Bake an additional 25 minutes, or until knife inserted in center comes out clean.

6. Serve warm topped with whipped cream, whipped topping, or vanilla ice cream.

SWEET POTATO PIE

MAKES 6–8 SERVINGS

4–6 medium-sized sweet potatoes
½ pound (2 sticks) butter, softened
1½ cups sugar
4–6 eggs
2 tablespoons flour
½ cup milk
ground nutmeg to taste
9" unbaked piecrust

1. Boil potatoes until soft. Peel, then mash to smooth consistency.

2. Add butter, sugar, eggs, and flour. Mix well.

3. Add milk and nutmeg. Mix well.

4. Pour into piecrust.

5. Bake at 350°F for 1¾–2 hours, until lightly browned and set. Cool before slicing.

PECAN PIE

Brothers and Sisters Cafe
MAKES 1 9" PIE

½ cup brown sugar
½ cup sugar
4 tablespoons flour
1 cup corn syrup
3 eggs
1 teaspoon vanilla
1 tablespoon butter, softened
2 cups pecans
9" piecrust, unbaked

1. Combine sugars and flour.

2. Stir in remaining ingredients. Mix well. Pour into piecrust.

3. Bake at 350°F until firm, 55–60 minutes. If edge of crust begins to brown too much, cover it with a rim of tinfoil, while center of pie bakes sufficiently.

———◆◆◆◆———

One of my fondest memories of cooking with my mother (Margaret Bailey) is the first time she taught me to make pudding, the kind you had to stir and stir. I wasn't tall enough, so she pulled a chair up to the stove for me to stand on. I felt like a giant!

—PHOEBE BAILEY

PECAN PIE

MAKES 1 9" PIE

¾ cup light corn syrup
¼ cup light molasses
1 cup light brown sugar
1 tablespoon butter, at room temperature
¼ teaspoon salt
1 teaspoon vanilla
3 eggs, slightly beaten
1 cup coarsely chopped pecans
9" unbaked piecrust

1. Combine syrup, molasses, brown sugar, and butter. Blend well, but do not overmix.

2. Add salt, vanilla, and eggs.

3. Fold in pecans.

4. Pour into piecrust.

5. Bake at 350°F for 45–50 minutes, or until knife inserted in center comes out clean.

PUMPKIN PIE

MAKES 1 9" PIE

1½–2 cups mashed, cooked pumpkin
½ teaspoon salt
½ teaspoon ground nutmeg
2 eggs, beaten
12-ounce can evaporated milk
⅔ cup brown sugar
½ teaspoon cinnamon
3 tablespoons molasses
9" unbaked piecrust
whipped cream
cinnamon

1. Combine pumpkin, salt, nutmeg, eggs, evaporated milk, brown sugar, cinnamon, and molasses. Mix until smooth.

2. Pour into piecrust.

3. Bake at 500°F for 8 minutes. Reduce heat to 325°F. Bake for 50–60 minutes.

4. Cool to room temperature. Top with whipped cream before serving. Sprinkle with cinnamon.

PEACH COBBLER

MAKES 12–15 SERVINGS

½ cup (1 stick) butter, melted
½ cup milk
½ cup sugar
scant 1 cup flour
1½ teaspoons baking powder
½ teaspoon salt
¾ cup sugar
½ teaspoon ground nutmeg
½ teaspoon cinnamon
3 15-ounce cans sliced peaches, drained

1. Pour butter into 9" x 13" pan.

2. Combine milk, ½ cup sugar, flour, baking powder, and salt until a paste is formed. Pour over butter. Do not stir together.

3. Arrange sliced peaches in baking pan. Sprinkle ¾ cup sugar, nutmeg, and cinnamon over peaches. Spoon on top of batter. Do not stir together.

4. Bake at 350°F for 40 minutes or longer, until brown.

5. Serve warm with milk or ice cream.

SWEETS *Other Favorites*

BAKED HONEY PEARS

MAKES 4 SERVINGS

4 firm pears
2 tablespoons brandy or pear liqueur
2 tablespoons honey
3 tablespoons butter, melted
3 tablespoons half-and-half

1. Place pears in small baking dish.

2. Combine brandy and honey. Brush over pears.

3. Bake at 325°F for 45–60 minutes, until tender, brushing pears with brandy/honey mixture every 15 minutes.

4. Place pears on serving dish.

5. Combine butter and half-and-half. Briefly cook over medium heat. Pour over pears. Serve warm.

POACHED PEARS

Rina Mckee
MAKES 2 SERVINGS

2 firm medium-sized pears, peeled
1½ cups red wine
¼ cup sugar
⅛ tsp cinnamon
1 tablespoon brandy, optional

1. Combine all ingredients in small saucepan. Simmer for about 15 minutes, until pears are just soft.

2. Remove pears to bowl. Cool to room temperature.

3. Raise flame to medium heat. Reduce sauce by half, simmering uncovered for about 10 minutes. Cool. Pour over pears.

4. Cover and refrigerate for at least 2 hours before serving.

BAKED PEARS

Mrs. Margaret Bailey
MAKES 4 SERVINGS

4 small ripe pears, halved and cored
½ cup water
½ teaspoons vanilla
sprinkle of ground cinnamon

1. Arrange pears in shallow baking pan.

2. Combine water and vanilla. Pour over pears.

3. Sprinkle with cinnamon.

4. Bake at 350°F for 40–45 minutes or until tender.

NOTE: For a sweeter dessert, sprinkle pears lightly with sugar before baking.

PEAR AU CHOCOLATE

MAKES 8 SERVINGS

32-ounce can pear halves, chilled and drained
1 can chocolate frosting, or your favorite
    homemade frosting
whipped cream
cherries

1. Spread 1 tablespoon frosting in each pear cavity. Top with another pear. Stand upright in serving dish. Keep pears cool while melting frosting.

2. Melt remaining chocolate frosting in top of double boiler. Pour over pears.

3. Garnish each with whipped cream and a cherry and serve immediately.

GLAZED APPLE RINGS

MAKES 6–8 SERVINGS

¼ cup margarine or butter
4 apples, cored, peeled or unpeeled
½ cup dry white wine or apple juice
1 tablespoon lemon juice
¼ teaspoon ginger
¼ teaspoon cinnamon
½ cup sugar, or less, according to your taste
    preference
whipped cream, whipped topping, or vanilla ice
    cream

1. Melt margarine in 10" skillet over medium heat.

2. Slice apples in ½"-thick rings. Fry apple slices, a few at a time, in margarine until golden brown, adding more margarine if necessary.

3. When all slices have been browned, return all apples to skillet.

4. Combine wine, lemon juice, ginger, and cinnamon. Pour over apples. Sprinkle with sugar.

5. Cover and cook over medium heat, turning once, until apples are tender and glazed, about 5 minutes.

6. Serve warm, drizzled with remaining syrup, and with topping of your choice.

FRIED APPLES

MAKES 4 SERVINGS

4 apples, preferably still green
2 tablespoons butter
⅓ cup brown sugar
2 tablespoons water

1. Core apples. Cut into circles or slices.

2. Sauté in butter, turning often until soft, but still holding their shape.

3. Stir in brown sugar and water. Continue cooking until apples are coated wtih syrup.

———◆✕◆———

NOTES:
1. You may choose whether or not to peel the apples.

2. If you like more syrup, double the amount of water.

———◆✕◆———

My mother used to make cherry dumplings, and I helped her make them, too. You'd put them in cloth napkins and dip them in hot water and that's the way you cooked them. We didn't make them in the oven.

—NELSON POLITE, SR.,
a member of Bethel AMEC,
Lancaster, PA

FLUFFY CREAM SAUCE OVER FRUIT

MAKES 4–5 SERVINGS

⅔ cup whipping cream, unwhipped
⅓ cup sour cream
2–3 cups assorted fresh fruit (strawberries, sliced peaches, pineapple, or raspberries)
nutmeg or sugar

1. Whip cream, then gently fold into sour cream. Cover and refrigerate until ready to serve.

2. Prepare fruit in individual serving dishes, dollop with cream sauce, and sprinkle with nutmeg or sugar.

CHOCOLATE-COVERED STRAWBERRIES

MAKES 8–10 SERVINGS

1 quart fresh strawberries with stems
8 ounces sweet chocolate
1½ tablespoons Grand Marnier, optional

1. Melt chocolate in double boiler. Whisk in Grand Marnier.

2. Hold each strawberry by its stem and dip its lower half, or more, into chocolate. Place on sheet of waxed paper. Cool.

FRUIT PIZZA COOKIES

MAKES AS MANY SERVINGS AS YOU HAVE COOKIES

sugar cookies
frozen whipped topping, thawed
fruit, such as apples, kiwi, strawberries, blueberries, mangoes, peaches, grapes, bananas

1. Spread cookies with whipped topping.

2. Cut fruit into bite-sized pieces.

3. Arrange fruit on top of frosted cookies and serve.

FRESH STRAWBERRY MOUSSE

MAKES 8–10 SERVINGS

1 pint fresh strawberries
2 (3-ounce) packages strawberry gelatin
¼ cup sugar
1 pint whipping cream

1. Crush strawberries. Drain, reserving juice.

2. Add enough water to juice to make 1½ cups. Bring to a boil.

3. Add gelatin. Stir until dissolved. Cool.

4. Fold in crushed strawberries and sugar.

5. Whip cream until it stands in soft peaks. Fold into strawberry mixture.

6. Pour into 1½-quart soufflé dish with 2" collar and serve immediately.

DELUXE STRAWBERRY PIE

MAKES 6-8 SERVINGS

1 quart fresh whole strawberries, stemmed
9" baked piecrust
3-ounce package cream cheese, softened
8-ounce container frozen whipped topping, thawed

1. Stand whole strawberries upright in piecrust.

2. Combine cream cheese and whipped topping. Spread over strawberries.

3. Chill until serving time.

BAKED CHERRIES AND CUSTARD

MAKES 8 SERVINGS

2 cups pitted dark sweet cherries
3 eggs
1 cup milk
½ cup flour
¼ cup sugar
1 teaspoon vanilla
powdered sugar

1. Spread cherries in lightly greased 6" x 10" or 8" x 8" baking dish.

2. Beat together eggs, milk, flour, sugar, and vanilla until smooth. Pour over cherries.

3. Bake at 350°F for 45–60 minutes.

4. Sprinkle with powdered sugar. Serve warm.

CHERRIES AND CREAM ROLL

MAKES 12 SERVINGS

3 eggs
¾ cup sugar
1 tablespoon frozen orange juice concentrate, thawed
2 tablespoons water
1 cup cake flour
1 teaspoon baking powder
¼ teaspoon salt
powdered sugar
21-ounce can red cherry pie filling
2 cups heavy whipping cream
½ cup powdered sugar
½ teaspoon almond extract
fresh mint, optional

1. Beat eggs until thickened. Beat in sugar, 1 tablespoon at a time. Continue to beat until mixture is very thick and creamy.

2. Slowly add orange juice concentrate and water.

3. Sift together flour, baking powder, and salt. Gradually add to batter. Beat until smooth.

4. Grease 15" x 10" jelly-roll pan. Line bottom with waxed paper. Grease paper.

5. Pour batter into prepared pan, spreading gently to corners.

6. Bake at 375°F for 12 minutes.

7. Dust clean towel with powdered sugar. Loosen cake around edges with paring knife. Invert onto towel. Trim ¼" from all sides for easier rolling. Roll up cake and towel together. Cool completely on wire rack.

8. Drain cherry filling. Reserve cherries.

9. Beat cream until stiff. Fold in powdered sugar and almond extract.

10. Unroll cake. Spread with half of cream. Spoon ¾ of cherries over cream. Roll up cake. Place roll seam down on plate. Spread with remaining cream. Garnish with cherries and mint.

11. Slice and serve.

NOTE: Substitute blueberries or sliced peaches for cherries, if you wish.

PUMPKIN CHEESE ROLL

MAKES 10–12 SERVINGS

⅔ cup chopped nuts
3 eggs
1 cup sugar
⅔ cup cooked pumpkin
¾ cup flour
1 teaspoon baking soda
2 heaping teaspoons cinnamon

FILLING:
8-ounce package cream cheese, at room temperature
1 cup powdered sugar
4 tablespoons (½ stick) butter, softened
2 teaspoons vanilla

1. Sprinkle greased jelly-roll pan with nuts.

2. Combine eggs, sugar, pumpkin, flour, baking soda, and cinnamon. Spread over nuts.

3. Bake at 375°F for 15 minutes.

4. Loosen sides with knife and turn upside down on 2 sections of paper towels. Roll up. Cool for 1 hour. Unroll. Remove towels.

5. Combine cream cheese, powdered sugar, butter, and vanilla. Beat well. Spread over cake. Roll up.

6. Refrigerate until ready to slice and serve.

STRAWBERRY ROLL

MAKES 12 SERVINGS

4 eggs, separated
½ cup granulated sugar
1 tablespoon lemon juice
1 tablespoon water
¾ cup cake flour
¼ teaspoon salt
¾ teaspoon baking powder
1 teaspoon vanilla
¼ cup granulated sugar
powdered sugar
1 cup heavy whipped cream
2 cups fresh sliced strawberries
several whole strawberries

1. Beat egg yolks until thick and lemon-colored. Beat in ½ cup granulated sugar, lemon juice, and water until well mixed.

2. Sift together flour, salt, and baking powder. Mix into egg-sugar mixture. Stir in vanilla.

3. In separate bowl beat egg whites until soft peaks form. Gradually add ¼ cup granulated sugar, beating until stiff peaks form. Fold egg whites into batter.

4. Pour onto jelly-roll pan lined with greased and floured waxed paper.

5. While cake is baking, spread out towel and sprinkle with powdered sugar.

6. Bake cake at 350°F for 15 minutes, or until cake springs back when touched in center.

7. Immediately loosen cake from baking pan and turn onto towel. Cut rough edges off cake. Roll cake up in towel. Cool for at least an hour.

8. Unroll cake and remove towel. Spread cake with whipped cream. Sprinkle with sliced strawberries. Roll up again (without towel).

9. Refrigerate until ready to slice and serve. Place slices on individual plates and garnish each with whole strawberries.

PRUNE TARTS IN EGG PASTRY

Wanda Davis
MAKES 6-8 SERVINGS

3 cups flour
1 teaspoon salt, optional
1 cup shortening
1 egg, beaten
1 tablespoon cold water
1 teaspoon vinegar
flour
16-ounce package dried prunes
sugar to taste
evaporated milk or whipping cream

1. Combine flour and salt.

2. Cut in shortening until mixture crumbles coarsely.

3. Add egg, cold water, and vinegar until mixture forms a ball of dough.

4. Sprinkle flat surface with flour. Pat down pastry. Sprinkle flour on top of dough. Roll to ¼" thick. Cut into 6-8 rounds with cookie cutter or large glass. Shape into tarts and place on greased cookie sheet.

5. Bake at 350°F until browned. Remove from oven and cool.

6. Cook prunes and sugar in saucepan until thick and syrupy. Remove from heat and cool.

7. Cut up fruit.

8. Spoon fruit into tart pastries. Drizzle with evaporated milk or garnish with whipping cream.

APPLE DUMPLINGS

MAKES 8 SERVINGS

2 cups flour
1 teaspoon salt
2 teaspoons baking powder
½ cup shortening
½ cup milk
8 small apples
¼ cup brown sugar
¼ teaspoon ground nutmeg
2 tablespoons butter

1. Sift together flour, salt, and baking powder.

2. Cut in shortening. Add milk to make soft dough.

3. Roll out fairly thin. Cut into 4" squares.

4. Peel and core apples, but keep them whole. Place an apple on each square.

5. Combine sugar and nutmeg. Divide sugar mixture and butter evenly into centers of apples.

6. Pull corners of dough squares up over apples. Seal.

7. Bake at 375°F for 40 minutes. Serve hot or cold.

BAKED APPLE PUDDING

Minnie Wilson
MAKES 8-10 SERVINGS

⅓ cup margarine, softened
1 cup sugar
1 egg
1 cup unsifted flour
1 teaspoon baking soda
¼ teaspoon salt
¼ teaspoon ground nutmeg
¼ teaspoon cinnamon
1 teaspoon vanilla
2 cups grated unpared apples
½ cup chopped walnuts

1. Combine margarine, sugar, and egg. Beat until light and syrupy.

2. Mix together flour, baking soda, salt, nutmeg, and cinnamon in a separate bowl.

3. Gradually blend dry ingredients into wet ones.

4. Stir in vanilla, apples, and walnuts.

5. Pour into ungreased 8" x 8" baking pan.

6. Bake at 350°F for 35 minutes. Serve warm or cold, topped with whipped cream or ice cream.

BAKED APPLE PUDDING

Colleen Porter
MAKES 9 SERVINGS

½ cup shortening
1 cup sugar
1 egg
1 cup flour
½ teaspoon cinnamon
½ teaspoon allspice
½ cup buttermilk
½ teaspoon baking soda
1¼ cups pared, diced apples
½ cup broken nuts

1. Cream together shortening and sugar. Add egg. Beat well until creamy.

2. Sift together flour, cinnamon, and allspice.

3. Combine buttermilk and baking soda. Alternately add dry mixture and wet mixture to creamed mixture.

4. Fold in apples and nuts.

5. Pour into 8" or 9" square baking pan.

6. Bake at 300°F for 45–50 minutes, until a tester inserted in the center comes out clean.

{ Oh my, my mom made some slamming apple dumplings! I tried to learn how to make the crust and I could never do it and I watched her every time.
—BETTY CUNNINGHAM,
a member of Bethel AMEC, Lancaster, PA }

SWEETS & Other Favorites

FRESH APPLE SQUARES

MAKES 20 SERVINGS

1¾ cups sugar
3 eggs
1 cup oil
2 cups flour
1 teaspoon baking soda
1 teaspoon cinnamon
¼ teaspoon salt
1 cup chopped nuts
2 cups pared, chopped apples
powdered sugar

1. Combine sugar, eggs, and oil. Mix well.
2. Stir together flour, baking soda, cinnamon, and salt. Mix into wet ingredients.
3. Fold in apples and nuts.
4. Spread into greased 9" x 13" pan.
5. Bake at 350°F for 60 minutes. Cool.
6. Dust with powdered sugar.

BLUEBERRY DELIGHT

MAKES 15–18 SERVINGS

20-ounce can crushed pineapple, drained
1 can blueberry pie filling
1 box deluxe yellow cake mix
¼ pound (1 stick) butter, melted

1. Layer ingredients in greased 9" x 13" baking dish in order given.
2. Bake at 325°F for 45-–55 minutes, until lightly browned.

ORANGE PINEAPPLE DELIGHT

MAKES 16 SERVINGS

3-ounce package orange gelatin
1 cup hot water
1-ounce package dry whipped topping
3-ounce package instant vanilla pudding
1 cup milk
20-ounce can crushed pineapple, well drained

1. Dissolve gelatin in hot water. Cool until room temperature.
2. In a separate bowl, prepare whipped topping according to package directions.
3. In a large bowl, combine pudding and 1 cup milk. Mix well.
4. Fold gelatin and whipped topping into pudding. Mix well.
5. Fold in pineapples.
6. Refrigerate until firm.

BANANA SPLIT DELIGHT

MAKES 15–18 SERVINGS

2 cups graham cracker crumbs
5 tablespoons butter, melted + ½ cup (1 stick) butter, softened, divided
2 cups powdered sugar
2 eggs, beaten
5 bananas
20-ounce can crushed pineapples, drained
16-ounce container frozen whipped topping, thawed
½ cup chopped nuts
¼ cup maraschino cherries, halved or quartered

1. Combine crumbs and 5 tablespoons butter. Press firmly in bottom of 9" x 13" pan.
2. Bake at 350°F for 8 minutes. Cool.
3. Combine powdered sugar, eggs, and ¼ pound butter. Beat well. Spread over crumbs.
4. Slice bananas lengthwise. Arrange over creamed mixture.
5. Top with pineapples. Spread with whipped topping.
6. Sprinkle with nuts and cherries.
7. Refrigerate for 8 hours before cutting and serving.

FAVORITE FLAVORS IN LAYERS

MAKES 12-18 SERVINGS

2 cups graham cracker crumbs
5 tablespoons butter, melted
8-ounce package cream cheese, at room
   temperature
⅓ cup peanut butter
1 cup powdered sugar
1 cup frozen whipped topping, thawed
1 small box vanilla instant pudding
1 small box chocolate instant pudding
2½ cups milk
frozen whipped topping, thawed

1. Combine crumbs and butter. Press firmly in bottom of 9" x 13" pan.
2. Bake at 350°F for 8 minutes. Cool.
3. Combine cream cheese and peanut butter, mixing until well combined. Stir in powdered sugar. Fold in 1 cup whipped topping. Spread over crust.
4. Combine puddings and milk. Beat until thickened. Spread over cream cheese mixture.
5. Spread top with additional whipped topping. Refrigerate until ready to cut and serve.

BUTTERSCOTCH DELIGHT

MAKES 12-18 SERVINGS

¼ pound (1 stick) margarine, softened
1 cup flour
½ cup chopped walnuts or pecans
8-ounce package cream cheese, softened
1 cup powdered sugar
1 cup frozen whipped topping, thawed
2 small boxes butterscotch pudding
9-ounce container frozen whipped topping,
   thawed
½ cup chopped nuts

1. Combine margarine, flour, and ½ cup nuts. Press into bottom of 9" x 13" pan.
2. Bake at 350°F for 15 minutes. Cool.
3. Beat together cream cheese and sugar. Fold in 1 cup whipped topping. Spread over baked crust.
4. Prepare pudding as directed on box. Spread over cream cheese layer.
5. Spread 9-ounce container whipped topping over pudding. Sprinkle with nuts. Chill until ready to serve.

———◆◆◆———

Selfishness is the most constant of human motives. Patriotism, humanity, or the love of God may lead to sporadic outbursts which sweep away the heaped-up wrongs of centuries; but they languish at times, while the love of self works on ceaselessly, unwearyingly, burrowing always at the very roots of life, and heaping up fresh wrongs for other centuries to sweep away.

—FREDERICK DOUGLASS

HOLIDAY SQUARES

MAKES 28 PIECES

1½ cups sugar
1 cup (2 sticks) butter or margarine, at room
   temperature
4 eggs
2 cups flour
1 tablespoon lemon juice or vanilla
1 can pie filling, flavor of your choice
powdered sugar

1. Cream together sugar and butter until fluffy.

2. Add eggs, one at a time, beating well.

3. Add flour and lemon juice. Beat well.

4. Pour into greased jelly-roll pan.

5. Lightly mark off 2" squares. Place 1 tablespoons pie filling in center of each square.

6. Bake at 350°F for 35 minutes.

7. Sift powdered sugar over warm cake. Cool. Cut in squares.

LEMON SQUARES

MAKES 20 PIECES

½ cup (1 stick) butter or margarine, softened
1 cup flour
½ cup finely chopped salted cashews
1 cup powdered sugar
8-ounce package cream cheese, softened
½ cup chilled whipping cream, unwhipped, or
   frozen whipped topping, thawed
2 small packages instant lemon pudding
3 cups milk
1 tablespoon lemon zest
¼ cup whipping cream
lemon-peel curls

1. Combine butter, flour, and cashews. Press into 9" x 13" pan.

2. Bake at 375°F for 15 minutes. Cool.

3. Beat ½ cup powdered sugar and cream cheese together until fluffy.

4. Beat ½ cup whipping cream. Fold into creamed mixture. Spread over crust. Refrigerate.

5. Combine pudding, milk, and lemon zest. When thickened, spread over cream cheese mixture.

6. Whip ¼ cup whipping cream. Drop over tops of squares and garnish with lemon-peel curls.

CHOCOLATEY COCONUT SQUARES

Rebecca Carter
MAKES 25 SQUARES

¼ cup (½ stick) melted butter
1 cup graham cracker crumbs
1 cup flaked coconut
1 cup chocolate chips
12-ounce can evaporated milk
1 cup chopped nuts

1. Combine butter and graham cracker crumbs. Press into 8" x 8" or 9" x 9" baking pan.

2. Combine coconut, chocolate chips, milk, and nuts. Pour over cracker-crumb crust.

3. Bake at 350°F for 30 minutes. Cut into squares. Cool.

CHEESECAKE COOKIES

MAKES 25 BARS

⅓ cup brown sugar
1 cup flour
½ cup chopped black walnuts
⅓ cup (5⅓ tablespoons) butter
8-ounce package cream cheese, at room temperature
¼ cup sugar
1 egg
1 tablespoon lemon juice
2 tablespoons cream
1 teaspoon vanilla

1. Combine brown sugar, flour, and nuts. Cut in butter until mixture is crumbly. Reserve 1 cup mixture for topping. Place remaining crumbs in 8" x 8" pan. Press firmly.

2. Bake at 350°F for 12–15 minutes.

3. Cream together cream cheese and sugar. Beat in egg, lemon juice, cream, and vanilla. Pour over baked crust. Top with remaining crumbs.

4. Bake at 350°F for 20–25 minutes, until lightly browned. Cool.

5. Cut into squares. Refrigerate.

Today, slaves are too often portrayed as passive victims waiting to be led out of slavery. But long before the invisible Underground Railroad was organized, slaves in Colonial America had frequently escaped alone or with others from their owners to seek freedom.

—CHARLES BLOCKSON,
Hippogreen Guide to the Underground Railroad

SWEETS & Other Favorites

CZECHOSLOVAKIAN COOKIES

MAKES 4–5 DOZEN BARS

½ pound (2 sticks) butter, at room temperature
1 cup sugar
2 egg yolks
2 cups flour
1 cup chopped walnuts
1½ cups strawberry jam

1. Cream together butter and sugar. Add egg yolks. Mix well.

2. Gradually add flour. Mix well.

3. Fold in nuts.

4. Spread half of batter into pan. Press gently. Spread with jam. Spoon remaining batter over jam.

5. Bake at 350°F for 40–50 minutes, or until lightly browned.

6. Before bars cool, cut into squares.

SWEET POTATO PONE

MAKES 4–5 SERVINGS

½ cup sugar
½ cup (1 stick) butter, softened
2 cups grated uncooked sweet potatoes
½ cup milk
½ teaspoon salt
1 teaspoon ground ginger
¼ teaspoon cinnamon
¼ teaspoon nutmeg
grated rind of one orange

1. Combine sugar and butter.

2. Stir in sweet potatoes and milk. Mix well.

3. Add remaining ingredients.

4. Pour into shallow buttered baking pan.

5. Bake at 325°F for 60 minutes. Serve slightly warm.

William Parker (1821–1891)

Enslaved in Anne Arundel County, Maryland, William Parker escaped to freedom and likely settled in the area of Columbia, where he may have been involved in resistance to the efforts of Marylanders to recapture freedom seekers. Parker relocated to the vicinity of Christiana and on September 11, 1851, was the key player in the first armed resistance to the institution of slavery. Edward Gorsuch, a Marylander, had come to Parker's house to recapture men who had escaped his lands. Parker's wife Eliza alerted other Africans in the area and in the resultant melee, Gorsuch was killed and his son severely wounded. Parker escaped to Rochester, New York, where he found assistance from Frederick Douglass who was acquainted with him from his own years in Maryland. Parker settled in Buxton, Ontario, the community especially created for freedom seekers and became an agent for Douglass's newspaper. After the Civil War, Parker published his story in the *Atlantic* magazine.

SWEET POTATO SOUFFLÉ

1 (29-ounce) can sweet potatoes, drained
2 eggs
½ cup (1 stick) butter, melted
½–¾ cup sugar, according to your taste
    preference
1 teaspoon vanilla
⅓ cup evaporated milk

TOPPING:
¾ cup light brown sugar
½ cup flour
⅓ cup (5⅓ tablespoons) melted butter
¾ cup crushed pecans or walnuts
1 teaspoon cinnamon

1. Combine sweet potatoes, eggs, butter, sugar, vanilla, and milk. Mash together until smooth.

2. Pour into greased casserole dish.

3. Combine topping ingredients until crumbly. Sprinkle over casserole.

4. Bake at 350°F for 20–30 minutes.

BREAD PUDDING

2 cups bread cubes
2 cups milk
3 tablespoons butter, at room temperature or
    melted
¼ cup sugar
2 eggs, slightly beaten
½ teaspoon vanilla
dash of salt

1. Place bread cubes in buttered 1-quart baking dish.

2. Scald milk. Stir in butter and sugar.

3. Stir in eggs, vanilla, and salt. Pour over bread cubes.

4. Set baking dish in larger baking pan. Fill outer pan with water up to the level of the pudding.

5. Bake at 350°F for 60–65 minutes, or until knife inserted in middle of pudding comes out clean.

{
I remember my mother used to make rice pudding, and most people who make rice pudding nowadays don't bake it, but she used to always bake it with custard on top. None of us were able to make rice pudding like that. That's one thing I really miss.

—DORIS JOHNSON,
a member of Bethel AMEC,
Lancaster, PA
}

SWEETS & Other Favorites

CREPESELLE

Rina Mckee

Makes 4–6 servings

1 cup flour
2 eggs, lightly beaten
1 cup milk
2 tablespoons butter, melted
¼ teaspoon salt

1. Whisk flour into eggs.

2. Whisk in milk and butter. Add salt. Refrigerate for 30 minutes.

3. Oil or butter small skillet. Heat, then pour in batter, a scant ¼ cup at a time. Swirl immediately. Cook for 45 seconds. Turn and cook other side for 45 seconds, or until lightly browned.

4. Serve topped with syrup, jam, or cut-up fruit.

PECAN PIE

Mrs. Margaret Bailey

Makes 1 10" pie

¼ cup (½ stick) butter, softened
½ cup sugar
1 cup light corn syrup
¼ teaspoon salt
3 eggs, beaten
2 cups broken pecans
10" unbaked piecrust

1. Cream butter. Add sugar. Cream until well mixed.

2. Add syrup, salt, and eggs. Mix until smooth and blended.

3. Stir in pecans. Pour into piecrust.

4. Bake at 350°F for 55–60 minutes.

NECTARINE PIE

Mrs. Margaret Bailey

Makes 2 10" pies

6 cups sliced nectarines, peeled
1 teaspoon lemon juice
½ cup sugar
¼ cup flour
¼ cup water, or nectarine juice, or orange juice
¼ teaspoon nutmeg or mace
⅛ teaspoon powdered ginger or ½ teaspoon grated fresh ginger
2 10" unbaked piecrusts
1½ tablespoons butter

1. Combine all ingredients except piecrusts and butter. Mix gently but well.

2. Pour into piecrusts. Dot with butter. Top with pastry cutouts, lattice crust, or a crumb topping.

3. Bake at 450°F for 30 minutes, or until bubbly.

Your power is in your faith. Keep it and pass it on to other bloods.

—**MOLEFIKETE ASANTE**

MOIST 'N CHEWY BROWNIES

Marvin Murray
MAKES 40 BROWNIES

1 cup (6 ounces) semisweet chocolate chips
¼ cup (½ stick) butter or margarine
2 cups buttermilk baking mix
14-ounce can sweetened condensed milk
1 egg, beaten
1 cup chopped walnuts

1. Place chocolate chips and butter in greased saucepan. Stir over low heat until melted. Remove from heat.

2. Stir in baking mix, milk, and egg. Mix well.

3. Fold in nuts.

4. Pour into greased 9" x 13" baking pan.

5. Bake at 350°F for 20–25 minutes. Cool before cutting into bars.

SUGAR COOKIES

MAKES 7 DOZEN COOKIES

1¾ cups sugar
1 cup (2 sticks) margarine or butter, at room temperature
3 eggs
1 teaspoon baking soda
1 cup buttermilk or sour milk
1 teaspoon vanilla or coconut extract
4½ cups flour
2 teaspoons baking powder

1. Cream together sugar, butter, and eggs. Mix well.

2. Combine baking soda, milk, and vanilla. Add to creamed mixture. Mix well.

3. Sift together flour and baking powder. Add to creamed mixture. Mix well.

4. Drop by teaspoonfuls onto greased cookie sheet.

5. Bake at 400°F for 8–10 minutes.

SUGAR COOKIES

Minnie Wilson
MAKES APPROXIMATELY 6½ DOZEN COOKIES

2 cups (1 pound or 4 sticks) butter or margarine, softened
2 cups sugar
4 eggs
¼ cup milk
5 cups sifted flour
1 teaspoon baking powder
1 teaspoon salt
3 teaspoons vanilla
colored sugar, optional

1. Cream together butter and sugar. Blend in eggs. Add milk and mix well.

2. In separate bowl, stir together dry ingredients, except colored sugar.

3. Stir dry ingredients into creamed ones. Mix in vanilla.

4. Drop batter by teaspoonfuls onto greased cookie sheet. Sprinkle each with colored sugar, if desired.

5. Bake at 350°F for 12–15 minutes.

ENGLISH SEMIS

MAKES 3-4 DOZEN COOKIES

2½ cups flour
pinch of salt
1 teaspoon baking soda
2 teaspoons baking powder
½ cup (1 stick) butter, at room temperature
4 tablespoons sugar
2 eggs
1 cup sour milk
raisins

1. Mix together flour, salt, baking soda, and baking powder.

2. In separate bowl, cream together butter and sugar. Blend in eggs, and then milk.

3. Mix dry ingredients into creamed ingredients.

4. Roll out dough and cut with cookie cutter, or drop by teaspoonfuls onto greased cookie sheet. Place a raisin in the center of each cookie.

5. Bake at 350°F for 12–15 minutes.

MOLASSES CRUMBLES

Minnie Wilson
MAKES ABOUT 3 DOZEN COOKIES

¾ cup shortening
1 cup brown sugar
1 egg, beaten
¼ cup dark baking molasses
2¼ cups flour
⅛ teaspoon salt
1 teaspoon baking soda
½ teaspoon ground cloves
1 teaspoon cinnamon
½ teaspoon ground ginger
sugar

1. Cream together shortening, brown sugar, egg, and molasses.

2. Sift together flour, salt, baking soda, cloves, cinnamon, and ginger. Add to creamed mixture. Mix well.

3. Refrigerate for 60 minutes.

4. Shape into balls the size of walnuts. Roll in sugar. Place on greased cookie sheet. Do not flatten cookies.

5. Bake at 350°F for 8–9 minutes.

TOLL HOUSE COOKIES

MAKES 5–6 DOZEN COOKIES

1 cup shortening
¾ cup sugar
¾ cup brown sugar
1 teaspoon vanilla
1 tablespoon hot water
2 eggs
3 cups flour
1 teaspoon baking soda
1 teaspoon salt
12 ounces (2 cups) chocolate chips

1. Cream together shortening and sugars. Add vanilla, water, and eggs. Mix well.

2. Sift together flour, baking soda, and salt. Add to creamed mixture. Mix well.

3. Stir in chocolate chips.

4. Drop by teaspoonfuls onto greased cookie sheets.

5. Bake at 350°F for 10–12 minutes, being careful not to overbake.

MONSTER COOKIES

MAKES ABOUT 11 DOZEN 2" COOKIES

2 cups brown sugar
½ tablespoons corn syrup
1 cup (2 sticks) margarine, at room temperature
24 ounces peanut butter
6 eggs
½ tablespoons vanilla
4 teaspoons baking soda
2 cups flour
5 cups quick oats
8 ounces chocolate chips
8 ounces M&M's

1. Cream together brown sugar, corn syrup, margarine, and peanut butter. Add eggs and vanilla. Mix well.

2. Mix together baking soda, flour, and oats. Add to creamed mixture. Mix well.

3. Stir in chocolate chips and candy. Mix thoroughly.

4. Drop by tablespoonfuls onto greased cookie sheet.

5. Bake at 350°F for 10 minutes.

{ I remember my mother preparing the food to make jelly preserve. She had this bag she would put the fruit inside of and squeeze and squeeze, and we'd help her do that. She always made all types of preserves. We never ran out.

—ANNA GANTT,
a member of Bethel AMEC,
Lancaster, PA }

LASSERS COOKIES

Minnie Wilson
MAKES 2 DOZEN COOKIES

½ cup corn syrup
⅔ cup sugar
½ cup (1 stick) margarine or butter
1 cup flour
1 cup chopped nuts or flaked coconut

1. Bring corn syrup, sugar, and margarine to boil in double boiler. Remove from heat.

2. Stir in remaining ingredients.

3. Drop by teaspoonfuls onto greased cookie sheet.

4. Bake at 325°F for 12–15 minutes. Cool completely before lifting from cookie sheet. Use a metal spatula and work carefully to remove.

SAND TARTS

MAKES 2½ DOZEN COOKIES

½ cup (1 stick) butter, softened
1 cup and 1 tablespoon sugar, divided
2 eggs, separated
1 tablespoon milk
½ teaspoon vanilla extract
1½ cups flour
½ teaspoon salt
1 teaspoon baking powder
¼ teaspoon cinnamon
15 unblanched almonds, split

1. Cream together butter and 1 cup sugar. Add egg yolks, milk, and vanilla. Beat until light and fluffy.

2. Sift together flour, salt, and baking powder. Add to creamed mixture. Mix well. Chill for at least 3 hours.

3. Roll out dough very thinly. Cut with 3" cookie cutters. Place on greased cookie sheet.

4. Brush tops of cookies with reserved egg whites. Combine cinnamon and 1 tablespoon sugar. Decorate cookies with almonds and sprinkle with cinnamon/sugar mixture.

5. Bake at 375°F for 8 minutes.

RUM BALLS

MAKES ABOUT 28 PIECES

1 cup finely crushed vanilla wafers
1 cup powdered sugar
1 cup chopped nuts
2 tablespoons cocoa powder
2 tablespoons light corn syrup
3–4 tablespoons rum
½ cup fine granulated sugar
½ cup finely chopped nuts
6-ounce jar maraschino cherries, with cherries cut into halves
corn syrup

1. Combine crushed wafers, sugar, nuts, and cocoa powder.

2. Stir in 2 tablespoons syrup and rum. Mix well.

3. Shape into 1" balls.

4. Roll half the balls in sugar and the other half in nuts.

5. Spread cut sides of cherry halves with corn syrup. Press one cherry half on each ball.

FRENCH CREMES

MAKES ABOUT 4 DOZEN COOKIES

1½ cups (3 sticks) butter, at room temperature
1 cup powdered sugar
⅓ cup orange juice
2 tablespoons whiskey
1 teaspoon baking powder
2¾ cups flour
powdered sugar

1. Cream together butter and 1 cup sugar.

2. Add orange juice. Mix well.

3. Add whiskey. Mix well.

4. Stir together baking powder and flour. Mix into batter.

5. Drop by half-teaspoonfuls onto greased cookie sheet, or form into small balls and flatten on greased cookie sheet.

6. Bake at 325°F for 10–12 minutes, or until light brown. Cool.

7. Sift powdered sugar over cooled cookies.

DANISH COOKIES

MAKES ABOUT 2 DOZEN COOKIES

2 cups flour
¾ cup (1½ sticks) margarine or butter, softened
⅓ cup sugar
½ teaspoon salt
2 eggs
⅓ cup jam

VANILLA FROSTING:
1 cup powdered sugar
1 tablespoon margarine or butter
1 tablespoon plus 1 teaspoon milk
¼ teaspoon vanilla

1. Combine flour, ¾ cup margarine, ⅓ cup sugar, salt, and eggs.

2. Roll dough ⅛" thick on lightly floured board. Cut into 2" circles. Place on greased cookie sheet.

3. Bake at 375°F for 8–10 minutes. Cool.

4. Cream together powdered sugar, margarine, milk, and vanilla until smooth.

5. Spread jam between two cookies to form sandwich. Spread tops of each sandwich with frosting.

ITALIAN SWEETS

2½ cups flour
1 cup sugar
2 teaspoons baking powder
½ teaspoon salt
¼ cup (½ stick) margarine or butter, softened
1 egg, separated
1 teaspoon almond extract
½ cup whipping cream, unwhipped
1¾ cups powdered sugar
½ teaspoon almond extract
½ cup chopped almonds
¼ cup cut-up red candied cherries
¼ cup cut-up green candied cherries

1. Combine flour, 1 cup sugar, baking powder, salt, margarine, egg yolk, 1 teaspoon extract, and whipping cream. Mix well. Cover. Refrigerate for 60 minutes.

2. Divide dough in half. Roll each half into 8" x 6" rectangle on well-floured board. Square off corners. Lift onto greased cookie sheet.

3. Beat egg white until foamy. Fold in powdered sugar and 1/2 teaspoon extract. Beat until stiff and glossy. Spread over dough.

4. Arrange almonds and cherries over tops of two rectangles.

5. Bake at 375°F for 10 minutes, until edges are light brown.

6. Cut into strips 2" x 1". Cool.

SCOTCH SHORTBREAD

Lora C. Wayne
MAKES 2½ DOZEN COOKIES

1 cup (2 sticks) butter (no substitutions), at room temperature
½ cup brown sugar
2½ cups sifted flour

1. Cream together butter and sugar. Stir in flour. Mix well with hands. Chill.

2. Shape into 1" balls. Place on ungreased cookie sheet. Press crisscross design on top of each cookie with floured fork.

3. Bake at 300°F for 20–25 minutes.

The songs of the slave represent the sorrows of his heart; and he is relieved by them, only as an aching heart is relieved by its tears.

—FREDERICK DOUGLASS

HONEY ICE CREAM

Mrs. Margaret Bailey
MAKES 1 QUART ICE CREAM

2+ cups milk
1 vanilla bean, split open lengthwise
¼ cup honey
6 egg yolks
generous ⅔ cup granulated sugar
1+ cup heavy cream

1. Place milk, vanilla bean, and honey in saucepan. Slowly bring to a boil, stirring to dissolve the honey.

2. In a mixing bowl, beat egg yolks and sugar until mixture whitens and forms a ribbon.

3. Pour a bit of the hot liquid into egg/sugar mixture, whisking constantly. Remove saucepan from heat. Pour egg/sugar mixture into milk mixture, stirring constantly.

4. Return saucepan to low heat and cook, stirring constantly until temperature on candy thermometer reaches 185°F (5–10 minutes). Do not boil. Remove from heat. Continue stirring for 1–2 more minutes.

5. Remove vanilla bean.

6. Add heavy cream. Mix well.

7. Cool completely before pouring into ice cream freezer. Run the ice-cream maker according to manufacturer's directions.

CHOCOLATE FUDGE

MAKES 5–6 DOZEN PIECES

4½ cups sugar
12-ounce can evaporated milk
¼ cup (½ stick) butter
dash of salt
½ teaspoon vanilla
16-ounce chocolate bar, grated
2 packages chocolate chips
2 squares unsweetened chocolate
1 pint marshmallow cream
2 cups chopped walnuts

1. Combine sugar, milk, butter, and salt in saucepan. Boil 10 minutes.

2. Stir in vanilla.

3. Combine remaining ingredients. Pour hot ingredients over chocolate-marshmallow-nut mixture. Beat until completely melted together.

4. Pour onto lightly greased jelly-roll pan. Chill.

5. Cut and store in covered tins.

CHOCOLATE PEANUT BUTTER FUDGE

MAKES ABOUT 2 DOZEN PIECES

½ pound (2 sticks) butter
4 tablespoons peanut butter
1 teaspoon vanilla
1 pound powdered sugar, sifted
3 tablespoons cocoa powder

1. Melt butter. Stir in peanut butter and vanilla.
2. Add powdered sugar and cocoa powder. Mix well.
3. Pour into 9" x 13" pan. Refrigerate.
4. When well chilled, cut into pieces.

CREAM CHEESE FUDGE

Minnie Wilson
MAKES 20-25 PIECES

3-ounce package cream cheese, softened to room temperature
2½ cups sifted powdered sugar
2 tablespoons peanut butter
¼ teaspoon vanilla
dash of salt
¼ cup chopped salted peanuts, optional

1. Beat cream cheese until soft and smooth.
2. Slowly fold in sugar.
3. Stir in peanut butter. Mix well.
4. Add vanilla, salt, and nuts. Mix until just blended.
5. Press into well-greased 8" x 8" pan. Refrigerate for 15 minutes. Cut into squares.

BIG BATCH NO-COOK FUDGE

MAKES ABOUT 4 DOZEN PIECES

7 cups (about 2 1-pound boxes) powdered sugar
½ cup cocoa powder
3⅓ sticks margarine, melted
2 tablespoons vanilla
12-ounce jar peanut butter, crunchy or smooth

1. Combine sugar and cocoa powder.
2. Stir in margarine, vanilla, and peanut butter. Mix well.
3. Press into 9" x 13" greased pan.
4. Cool in refrigerator before cutting and serving.

OPERA FUDGE

MAKES ABOUT 5½ DOZEN PIECES

2 pounds powdered sugar
8-ounce package cream cheese, softened
¼ pound (1 stick) butter, softened
1 teaspoon vanilla
4 squares unsweetened chocolate
⅓ of a ¼-pound bar food-grade paraffin

1. Combine powdered sugar, cream cheese, butter, and vanilla.
2. Roll into small balls. Refrigerate for 8 hours.
3. Heat chocolate and paraffin over low heat until melted.
4. Dip candy into chocolate. Place on waxed paper to cool.

PEANUT BUTTER EASTER EGGS

MAKES ABOUT 4 DOZEN EGGS

18-ounce jar peanut butter
¼ pound (1 stick) butter or margarine, at room temperature
3 pounds powdered sugar
pinch of salt
1 tablespoon vanilla
½ cup evaporated milk, approximately
2¼ cups semisweet chocolate chips
⅔ of a ¼-pound bar food-grade paraffin
chopped peanuts, coconut flakes, or candy sprinkles, optional

1. In large bowl, knead together peanut butter, butter, sugar, salt, and vanilla. Add milk to soften dough to pliable texture, but firm enough to take egg-shape. Form into eggs, each about 2 tablespoons in size.

2. Melt chocolate chips and paraffin together in top of double boiler.

3. Spear eggs, one at a time, and quickly dip into chocolate to coat. Let cool, then dip a second time. Let cool, and dip a third time, so the coating is not too thin.

4. Before final chocolate coating sets, sprinkle each egg with chopped peanuts, coconut flakes, or candy sprinkles, if you wish.

PEANUT BRITTLE

MAKES 2 LARGE SHEETS

2 cups sugar
1 cup light corn syrup
½ cup water
½ teaspoons salt
1 teaspoon butter
3 cups raw Spanish peanuts or whole peanuts
2 teaspoons baking soda

1. In large saucepan, boil sugar, corn syrup, water, and salt together until mixture reaches 236°F and forms a thread.

2. Stir in butter and peanuts. Cook, stirring constantly, until mixture reaches 290°F and becomes golden brown.

3. Remove from heat. Stir in baking soda. Mix well until candy thickens.

4. Pour onto greased baking sheets. As mixture cools, spread as thinly as possible. Cool.

5. Break into pieces. Store in airtight container.

{ I remember the special luncheons my mother gave for her church friends. She would put out her finest china. She would fill the platters with wonderful delights, such as crepes filled with a fruit puree, topped with fresh fruit and homemade whipped cream. My favorite was her upside-down pineapple cake and watermelon boats.

—CORNELIA BYNUM }

SWEETS & Other Favorites

A NEWLY FREED MAN'S PRAYER

Dear Father, I come before you today with thanks in my heart for everything you have done for me. Thank you for allowing me to live as a free man just one more day. Thank you for all the things you have done for me in my life. I pray to you, Father, that I remain your humble servant and that I never think more of myself than I ought.

I pray, Father, that I will always remember that it was your grace and mercy which allowed me to reach the position I am currently in. I thank you, Father, for allowing Thomas Boude to set the price for my freedom at only 50 dollars. I thank you for giving me strength to work off my bondage in less than one year. I thank you for the gift of wisdom which enabled me to prosper in my first lumber business. I thank you for leading me to choose such an excellent wife as Harriet Lee.

Please, Father, keep fresh in my mind how it felt to be enslaved. If you do this, Father, I know I will continue with all of my strength and might to fight against this system for all of my people who are still being subjected to living as someone else's property. If you keep this fresh in my mind, Father, I will remember how it felt to work from "can't see in the morning" to "can't see in the night." This will remind me always to make sure I pay my workers a fair day's wage for a fair day's work.

Father, I thank you for not having to face this battle alone. I thank you, Father, for the countless number of fellow Christians who help to lift me up when I am down. Whose testimonies always inspire me to continue in this struggle, no matter how large or impossible it might seem to me that day. Father, I thank you for keeping it fresh in my mind that it is sin not skin, and that there are some whites who are willing to help us fight in the most holy war. I thank you, Father, for the gift of discernment which has allowed me to be able to recognize the evil one disguising himself as the truth.

Father, allow us to release all the pain, all the sorrow, we have endured during this life. We want to make sure these things are loosened here, because you said whatever is loosened on earth will be loosened in heaven, and what is bound on earth will be bound in heaven. Father, we ask you to bind up all our pain, all our misery, all our sorrow, all our fears, all our disappointments. We ask you, Father, to replace those things and let loose on this earth your love, your joy, your gentleness, your kindness, your peace, and your compassion. Once you have let loose these things, O heavenly Father, then please remind us daily that the world didn't give us these things, so the world can't take them away. Amen.

—BY STEPHEN SMITH IN *LIVING THE EXPERIENCE*

"Prayer is the key that unlocked the door of our bondage."
—REVEREND EDWARD M. BAILEY

CAKES

—◆◆◆—

I was an apron-string child, always staying very close to my mother as she worked in her kitchen. The benefit to me was that I got to see an incredible woman bake the finest cakes. She baked cakes for church, friends, and every one of her children's birthdays.

My oldest sister, Margaret, named after my mother, loved pineapple upside-down cake. Every birthday, that is what she got. Thankfully, she liked to share, so I always got a nice big piece.

Over time I began to realize that my mother made the majority of her recipes by memory. She measured when she needed to, but she was famous for a pinch of this or a sprinkle of that. What impresses me is that her dishes were often very complicated ones. All the information she needed was safely tucked away in her mind for future recall.

Our African ancestors, because of the perilous times, needed to memorize and retain every piece of information they heard or discovered, that would aid them in getting to freedom or preserving their lives on the plantation. Writing and reading were practices enslaved Africans could not display in mixed company. Exhibiting that knowledge would have cost them their lives. In fact, there were laws discouraging giving any African instructions in reading and writing. The intent was to hinder communication among Africans and to keep them in an ignorant, dependent state. Denmark Vessey, Frederick Douglass, and others understood differently—that if we as a people did not educate ourselves, the condition of slavery would never end.

— PHOEBE BAILEY

CAKES *Traditional*

POUND CAKE

Rebecca Carter
MAKES 16 SERVINGS

1 cup (2 sticks) butter or margarine, softened
½ cup vegetable oil
3 cups sugar
pinch of salt
4 eggs
3 cups flour
1 cup whole milk
1 teaspoon vanilla
1 teaspoon lemon extract

1. Cream together butter, oil, sugar, and salt. Mix well.

2. Add eggs, one at a time, beating well after each addition.

3. Alternately add flour and milk. Mix well.

4. Stir in flavorings. Beat well.

5. Pour into greased and floured tube pan.

6. Bake at 300°F for 90–95 minutes.

7. Invert pan and cool for 10 minutes before removing cake from pan. Serve pieces topped with fresh fruit or ice cream.

POUND CAKE

Alice Mack
MAKES 3 LOAVES

3½ cups sugar
1 pound butter (4 sticks),
    at room temperature
10 eggs
4 cups flour
1½ teaspoons nutmeg
2 cups nuts

1. Cream together sugar, butter, and eggs.

2. Add flour and nutmeg. Mix well.

3. Fold in nuts.

4. Pour into 3 greased and floured loaf pans.

5. Bake at 325°F for 60 minutes.

BUTTERMILK POUND CAKE

Shirley C. Owens
MAKES 16–20 SERVINGS

1 cup (2 sticks) butter or margarine, at room
   temperature
2 cups sugar
4 eggs
2 teaspoons vanilla
3 cups flour
½ teaspoon baking soda
½ teaspoon salt
1 cup buttermilk

GLAZE:
1 cup sifted powdered sugar
1 or 2 tablespoons evaporated milk
½ teaspoon vanilla

1. Cream together butter and sugar until light and
   fluffy.

2. Add eggs and vanilla. Mix well.

3. Combine flour, baking soda, and salt.

4. Alternately add dry ingredients and buttermilk
   to creamed mixture. Mix well.

5. Pour into greased and floured 10" tube pan.

6. Bake at 325°F for 65 minutes.

7. Combine glaze ingredients. Pour over
   warm cake.

SHORTBREAD

MAKES 16 SERVINGS

2 cups flour
½ teaspoon salt
½ cup brown sugar, packed
1 cup (2 sticks) butter, chilled

1. Sift together flour and salt.

2. Add brown sugar. Mix well.

3. Cut butter into dry mixture, until pea-sized
   lumps form. Use your fingertips to work the
   butter into the flour unitl the mixture is smooth.

4. Pat shortbread into 9" x 13" baking pan. Press
   down until dough is spread evenly.

5. With fork, prick shortbread all over.

6. Bake at 350°F for 20 minutes, until shortbread
   turns brown and pulls away from the pan.

7. Cut in squares while still warm. Cool in pan.

I always worked in the kitchen with my mother. I can
remember mixing the cake up and licking the batter
off the spoon!

—NELSON POLITE, SR.,
a member of Bethel AMEC,
Lancaster, PA

CAKES *Other Favorites*

———— ◆ ————

DEVIL'S FOOD CAKE

Minnie Wilson
MAKES 16–20 SERVINGS

2 cups sugar
½ cup vegetable oil
3 squares baking chocolate, melted
¾ cup sour milk or buttermilk
2 cups flour
1 teaspoon salt
1⅓ teaspoons baking soda
½ teaspoon baking powder
½ cup buttermilk or sour milk
3 eggs
1 teaspoon vanilla

1. Combine sugar, oil, chocolate, and 3/4 cup milk. Mix well.

2. In separate bowl, mix together dry ingredients.

3. In a third bowl, mix together 1/2 cup milk, eggs, and vanilla.

4. Add dry ingredients to creamed chocolate mixture, alternately with egg mixture. Beat well after each addition until well blended.

5. Pour into greased and floured 9" x 13" pan.

6. Bake at 350°F for 30–45 minutes.

CLASSIC CHOCOLATE CAKE

Jean Townsend
MAKES 9–12 SERVINGS

¼ cup (½ stick) butter, softened
¼ cup oil
2 cups sugar
1 teaspoon vanilla
2 eggs
¾ teaspoon baking soda
¾ cup unsweetened cocoa powder
1¾ cups flour
¾ teaspoon baking powder
⅛ teaspoon salt
1¾ cups milk

1. Cream together in stand mixer the butter, oil, and sugar. Then blend in vanilla and eggs.

2. In separate bowl, stir together dry ingredients. Add alternately to creamed mixture with milk. Beat well after each addition until well combined.

3. Spread batter into greased 9" square baking dish.

4. Bake at 350°F for 30–35 minutes, or until pick inserted into center of cake comes out clean.

CHOCOLATE CHIP PEANUT BUTTER CAKE

MAKES 16–20 SERVINGS

2¼ cups flour
2 cups brown sugar
1 cup peanut butter
½ cup (1 stick) margarine, softened
1 teaspoon baking powder
½ teaspoon baking soda
1 cup milk
1 teaspoon vanilla
3 eggs
1½ cups chocolate chips, divided

1. Combine flour, sugar, peanut butter, and margarine in bowl of stand mixer. Blend at low speed until crumbly. Set aside 1 cup.

2. Add remaining ingredients, except chocolate chips, to crumb mixture. Mix well.

3. Stir in 1 cup chocolate chips.

4. Pour into greased 9" x 13" pan. Sprinkle with reserved crumbs and remaining chocolate chips.

5. Bake at 350°F for 30 minutes.

CHOCOLATE TEXAS SHEET CAKE

Christel Wayne
MAKES 24 SERVINGS

CAKE:
1 cup (2 sticks) butter or margarine
7 tablespoons unsweetened cocoa powder
1 cup water
2 cups sifted flour
2 cups sugar
2 eggs, slightly beaten
1 teaspoon baking soda
½ cup buttermilk
1 teaspoon vanilla extract

FROSTING:
½ cup (1 stick) butter or margarine
4 tablespoons unsweetened cocoa powder
6 tablespoons milk
16-ounce box powdered sugar
1 teaspoon vanilla
1 cup chopped pecans

1. In large saucepan, combine butter, cocoa powder, and water. Bring mixture to boil, stirring constantly.

2. Combine flour and sugar. Add to cocoa mixture. Mix well.

3. Beat eggs. Add baking soda, buttermilk, and vanilla. Add to cocoa mixture. Mix well.

4. Pour into greased and floured 10" x 15" jelly-roll pan.

5. Bake at 400°F for 25 minutes.

6. Prepare frosting while cake is baking. Melt butter. Add cocoa powder and milk. Bring to a boil, stirring constantly. Remove from heat.

7. Immediately add powdered sugar, vanilla, and pecans. Mix well.

8. Pour hot frosting over hot cake, spreading evenly. Cool.

DIETERS' CHOCOLATE CHEESECAKE

Mrs. Margaret Bailey
MAKES 8 SERVINGS

¼ cup skim milk
1 package unflavored gelatin
⅔ cup skim milk
2 egg yolks (reserve egg whites)
3 tablespoons unsweetened cocoa powder
¼ cup sugar or the equivalent of sugar substitute
1½ teaspoons vanilla
1½ cups (12-ounce carton) creamed cottage cheese
2 egg whites
2 tablespoons sugar
⅓ cup graham cracker crumbs
⅛ teaspoon cinnamon
fresh or canned fruit, for garnish

1. Pour ¼ cup milk into blender. Add gelatin. Allow to stand for 5 minutes.

2. Heat ⅔ cup milk to boiling point. Pour into blender and process until gelatin dissolves.

3. Add egg yolks, cocoa powder, ¼ cup sugar, and vanilla. Process at medium speed until well blended.

4. Add cottage cheese. Blend on high until smooth.

5. Pour into bowl. Chill until mixture mounds from a spoon.

6. Beat egg whites until frothy. Gradually add 2 tablespoons sugar. Beat until stiff peaks form. Fold into chocolate mixture.

7. Combine graham cracker crumbs and cinnamon. Sprinkle onto bottom of 8" round springform pan.

8. Pour chocolate mixture into pan. Chill for several hours.

9. Arrange fruit on top just before serving.

CHOCOLATE SWIRL COFFEE CAKE

Minnie Wilson
MAKES 9 SERVINGS

⅓ cup flaked coconut
¼ cup chopped nuts
½ cup sugar, divided
1 tablespoon butter, softened + 2 tablespoons butter or margarine, melted, divided
2 cups buttermilk baking mix
1 egg
⅔ cup water or milk
⅓ cup semisweet chocolate pieces, melted

1. Mix coconut, nuts, ¼ cup sugar, and 1 tablespoon softened butter. Set aside.

2. Combine baking mix, ¼ cup sugar, 2 tablespoons melted butter, egg, and water or milk. Beat well for 30 seconds. Spread in bottom of greased 8" x 8" x 2" pan.

3. Spoon chocolate over batter. Lightly swirl batter several times for marbled effect.

4. Sprinkle coconut mixture over top.

5. Bake at 400°F for 20–25 minutes. Serve warm.

ONE BOWL
APPLE NUT CAKE

MAKES 16-20 SERVINGS

2 cups sugar
2 eggs, beaten slightly
¼ cup oil
¼ cup (½ stick) melted butter
½ teaspoon vanilla or almond extract
½ teaspoon lemon extract
2¼ cups flour
1 teaspoon baking soda
1 teaspoon baking powder
½ teaspoon salt
4 cups diced apples
1 cup chopped nuts, of your choice

1. Combine all ingredients in the order listed. Mix well.

2. Spread into ungreased 9" x 13" pan.

3. Bake at 350°F for 60 minutes, or until done in the center.

————◆————

We used to grow whole fields of sugarcane. We would go out into the field and break pieces off. We would peel them and cut them into little pieces. Then we'd chew them until we got all the juice out and spit out the skin.

—FRANCES MORANT,
Brothers & Sisters Cafe

JEWISH
APPLE CAKE

MAKES 16-20 SERVINGS

1 cup sifted flour
½ teaspoon salt
1½ teaspoons baking powder
3 tablespoons sugar
4 tablespoons (½ stick) butter, at room temperature
1 egg
¼ cup milk
4 cups peeled and sliced apples
1 teaspoon cinnamon
6 tablespoons sugar
¼ pound (1 stick) butter
½ cup currant jelly, optional

1. Sift together flour, salt, and baking powder. Add sugar. Work in 4 tablespoons butter until mixture is crumbly.

2. Beat together egg and milk. Add to flour mixture. Mix to form dough.

3. Pat into buttered 8" x 12" pan.

4. Arrange apples in rows on dough. Sprinkle with cinnamon and sugar.

5. Melt butter and pour over cake.

6. Bake at 400°F for 35–40 minutes. Brush with melted jelly while cake is hot.

JOHNNY APPLESEED COFFEE CAKE

Minnie Wilson
MAKES 8-10 SERVINGS

2 cups buttermilk baking mix
2 tablespoons sugar
1 egg
⅔ cup water or milk
1½ cups chopped apple

TOPPING:
¼ cup sugar
2 tablespoons buttermilk baking mix
2 teaspoons cinnamon
2 tablespoons firm butter or margarine

1. Combine baking mix, sugar, egg, and water or milk. Beat well.

2. Fold in apple. Batter will be stiff.

3. Spread batter in greased 9" round layer pan or 8" x 8" pan.

4. Make topping by combining sugar, baking mix, cinnamon, and butter until crumbly. Sprinkle over batter.

5. Bake at 400°F for 20–25 minutes. Serve warm.

OLD-FASHIONED APPLESAUCE CAKE

MAKES 16-20 SERVINGS

2½ cups flour, sifted
1½ cups sugar
¼ teaspoon baking powder
1½ teaspoons baking soda
½ teaspoon salt
1 teaspoon cinnamon
½ teaspoon ground cloves
½ teaspoon allspice
½ teaspoon nutmeg
½ cup shortening, melted
15-ounce can applesauce
3 eggs
1 cup seedless raisins (optional)
1 cup chopped walnuts

1. Combine flour, sugar, baking powder, baking soda, salt, and spices.

2. Add shortening and applesauce. Mix well.

3. Add eggs. Mix well.

4. Stir in raisins if using and walnuts.

5. Pour into greased and floured 9" x 13" pan.

6. Bake at 350°F for 45 minutes.

APPLESAUCE CAKE

MAKES 20-24 SERVINGS

⅔ cup (10⅔ tablespoons) butter, softened
2 cups sugar
4 egg yolks
¾ cup unsweetened applesauce
½ cup milk
2½ cups cake flour or 2¼ cups all-purpose flour
3 teaspoons baking powder
4 egg whites, stiffly beaten

1. Cream together butter and sugar.

2. Add egg yolks and applesauce. Mix well.

3. Add milk. Mix well.

4. Sift together flour and baking powder. Add to wet mixture. Mix well.

5. Fold in egg whites.

6. Bake at 350°F for 35-40 minutes.

NOTES:
1. To add flavor, mix 1 teaspoon cinnamon and ½ teaspoon nutmeg with dry ingredients in Step 4.

2. If you use sweetened applesauce, reduce the sugar to 1½ cups.

COWBOY COFFEE CAKE

Minnie Wilson
MAKES 8-10 SERVINGS

12-ounce jar apricot, peach, strawberry, or seedless raspberry preserves
2 cups buttermilk baking mix
2 tablespoons sugar
1 egg
⅔ cup water or milk

1. Spread preserves in greased 9" round layer pan.

2. Combine remaining ingredients. Beat well. Spread over preserves to edge of pan.

3. Bake at 400°F for 25-30 minutes.

4. Invert onto heatproof plate. Leave pan over cake a few minutes. Remove pan and serve warm.

BLUEBERRY AND PEACH SHORTCAKE

MAKES 12 SERVINGS

6.5-ounce sponge cake mix
8-ounce package cream cheese, softened
14-ounce can sweetened condensed milk
⅓ cup lemon juice
1 teaspoon vanilla extract
2 tablespoons sugar
2 teaspoons cornstarch
¼ cup water
1 tablespoon lemon juice
1 cup blueberries
3 medium peaches, peeled, seeded, and sliced

1. Prepare and bake sponge cake according to directions on package.

2. Beat cream cheese until fluffy.

3. Gradually beat in condensed milk until smooth.

4. Stir in ⅓ cup lemon juice and vanilla.

5. Spread on partially cooled cake. Chill.

6. In saucepan, combine sugar, cornstarch, water, and 1 tablespoon lemon juice. Cook, stirring constantly, until thickened. Add blueberries. Cook until bubbly. Chill.

7. Top cake with peach slices and blueberry sauce. Refrigerate leftovers.

SURPRISIN' CARROT CAKE

MAKES 16-20 SERVINGS

3 eggs
1½ cups sugar
¾ cup mayonnaise
8-ounce can crushed pineapple, undrained
2 cups flour
2 teaspoons baking soda
½ teaspoon ground cinnamon
½ teaspoon ground ginger
½ teaspoon salt
2 cups coarsely shredded carrots
¾ cup chopped walnuts

1. Mix together eggs, sugar, mayonnaise, and pineapple.
2. Combine flour, baking soda, cinnamon, ginger, and salt. Add to pineapple mixture. Mix well.
3. Fold in carrots and walnuts. Pour into greased and floured 9" x 13" pan.
4. Bake at 350°F for 35-40 minutes.
5. Cool and frost with Cream Cheese Icing.

CREAM CHEESE ICING

3-ounce package cream cheese, softened
2 tablespoons butter or margarine, softened
1 cup powdered sugar
1 teaspoon vanilla

1. Combine ingredients. Beat in electric mixer on high until smooth.
2. Use on cakes, cinnamon rolls, and cookies.

WILLIAMSBURG ORANGE CAKE

MAKES 16-20 SERVINGS

2½ cups flour
1½ cups sugar
1½ teaspoons baking soda
¾ teaspoon salt
1½ cups buttermilk
½ cup (1 stick) melted butter or margarine
¼ cup vegetable oil
3 eggs
1½ teaspoons vanilla
1 cup raisins
½ cup chopped nuts
1 tablespoon grated orange peel

1. Combine dry ingredients for cake in large mixing bowl. Mix well.
2. In separate bowl blend together milk, butter, oil, eggs, and vanilla. Stir into dry ingredients until thoroughly mixed. Stir in raisins, nuts, and orange peel.
3. Pour into greased and floured 9" x 13" pan, 2 9" round pans, or 3 8" round pans.
4. Bake 9" x 13" cake for 40-45 minutes at 350°F. Bake either of the round pans for 30-35 minutes at 350°F.
5. Cool and frost with Butter Frosting.

BUTTER FROSTING

⅓ cup (5⅓ tablespoons) melted butter or margarine
3 cups powdered sugar
3-4 tablespoons orange juice
2 teaspoons grated orange peel

1. Combine ingredients. Beat in electric mixer on high until smooth.
2. Use on cakes, cinnamon rolls, and cookies.

CRANBERRY ORANGE BUTTER CAKE

Dianne Prince
MAKES 15-20 SERVINGS

CAKE:
1 package butter cake mix
⅓ cup oil
2 tablespoons frozen orange juice, thawed
3 eggs
16-ounce can whole cranberry sauce (reserve 3 tablespoons for glaze)

GLAZE:
¼ cup firmly packed brown sugar
3 tablespoons reserved cranberry sauce
3 tablespoons frozen orange juice, thawed
3 tablespoons butter or margarine

1. Mix together cake ingredients in stand mixer. Beat well.

2. Pour into greased and floured tube pan.

3. Bake at 350°F for 35-45 minutes.

4. Combine glaze ingredients in saucepan. Heat until well combined.

5. Using a long-tined fork, prick cake at ½" intervals. Pour half of glaze over cake.

6. Let stand 10 minutes. Invert onto serving plate. Prick cake again. Spoon remaining glaze over cake. Serve warm or cold.

GOLD RUSH COFFEE CAKE

Minnie Wilson
MAKES 8-10 SERVINGS

2 cups buttermilk baking mix
2 tablespoons sugar
1 egg
1 tablespoon grated orange peel
⅔ cup orange juice
1 cup cut-up pitted prunes or cranberries

ORANGE GLAZE:
½ cup powdered sugar
1 teaspoon grated orange peel
2 teaspoons orange juice

1. Combine baking mix, sugar, egg, orange peel, and orange juice. Beat well.

2. Fold in prunes or cranberries. Spread in greased 9" round layer pan.

3. Bake at 400°F for 25-30 minutes.

4. To make glaze combine powdered sugar, orange peel, and orange juice. Drizzle over warm cake.

If something fell we picked it up, kissed it up to God, and ate it!

—**JANET GANTZ**

HESTER'S CAKE

Hester Prince
MAKES 16–20 SERVINGS

5 eggs
2 cups sugar
1 cup (2 sticks) melted butter or margarine
3 cups graham cracker crumbs
15-ounce can crushed pineapple, undrained
1 cup lightly packed flaked coconut
1 cup chopped nuts
whipped cream

1. Combine all ingredients except whipped cream. Mix well.

2. Pour into greased and floured 9" x 13" cake pan.

3. Bake at 325°F for 60 minutes, or until done in the center.

4. Serve topped with whipped cream.

DUMP CAKE

Makes 16–20 servings

21-ounce can cherry pie filling
20-ounce can crushed pineapple, undrained
1 box yellow or white cake mix
1 cup (2 sticks) butter, melted
3.5-ounce can flaked coconut
1¼ cups chopped pecans

1. Layer ingredients in order given in greased 9" x 13" pan.

2. Bake at 325°F for 60 minutes.

WATERGATE CAKE

MAKES 16–20 SERVINGS

CAKE:
18-ounce box white cake mix
3.4-ounce box instant pistachio pudding
1 cup vegetable oil, less 1 tablespoon
3 eggs, slightly beaten
1 cup ginger ale
½ cup chopped nuts

FROSTING:
2 envelopes Dream Whip
3.4-ounce box instant pistachio pudding
1¼ cups cold milk

grated coconut
maraschino cherries
chopped nuts

1. Combine all cake ingredients. Mix well.

2. Pour into greased and floured 9" x 13" pan.

3. Bake at 350°F for 30–35 minutes. Cool.

4. Combine Dream Whip mix, pistachio pudding, and milk. Mix well. Spread on cake.

5. Garnish with coconut, cherries, and nuts.

From my earliest recollection, I date the entertainment of a deep conviction that slavery would not always be able to hold me within its foul embrace.

—FREDERICK DOUGLASS

TOSSED BUTTER PECAN CAKE

Ann Beardan
MAKES 8–12 SERVINGS

2 cups pecans, chopped
¼ cup (½ stick) butter + 1 cup (2 sticks) butter, softened, divided
2 cups sugar
4 unbeaten eggs
3 cups sifted flour
2 teaspoons baking powder
½ teaspoon salt
1 cup milk
2 teaspoons vanilla

FROSTING:
¼ cup (½ stick) butter, softened
16 ounces powdered sugar, sifted
1 teaspoon vanilla
4–6 tablespoons evaporated milk or cream

1. Toast pecans in ¼ cup butter in 350°F oven for 20–25 minutes, stirring frequently.

2. Cream 1 cup butter. Gradually beat in sugar. Mix well.

3. Blend in eggs. Mix well.

4. Sift together flour, baking powder, and salt.

5. Alternately add dry mixture and milk to creamed mixture. Mix well.

6. Stir in vanilla and 1⅓ cups toasted pecans.

7. Grease and flour bottoms of three 8" or 9" round layer baking pans. Divide batter among the three pans.

8. Bake at 350°F for 20–30 minutes. Cool.

9. Make frosting by creaming ¼ cup butter. Add powdered sugar and vanilla. Add milk until of spreading consistency. Sir in remaining pecans.

10. Spread between layers of cake and over top and sides.

PECAN CAKE

Nancy C. Hill
MAKES 16–20 SERVINGS

1 pound butter, softened
2 cups sugar
6 eggs
1 tablespoon lemon extract
4 cups flour
1½ teaspoons baking powder
4 cups chopped pecans
6 cups white raisins

1. Cream together butter and sugar.

2. Add eggs, one at a time, beating well after each addition. Add lemon extract and mix well.

3. Sift flour and baking powder together three times.

4. Add pecans and raisins to flour.

5. Gradually add flour mixture to creamed mixture. Mix well.

6. Pour into greased and floured 10" tube pan.

7. Bake at 300°F for 1½–2 hours. Cool 15 minutes in pan before removing.

BUTTER CAKE

Rebecca Carter
MAKES 16–20 SERVINGS

1 cup (2 sticks) butter, softened
2 cups sugar
4 eggs
1 cup buttermilk
2 teaspoons vanilla
3 cups flour, sifted
1 teaspoon baking powder
½ teaspoon baking soda
1 teaspoon salt

SAUCE:
1 cup sugar
¼ cup water
½ cup (1 stick) butter
1 teaspoon vanilla

1. Cream together butter and sugar.

2. Add eggs, one at a time. Mix well after adding each one.

3. Add buttermilk and vanilla. Mix thoroughly.

4. Sift together flour, baking powder, baking soda, and salt. Gradually add to creamed mixture. Mix well.

5. Pour into greased and floured 10" tube pan.

6. Bake at 325°F for 60–65 minutes.

7. In saucepan, make sauce by combining sugar, water, and butter. Heat and stir until sugar is dissolved. Remove from heat. Add vanilla.

8. Poke holes in top of baked cake with a fork.

9. Pour glaze over hot cake. Cool. Remove cooled cake from pan.

EASY TWO-EGG CAKE

Linda Maison
MAKES 12–18 SERVINGS

2 cups self-rising flour
1 cup sugar
1 cup milk
2 eggs
½ cup (1 stick) butter or margarine, melted
1 teaspoon vanilla
butter or margarine
cinnamon sugar

1. Combine all ingredients except the last two. Beat until smooth.

2. Pour into greased and floured 8" x 10" pan.

3. Bake at 375°F for 20–25 minutes.

4. Rub hot cake with butter or margarine and sprinkle with cinnamon sugar.

5. Cool on wire rack for 10 minutes before cutting to serve.

CHERRY ZIP UP

MAKES 9 SERVINGS

21-ounce can cherry pie filling
2 cups white or yellow cake mix
½ cup (1 stick) melted butter
⅓ cup grated coconut
½ cup chopped nuts

1. Spread filling in bottom of 9" glass pie dish.

2. Sprinkle cake mix over pie filling. Pour butter over top. Do not mix together.

3. Bake at 350°F for 40 minutes.

4. Sprinkle on coconut and nuts.

5. Serve warm with ice cream.

OLD-FASHIONED SHORTCAKE

MAKES 18–24 SERVINGS

2 cups sugar
½ cup shortening
2 eggs
1 cup milk
2½ cups flour
3 teaspoons baking soda
⅛ teaspoon nutmeg
1 teaspoon vanilla

1. Cut shortening into sugar in mixing bowl until crumbly. Stir in eggs and milk.

2. Mix dry ingredients together in separate bowl. Stir into wet ingredients until well blended. Add vanilla and mix thoroughly.

3. Pour into greased 9" x 13" pan.

4. Bake at 350°F for 35–40 minutes, or until toothpick tests clean in the middle of the cake.

NOTE: This is absolutely delicious topped with sliced fresh strawberries.

MILLION-DOLLAR POUND CAKE

Rebecca Carter
MAKES 16–20 SERVINGS

3 cups sugar
1 pound butter, softened
6 eggs, at room temperature
4 cups flour
¾ cup milk
1 teaspoon almond extract
1 teaspoon vanilla extract

1. Cream together sugar and butter until light and fluffy.

2. Add eggs, one at a time, beating well after each addition.

3. Add flour and milk alternately to creamed mixture, beating well after each addition.

4. Stir in flavorings. Mix well.

5. Pour batter into greased and floured 10" tube pan.

6. Bake at 300°F for 1 hour, 40 minutes. Invert pan to cool.

{ Human rights are mutual and reciprocal . . . If you take my liberty and life you forfeit your own.

—WILLIAM PARKER }

SOUR CREAM POUND CAKE

Rebecca Carter
MAKES 16–20 SERVINGS

1½ cups (3 sticks) butter, at room temperature
2 cups sugar
8 eggs
1 cup sour cream
4 cups self-rising flour
strawberries or blueberries for topping

1. Cream together butter and sugar until light and fluffy.

2. Add eggs, one at a time, beating well after each addition.

3. Alternately add flour and sour cream.

4. Pour into greased and floured 10" tube pan.

5. Bake at 350°F for 60 minutes. Invert and cool in pan 10 minutes. Remove from pan.

6. Serve with a topping of strawberries or blueberries.

———— ✦✦✦ ————

Africans, who were known to be great barterers and vendors, continued to use their industrious talents in America. Many free Africans would vend, even at auction blocks. It is said that Harriet Tubman sold pies as a source of income.

COCONUT POUND CAKE

MAKES 16–20 SERVINGS

2½ cups sugar
1 cup (2 sticks) butter or margarine, softened
⅔ cup shortening
5 eggs
3 cups flour, sifted
1 teaspoon baking powder
⅛ teaspoon salt
1 cup milk
1 teaspoon vanilla
1 teaspoon coconut flavoring
1 teaspoon butter flavoring
2⅔ cups or 1 (7-ounce) can flaked coconut

1. Cream together sugar, butter, and shortening.

2. Add eggs, one at a time, beating after each addition.

3. Sift together flour, baking powder, and salt.

4. Alternately add dry mixture and milk to creamed mixture. Mix well.

5. Stir in flavorings and coconut.

6. Pour into greased and floured tube pan.

7. Bake at 325°F for 90 minutes. Invert pan until cake cools.

FIVE-FLAVOR POUND CAKE

Patricia Washington
MAKES 16–20 SERVINGS

1 cup (2 sticks) butter or margarine,
    at room temperature
½ cup shortening
3 cups sugar
4 eggs, beaten
3 cups flour
½ teaspoon baking powder
1 cup milk
1 teaspoon coconut extract
1 teaspoon lemon extract
1 teaspoon rum flavoring
1 teaspoon butter flavoring
1 teaspoon vanilla

1. Cream together butter, shortening, and sugar until light and fluffy.

2. Add eggs one by one. Mix well after each addition.

3. Combine flour and baking powder.

4. Alternately add dry ingredients and milk to creamed mixture.

5. Stir in flavorings until well blended.

6. Pour into greased and floured tube pan.

7. Bake at 300°F for 90 minutes. Invert pan and cool 10 minutes before removing cake from pan.

BEST YET POUND CAKE

Patricia Washington
MAKES 16 SERVINGS

8 ounces cream cheese, at room temperature
1½ cups (3 sticks) butter, at room temperature
3 cups sugar
5 eggs
3 cups cake flour
1 tablespoon butter flavoring

1. Cream together cream cheese and butter.

2. Add sugar. Beat well.

3. Add eggs, one at a time, beating well after each addition.

4. Gradually add flour. Mix well.

5. Stir in flavoring.

6. Pour into greased and floured tube pan.

7. Bake at 300°F for 1 hour, 30 minutes to 1 hour, 40 minutes minutes, until cake tests done. Invert pan and cool for 10 minutes before removing from pan.

8. Cover slices with fruit topping before serving.

NOTE: You can substitute 1 teaspoon vanilla extract for the butter flavoring.

—GERMAINE W. PICKNEY

PINEAPPLE POUND CAKE

MAKES 16–20 SERVINGS

½ cup shortening
1 cup (2 sticks) butter, softened
2¾ cups sugar
6 large eggs
3 cups flour
1 teaspoon baking powder
¼ cup milk
¾ cup crushed pineapple, undrained
1 teaspoon vanilla

TOPPING:
¼ cup (½ stick) butter, softened
1½ cups powdered sugar
1 cup crushed pineapple, drained

1. In large bowl, cream together shortening, butter, and sugar.

2. Add eggs, one at a time, beating well after each addition.

3. In separate bowl, sift together flour and baking powder. Add alternately with milk to creamed mixture.

4. Stir in pineapple and vanilla. Mix well.

5. Pour into greased and floured 10" tube pan. Place in cold oven.

6. Turn oven to 325°F. Bake for 1½ hours, or until top springs back when lightly touched. Let stand for a few minutes before removing from pan.

7. Prepare Topping by combining butter, powdered sugar, and pineapple. Pour over cake while cake is still hot.

7-UP POUND CAKE

Shirley C. Owens
MAKES 16–20 SERVINGS

1 cup (2 sticks) butter or margarine, softened
½ cup vegetable oil
3 cups sugar
5 eggs
3 cups flour
¾ cup 7-Up
1 teaspoon vanilla or lemon flavoring

1. Cream together butter, oil, and sugar.

2. Add eggs one at a time, beating well after each addition.

3. Alternately add flour and 7-Up. Mix well.

4. Stir in vanilla.

5. Pour into greased and floured tube pan.

6. Bake at 325°F for 60–90 minutes, or until done. Invert pan to cool for 10 minutes before removing cake.

7. Serve slices topped with fruit sauce or ice cream.

COOL WHIP POUND CAKE

Rebecca Carter
MAKES 16-20 SERVINGS

1 cup (2 sticks) butter or margarine, softened
3 cups sugar
6 eggs
3 cups flour
1½ teaspoons vanilla
1 tablespoon lemon extract
8-ounce container frozen whipped topping, thawed

1. Cream together butter and sugar.

2. Add eggs, one at a time. Beat well after each addition.

3. Gradually add flour. Mix well.

4. Fold in vanilla, lemon extract, and whipped topping until well blended.

5. Pour into greased and floured 10" tube pan.

6. Bake at 325°F for 75 minutes. Invert pan to cool.

SPICE CAKE

Minnie Wilson
MAKES 16-20 SERVINGS

2 cups brown sugar
½ cup (1 stick) butter, softened
3 eggs
2 cups flour
1 teaspoon ginger
1 teaspoon ground cloves
1 teaspoon cinnamon
½ teaspoon nutmeg
1 teaspoon baking soda
1 cup sour milk
1 teaspoon vanilla

1. Cream together brown sugar and butter in large mixing bowl.

2. Add eggs and beat until well mixed.

3. In separate bowl, stir together dry ingredients.

4. Add dry ingredients alternately with sour milk to creamed mixture, beating well after each addition. Stir in vanilla thoroughly.

5. Pour into greased and floured 9" x 13" pan.

6. Bake at 350°F for 30–45 minutes.

7. When cooled, but still warm, frost with your favorite Cream Cheese Icing (see page 240).

Daniel Hughes (1804–1880)

Daniel Hughes was an abolitionist and entrepreneur who lived in Lycoming County near Williamsport. He engaged in the lumbering business and used the Susquehanna River to transport his goods from Havre de Grace to Williamsport. As was the case with William Whipper and his partners, Hughes had a hiding space on his barges that were used to smuggle freedom seekers north to Williamsport. From there he sent them on to Canada. It is very likely that Hughes worked together with individuals in Black enclaves along the Susquehanna in towns such as Wrightsville, Port Deposit, and Havre de Grace.

CAKES & Other Favorites

249

GINGERBREAD

Hester Prince

MAKES 16–20 SERVINGS

¾ cup honey
¾ cup vegetable oil
1¼ cups molasses
3 eggs
2 cups flour
1 cup whole wheat flour
½ teaspoon salt
½ teaspoon ground cloves
1 teaspoon baking powder
1 teaspoon ginger
1½ teaspoons cinnamon
¾ cup scalded milk

1. In large bowl, combine honey, oil, molasses, and eggs.

2. Sift together flours, salt, cloves, baking powder, ginger, and cinnamon.

3. Add dry ingredients alternately with hot milk to creamed mixture.

4. When smooth, pour into greased 9" x 13" baking pan.

5. Bake at 350°F 40–45 minutes.

GRAND CHAMPION SPONGE CAKE

MAKES 16–20 SERVINGS

1¼ cups sifted flour
1 cup sugar
1½ teaspoons baking powder
½ teaspoon salt
6 egg yolks
¼ cup water
1 teaspoon vanilla
6 egg whites
1 teaspoon cream of tarter
½ cup sugar

1. Sift together flour, 1 cup sugar, baking powder, and salt.

2. In small electric mixer bowl, combine egg yolks, water, vanilla, and sifted dry ingredients. Beat at medium-high speed for 4 minutes, or until mixture is light and fluffy.

3. In large electric mixer bowl, beat egg whites until frothy. Gently add cream of tartar.

4. Gradually beat in ½ cup sugar, 1 tablespoon at a time. Beat until whites form stiff, not dry, peaks. Fold batter gently, but thoroughly, into the beaten egg whites.

5. Turn into an ungreased 10" tube pan. Bake at 350°F for about 45 minutes. Invert pan to cool.

❖━━◆✕◆━━❖

NOTE: For a change of flavor, substitute 1 teaspoon lemon extract for 1 teaspoon vanilla.

JELLO CAKE

18½-ounce box yellow cake mix
3¼-ounce box gelatin
4 eggs, slightly beaten
⅔ cup oil
⅔ cup water
1 teaspoon vanilla

1. Combine all ingredients. Mix well.

2. Pour into greased and floured 9" x 13" pan.

3. Bake at 325°F for 45–60 minutes.

WINE CAKE

MAKES 16-20 SERVINGS

18½-ounce box yellow cake mix
3¼-ounce box instant vanilla pudding
4 eggs
1 cup oil
1 cup wine
1 teaspoon nutmeg

1. Combine all ingredients. Mix well.

2. Pour into greased and floured 9" x 13" pan.

3. Bake at 325°F for 45–50 minutes.

RUM CAKE

MAKES 12-15 SERVINGS

½ cup chopped pecans
18½-ounce box golden butter cake mix
3¼-ounce box instant vanilla pudding
½ cup water
½ cup vegetable oil
4 eggs, slightly beaten
½ cup light rum

GLAZE:
¾ cup sugar
½ cup (1 stick) butter or margarine
¼ cup light rum
pinch of salt

1. Grease and flour Bundt pan. Sprinkle nuts in bottom of pan.

2. Combine cake mix and dry pudding mix.

3. Add remaining cake ingredients. Mix well. Pour into Bundt pan.

4. Bake at 325°F for 60 minutes.

5. Combine glaze ingredients in saucepan. Boil for 2–3 minutes. Pour over hot cake. Let cake cool for 30 minutes, then remove from pan.

{ Harriet Tubman and the runaways she assisted would often travel without eating until they reached their next station. There they were given food and shelter. }

CAKES & Other Favorites

WE ARE CLIMBING JACOB'S LADDER

We are climbing Jacob's ladder.
We are climbing Jacob's ladder.
We are climbing Jacob's ladder,
Soldiers of the cross.

Every round goes higher, higher.
Every round goes higher, higher.
Every round goes higher, higher,
Soldiers of the cross.

Sinner do you love my Jesus?
Sinner do you love my Jesus?
Sinner do you love my Jesus?
Soldiers of the cross.

If you love Him, why not serve Him?
If you love Him, why not serve Him?
If you love Him, why not serve Him?
Soldiers of the cross.

We are climbing higher higher.
We are climbing higher higher.
We are climbing higher higher,
Soldiers of the cross.

Through this spiritual, a conductor learned that an enslaved African was running and wanted to go North, as far as Canada.

SNACKS, APPETIZERS, AND DRINKS

My mother's famous homemade eggnog was so rich and creamy. Our friends loved to come over to our house for food, because they never knew what special treat Mrs. Bailey was going to serve. My mother never refused anyone a meal; she welcomed everyone into our home, a tradition her children maintain in their homes today.

The enslaved Africans used the earth around them to make teas, to be shared with guests and used for medicinal purposes. First- and second-generation African immigrants were faced with unfamiliar plants—and new diseases—when they were brought to this country. Many adapted the foliages and tree barks they found in America to recipes they remembered and were taught by their grandmothers.

—PHOEBE BAILEY

SNACKS, APPETIZERS, AND DRINKS

BEGGARS PURSES WITH CRABMEAT

Rina Mckee
MAKES 6 APPETIZER SERVINGS

½ pound lump crabmeat
1 tablespoon mayonnaise
1 teaspoon lemon juice
1 teaspoon Dijon mustard
2 teaspoons minced green onion
1 teaspoon minced parsley
½ teaspoon salt
¼ teaspoon cayenne pepper
6–8 small crepes
6 whole chives, blanched

1. Gently mix together all ingredients except crepes and whole chives.

2. Place heaping tablespoon of crabmeat salad in center of each crepe. Draw up crepe as though making a bundle, twisting the crepe gently to enclose the crabmeat. Tie a chive around the top of the bundle to close.

3. Serve immediately or store in refrigerator, tightly wrapped, for no longer than an hour.

NOTE: The crab mixture can also be used as a salad, served on top of lettuce leaves, as a dip on small snack bread slices or crackers, or as a spread on thinly sliced baguettes.

SHRIMP HORS D'OEUVRES

Nancy Perkins
MAKES 36 SERVINGS

1 pound fresh shrimp, cleaned and cooked
1 tablespoon minced onion
1 teaspoon minced celery
1 teaspoon minced green pepper
2 teaspoons lemon juice
½ teaspoon grated lemon rind
¼ teaspoon salt
4 or 5 drops Tabasco sauce
dash of pepper
¾ cup mayonnaise
36 snack bread slices or full-sized bread slices
fresh parsley

1. Cut shrimp into very fine pieces. (A food processor works well with the shrimp and fresh vegetables.)

2. Combine all ingredients except bread and parsley.

3. If using full-sized bread slices, cut a round from each slice about the size of a half dollar. Pile a heaping teaspoon of shrimp mix on each round or snack bread slice. Garnish with parsley.

MUSHROOMS OREGANO

MAKES 10-12 APPETIZER SERVINGS

50 small mushrooms
2 cloves garlic, minced
1½ tablespoons olive oil
1 teaspoon salt
1 tablespoon Romano cheese
1 teaspoon dried oregano
snack bread or crackers

1. Wash mushrooms and pat dry.

2. In frying pan, heat minced garlic, olive oil, salt, Romano cheese, and oregano until warm. Add mushrooms.

3. Cover and simmer for 15–20 minutes.

4. Serve on top of snack bread slices or crackers.

ITALIAN-STYLE FINGER SANDWICHES

Rina Mckee
MAKES 20-25 APPETIZER SERVINGS

focaccia
½ pound Genoa salami, sliced
1 pound provolone cheese, sliced
½ pound pepperoni, sliced
2 medium tomatoes, cut into half slices
Italian dressing or mayonnaise, optional

1. Split focaccia in half lengthwise, then cut into 2" squares.

2. Layer meat, cheeses, and tomatoes on focaccia. Drizzle with dressing or dollops of mayonnaise.

3. Serve at room temperature.

SWEET AND SOUR TURKEY BALLS

Doris Harvey
MAKES 8-10 APPETIZER SERVINGS

1 pound ground turkey
½ cup Italian bread crumbs
1 egg
1 cup ketchup
2 teaspoons cider vinegar
¾ cup brown sugar

OPTIONAL SAUCE:

8-ounce can pineapple chunks with juice
green peppers, chopped
red peppers, chopped
mushrooms, sliced

1. Combine turkey, bread crumbs, and egg. Form into 1" balls. Place on cookie sheet.

2. Bake at 350°F for 20–30 minutes.

3. In large saucepan, combine ketchup, vinegar, and brown sugar. (Add pineapple chunks, peppers, and mushrooms, if desired.) Bring to a boil. Pour over meatballs and serve.

❖

NOTE: Serve with rice as a main dish.

❖

I can remember my mom taking peach skin and making peach wine and peach brandy in the yard. The bees would be around so you had to strain it, oh yes! It was potent!

—BETTY CUNNINGHAM,
a member of Bethel AMEC,
Lancaster, PA

MEATBALLS IN SWEET-AND SOUR-SAUCE

Alice Dabney
MAKES 10–15 APPETIZER SERVINGS

1½ pounds lean ground beef
1½ cups cornflake crumbs
⅓ cup dried parsley flakes
¼ teaspoon pepper
3 tablespoons soy sauce
¾ teaspoon garlic powder
⅓ cup ketchup
2 tablespoons minced onions
9-ounce can whole cranberry sauce
butter or bacon drippings

SAUCE
½ cup brown sugar
12-ounce bottle chili sauce
1½ teaspoons lemon juice

1. Combine ground beef, cornflake crumbs, parsley flakes, pepper, soy sauce, garlic powder, ketchup, onions, and cranberry sauce.

2. Roll into walnut-sized balls. Brown in batches in skillet in butter or bacon drippings. Place browned meatballs in baking dish; continue until all meatballs are browned.

3. Combine sauce ingredients. Pour over meatballs.

4. Bake uncovered at 350°F for 30 minutes.

SOUTHWEST CHEESECAKE

MAKES 8–12 APPETIZER SERVINGS

1 cup finely crushed tortilla chips
3 tablespoons butter or margarine, melted
2 (8-ounce) packages cream cheese, softened
2 eggs
1 package dry taco seasoning
8 ounces shredded Colby or Monterey Jack cheese
4-ounce can chopped green chilies, drained
1 cup sour cream
1 cup chopped bell pepper
½ cup sliced green onions
⅓ cup chopped tomatoes
¼ cup pitted ripe olive slices

1. Stir chips and butter together in small bowl. Press into 9" springform pan.

2. Bake at 350°F for 15 minutes.

3. Beat cream cheese, eggs, and taco seasoning in large bowl at medium speed until well blended.

4. Fold in shredded cheese and chilies. Pour over crust.

5. Bake at 350°F for 30 minutes.

6. Spread sour cream over cheesecake.

7. Loosen cake from rim of pan. Cool before removing rim.

8. Refrigerate for at least 30 minutes.

9. Top with remaining ingredients just before serving.

SARA'S CHEESE BALL

Sara Flack
MAKES 8-10 SERVINGS

2¼-ounce jar dried beef
2 (8-ounce) packages cream cheese, softened
1 tablespoon mayonnaise or salad dressing
¼ teaspoon dry mustard
¼ teaspoon cayenne pepper
4 green onions, chopped
¼ cup chopped nuts, optional

1. Drain dried beef and tear into shreds.

2. Combine all ingredients except nuts. Refrigerate until very firm.

3. Form into ball.

4. Roll in nuts. Chill until ready to serve. Bring to table with a variety of snack crackers.

CHEESE BALL

MAKES 12-14 SERVINGS

2 (8-ounce) packages cream cheese, softened
5-ounce jar blue cheese, softened
5-ounce jar Old English cheese, softened
1 tablespoon Worcestershire sauce
crushed pecans
parsley (optional)

1. Combine cream cheese, blue cheese, Old English cheese, and Worcestershire sauce with fork until well blended.

2. Refrigerate until very firm.

3. Shape into ball.

4. Mix together crushed pecans and parsley; then roll cheese in mixture until well coated.

VEGETABLE SPREAD

Cormylene Williams
MAKES 1½ CUPS

2 carrots
half a sweet red pepper
1 rib celery
½ cup walnuts
1 teaspoon freshly grated ginger
1 teaspoon freshly grated lemon rind
3-4 tablespoons mayonnaise

1. In food processor, grate carrots. Remove and set aside. Then chop red pepper, celery, and walnuts until of a coarse consistency.

2. Stir in grated carrots, ginger, lemon rind, and enough mayonnaise to hold mixture together.

3. Chill before serving.

4. Spread on snack crackers, celery sticks, or bread squares.

. . . One universal Father hath given being to us all, and that he hath not only made us all of one flesh, but that he hath also without partiality afforded us all the same sensations and endued us all with the same faculties, and that however variable we may be in society or religion, however diversified in situation or colour, we are all of the same family, and stand in the same relation to Him.

—BENJAMIN BANNEKER,
excerpt from letter to
Thomas Jefferson

SOUTHERN CAVIAR

Mrs. Margaret Bailey
MAKES 4 TO 6 SERVINGS

8 ounces dried black-eyed peas
¾ cup oil
¼ cup vinegar
1 whole clove garlic, smashed
½ onion, chopped
ground black pepper to taste

1. Rinse peas under cold water. Place in saucepan and cover with water. Boil for 2 minutes. Remove from heat. Let soak for 60 minutes.

2. Drain peas. Rinse well. Cover with water and cook until peas are tender but still whole, about 15 minutes. Drain. Place peas in bowl.

3. Add oil, vinegar, garlic, onion, and pepper. Mix well. Cover and refrigerate for 3 days. Remove garlic after first day. Drain before serving.

ANCHOVY SPREAD

MAKES SPREAD FOR 16–20 SNACK CRACKERS

3-ounce package cream cheese, softened
2 teaspoons capers
½ teaspoon grated onion
1 teaspoon anchovy paste
few drops Worcestershire sauce
2 tablespoons mayonnaise, approximately

1. Mash cream cheese.

2. Stir in capers, onion, anchovy paste, and Worcestershire sauce. Mix well.

3. Stir in mayonnaise until thin enough to spread.

NOTE: Add ½ teaspoon of your favorite herb to add color and flavor.

ASIAN SALMON DIP

Mrs. Margaret Bailey
MAKES 1¾ CUPS

1 tablespoon sesame seeds
1 scant teaspoons oil
7¾-ounce can salmon, drained and flaked
2 tablespoons minced green onions
½ cup sour cream
½ cup mayonnaise
1 tablespoon soy sauce
¼ teaspoon freshly grated, peeled, fresh ginger
raw broccoli florets
sliced zucchini, celery, and carrots
fresh pea pods

1. Toast sesame seeds by heating in oil in skillet until light brown, or by placing on tray in 350°F toaster oven for 2 minutes or until light brown.

2. Combine all ingredients, except raw vegetables and pea pods. Mix well. Refrigerate for at least an hour.

3. Serve with vegetables.

We ate so much apple butter that I won't eat it now. My children don't even know what it tastes like.

—DORIS JOHNSON

SHRIMP DIP

Hester Prince
MAKES 6–8 SERVINGS

8-ounce package cream cheese, softened
½ cup mayonnaise
1 tablespoon lemon juice
1 tablespoon ketchup
¼ medium onion, grated
½ teaspoon seasoned salt
½ pound cooked shrimp

1. Cream together cheese and mayonnaise.

2. Stir in lemon juice, ketchup, onion, and seasoned salt.

3. Fold in shrimp. Chill.

4. Serve with chips.

NOTES:

1. To reduce calories, substitute Neufchâtel in place of cream cheese, and light mayonnaise or salad dressing instead of regular mayonnaise.

2. You can use small salad shrimp in place of larger cooked shrimp.

TACO DIP

Bernadette Zone
MAKES 10–12 SERVINGS

16 ounces cottage cheese
8-ounce package cream cheese, softened
1 package dry taco seasoning
Mexican cheese, shredded
lettuce, shredded
tomatoes, chopped
taco chips

1. Combine cottage cheese, cream cheese, and taco seasoning. Pour into dish.

2. Top with a layer of Mexican cheese, followed by a layer of lettuce, and then a layer of tomatoes.

3. Serve with taco chips.

CRACKLINS

fresh pork skin or 1 cup salt pork or
    slab bacon
salt

1. Cut pork skin into small pieces. Cook in heavy pot until skin is crispy. Stir frequently so the skin doesn't burn.

2. Drain drippings. (Reserve for browning chopped onions or minced garlic or other vegetables.)

3. Sprinkle cracklins with salt. Cool.

The Notorious Gap Gang

The Gap Gang was named for an area in Pennsylvania called the Gap Hills. They normally met in the Gap Tavern, where they developed many of their schemes for ambushing and kidnapping both enslaved freedom seekers, as well as free Africans, and reselling them back into the slavery of the south. They primarily operated throughout eastern and western Lancaster County. The gang maintained a presence from the late years of the 1830s until the early 1870s. After the Civil War, they were mainly a gang of thieves causing trouble and stealing until they were finally stopped and made to disband by the local community.

GARLIC SPREAD

Nancy Perkins

MAKES SPREAD FOR ONE LOAF ITALIAN BREAD

1¼ cups (1½ sticks) butter
3 tablespoons grated Parmesan cheese
½ teaspoon garlic powder
loaf of Italian bread, sliced

1. Warm butter to room temperature.

2. Combine all ingredients except bread.

3. Spread on slices of Italian bread.

4. Wrap bread in foil and heat in 350°F oven for 15–20 minutes.

CARAMEL POPCORN

MAKES 12–15 SERVINGS

1 cup (2 sticks) margarine or butter
½ cup white corn syrup
2 cups brown sugar
¼ teaspoon cream of tartar
1 teaspoon salt
1 teaspoon baking soda
6 quarts popped popcorn
peanuts, optional

1. In saucepan, combine butter, syrup, and sugar. Boil for 6 minutes, stirring constantly. Remove from heat.

2. Stir in cream of tartar, salt, and baking soda. In large mixing bowl, pour over popcorn and peanuts and stir well. Spread on greased cookie sheet.

3. Bake at 200°F for 60 minutes.

4. Allow to cool; then break apart into bite-sized pieces.

CRANBERRY FRUIT PUNCH

MAKES 8–12 SERVINGS

1 quart cranberry juice cocktail
2 cups orange juice
½ cup lemon juice
1 cup pineapple juice
½ cup sugar
1–2 cups water

1. Combine all ingredients.

2. Serve over crushed ice or cubes.

HOT CRANBERRY PUNCH

MAKES ABOUT 24 6-OUNCE SERVINGS

½ cup packed brown sugar
7 cups water, divided
½ teaspoon ground cinnamon
½ teaspoon ground nutmeg
¼ teaspoon ground cloves
2 (16-ounce) cans jellied cranberry sauce
12-ounce can frozen orange juice concentrate
2 tablespoons fresh lemon juice

1. Combine brown sugar, 1 cup water, cinnamon, nutmeg, and cloves in Dutch oven. Heat over high heat until mixture boils, stirring constantly. Cook and stir until sugar is dissolved. Remove from heat.

2. Stir in cranberry sauce. Mix well.

3. Stir in remaining water, orange juice, and lemon juice. Heat to boiling. Reduce heat. Simmer, uncovered, for 5 minutes.

4. Serve hot.

PARTY PUNCH

MAKES 24 SERVINGS

3 cups orange juice
fresh whole small strawberries
1 quart apple juice
1 quart orange soda
1 quart ginger ale
2 cups cranberry juice
2 cups pineapple juice
3 cups orange juice

1. Combine 3 cups orange juice and strawberries. Freeze in container to make large ice cube.

2. Chill apple juice, orange soda, ginger ale, cranberry juice, pineapple juice, and 3 cups orange juice.

3. Combine chilled ingredient in punch bowl. Add orange juice–strawberry ice cube.

HAWAIIAN FRUIT PUNCH

MAKES 45 6-OUNCE SERVINGS

2 (46-ounce) cans unsweetened pineapple juice
2⅔ cups orange juice
1½ cups lemon juice
⅔ cup lime juice
2 cups sugar
2-liter bottle ginger ale, chilled
2-liter bottle club soda, chilled
orange and lemon slices

1. Combine fruit juices and sugar. Chill.

2. Pour over ice in punch bowl. Slowly pour ginger ale and club soda down the side of the bowl.

3. Garnish with orange and lemon slices.

WEDDING PUNCH

MAKES 25 SERVINGS

3-ounce package gelatin, any flavor for desired color
¾ cup sugar
1 gallon hot water
12-ounce can frozen lemonade
46-ounce can unsweetened pineapple juice

1. Dissolve gelatin and sugar in hot water. Freeze.

2. When ready to serve, partially thaw punch and stir until slushy. Add frozen lemonade and pineapple juice.

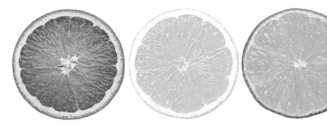

MOCK CHAMPAGNE PUNCH

MAKES 18–20 SERVINGS

32 ounces white grape juice
sliced fruit—lemon, lime, oranges, cherries
25.4 ounces non-alcoholic sparkling white
    grape juice
2 liters ginger ale
32 ounces white grape juice
6-ounce can frozen lemonade concentrate

1. Make ice ring with sliced fruit and 32 ounces
   white grape juice.

2. Chill remaining ingredients.

3. Combine sparkling grape juice, ginger ale,
   32 ounces grape juice, and lemonade in punch
   bowl. Add ice ring just before serving.

NOTE: If you prefer a less-sweet beverage,
substitute sparkling water in place of the ginger ale.

INSTANT RUSSIAN TEA

MAKES MANY SERVINGS

18-ounce jar Tang instant breakfast drink
2 (3-ounce) packages instant lemonade mix
2 teaspoons ground cinnamon
2 teaspoons ground cloves
¾ cup instant dry tea
2½ cups sugar

1. Mix all ingredients together thoroughly.

2. Place in tightly covered jar or plastic container
   and use as needed.

3. To make a cup of hot tea, place 2 heaping
   tablespoons dry mix in cup and add boiling
   water. Stir well.

PEACH TEA

MAKES 6–8 SERVINGS

3 cups chilled iced tea
6 tablespoons sugar
½ cup lemon juice
2 (12-ounce) cans peach nectar
orange slices
whole cloves
fresh mint sprigs

1. Combine all ingredients and chill.

2. Just before serving, remove whole cloves.

DRIED PEACH
(OR APRICOT) WINE

3 pounds dried peaches (or apricots)
1½ gallons cold water
4½ pounds sugar
1 package wine yeast or one ¼-ounce package
   active dry yeast

1. Soak peaches in cold water overnight.

2. Place peaches and water in large cooking vessel.
   Bring to a boil. Simmer for 5 minutes. Cool
   mixture until it is just cool enough to handle.

3. Strain through cheesecloth bag into a crock,
   using your hands to press out as much liquid as
   possible.

4. Stir in sugar while liquid is still warm. Cool to
   room temperature.

5. Sprinkle yeast on top. Cover. Let stand for
   12 hours.

6. Stir yeast into mixture.

7. Let stand for 7 days, stirring daily.

8. Transfer to gallon jugs. Place fermentation locks
   or corks on the jugs and allow wine to continue
   fermentation undisturbed.

9. Rack after 3 months.

10. Bottle when wine has cleared and fermentation
    has ceased. Age for 9–12 months.

VANILLA COKE

MAKES 1 SERVING

scoop of ice cream
2 ounces vanilla syrup
cola soda
maraschino cherry

1. Place scoop of ice cream in mason jar.

2. Combine vanilla syrup and cola soda. Pour over
   ice cream.

3. Garnish with cherry.

4. Serve immediately.

NOTE: Multiply as often as you want to make
more servings.

Every year in the summertime my mother and
father would make root beer. We would pour it into
the bottles and close them with metal caps. It was
my job to squeeze the caps on. Then we'd take them
down in the yard and lay them in the sun. When
they were ready to drink, the caps would pop off.
If you didn't put the caps on right they wouldn't
pop off.

— NELSON POLITE, SR.,
a member of Bethel AMEC,
Lancaster, PA

ETC.

———◆———

DUSTING POWDER

Sandy Cornish

2 cups cornstarch
1 cup baking soda
20 drops essential oil of any fragrance (no substitutes)
wooden boxes or containers of any size
powder puffs

1. Mix cornstarch and baking soda together.

2. Add drops of essential oil and mix.

3. Place powder in containers.

4. Give as gifts with powder puffs.

BATH SALT

Sandy Cornish

box of Epsom salt or rock salt
1 drop food coloring, optional
15 drops essential oil per cup of salt
empty jars or containers of any size

1. Mix Epsom salt with choice of food coloring.

2. Add drops of essential oil and mix.

3. Pour salt into jars or containers.

BATH OIL

Sandy Cornish

12-ounce or 16-ounce bottle baby oil
15 drops essential oil
empty jars or containers of any size

1. Place drops of essential oil inside baby oil bottle and shake.

2. Pour bath oil mixture into jars or containers. Seal and enjoy.

———◆———

A wise person speaks carefully and with truth, for every word that passes between one's teeth is meant for something.

—MOLEFIKETE ASANTE

STORY AND SONG

BY REVEREND EDWARD M. BAILEY

Oh! This is my story, this is my song,
Praising my Savior all the day long;
This is my story, this is my song,
Praising my Savior all the day long.

As a youngster, I was very proud of my knowledge of history. I read books and pamphlets, attended seminars, and took history courses in college. I felt competent discussing American history, especially the history of my people, sun-kissed African Americans. In fact, I was downright arrogant and insufferably rude in my assessment of how bright and knowledgeable I was about African history and about how ignorant others were.

But in 1987, in a workshop facilitated by Dr. Leroy Hopkins, a student of local African and German history, I began hearing a story of the Africans of America that I knew nothing about. I could not believe my ears nor my ignorance. I learned for the first time that there were African Civil War soldiers, scouts, and nurses. I also discovered that underneath my bravado I carried shame about my people and my history, because I had never heard of the full-scale resistance by Africans. I realized that my knowledge was based on half-truths and untruths.

I wondered how many other African Americans were as limited in their knowledge and as filled with shame about their history as I was. From my conversations with folk who looked like me, I began to realize that others were suffering under these same delusions.

Bethel Harambee Historical Services was born out of this personal struggle. In the Bible the word Bethel means "house of God." For Richard Allen, an enslaved African who helped to found the African Methodist Episcopal Church in the early nineteenth century, Bethel also meant "a place of refuge and comfort." Harambee comes from the Swahili language and means "Let's pull together."

That is exactly what Richard Allen and the founding parents of the African Methodist Episcopal Church did when they formed the denomination. They pulled together and provided a house of God that was a place of refuge and comfort for both free Africans and enslaved Africans. Almost all of the churches founded by Allen and others in Pennsylvania were called Bethel. These Bethels were active in the fight for freedom, and by their locations were strategically placed milestones on the trail to freedom. In fact, many who "followed the drinking gourd" and traveled the Underground Railroad in Pennsylvania stopped at stations called Bethel.

Bethel Harambee, a not-for-profit corporation, has a vision for freeing those of African descent who have no knowledge of the real African story in America.

Many who are captives of old assumptions also do not know about the triumphs of an ordinary people who trusted in the God of Abraham, Isaac,

and Jacob. Through Him and by Him ordinary people did extraordinary acts. Rev. Steven Smith, an African Methodist preacher, was a conductor on the Underground Railroad. William Whipper, a wealthy businessman, helped fund the work of the Africans' underground resistance. These and many others are virtually unknown and until recently were not mentioned in school textbooks.

Bethel Harambee produces "Living the Experience," a spiritual reenactment of the Underground Railroad, which includes the lives and times of enslaved Africans. Along with telling the story, we sing the songs of freedom, without which the story would be incomplete.

Fannie Crosby, in the chorus of "Blessed Assurance," a beloved hymn, captures a profound truth:

This is my story, this is my song,
Praising my Savior all the day long.

The Christian walk is both a song and a story. Having one without the other is being, as Paul of the Bible wrote, "a resounding gong or a clanging cymbal." No one wants to hear the testimony or the song of a Christian who does not have a story and a life that are in agreement. For we not only want to hear a sermon preached, we want to see the sermon lived, with full evidence that both are real.

We at Bethel Harambee find it necessary to hear the story and the song of Africans who have experienced the God who does deliver. It is essential for those of us who have been sun-kissed and who trace our heritage back to a lost time, to lost shores, and to a lost culture.

Our best and our most popular preachers were those who could tell the story—with the

MANY WHO FOLLOWED THE DRINKING GOURD AND TRAVELED THE UNDERGROUND RAILROAD IN PENNSYLVANIA STOPPED AT STATIONS CALLED BETHEL.

rhythm of the song. Those preachers who gave the "whoop" or the song without the story found out very quickly during the "call and response" that this was unacceptable. Someone in the congregation would say, "Bring it on in, Rev." That meant, "It is time to sit down and shut up because all you're doing is making noise." In other words, you're singing but you don't have a story.

The old favorite Negro spirituals had both song and story. "Go Down Moses," "Ezekiel Saw a Wheel Way Up in the Middle of the Air," "Joshua Fought the Battle of Jericho," and many others, are biblical stories set to the rhythm of song.

The spirituals that endured are those Bible stories that became the songs and stories of enslaved Africans.

Enslaved Africans adapted the stories of the Bible to tell their story. These songs and stories became their way of communicating and relating with one another. These folks were taken captive from the continent of Africa, where there are more languages and dialects than any of the other continents. Yet these Africans met, sent messages, asked for help, and gave warning to each other through these stories and songs.

These songs endured because the people who sang the songs also lived their stories. They identified with the bondage of the children of

"Living the Experience," a spiritual interactive reenactment, was developed to share the story of free and enslaved Africans who lived, pioneered, and carved out a place for themselves in the Americas. Told from the point of view of Africans of the 1800s, it highlights the contribution Africans made in demanding, obtaining, and securing their freedom. Using the first person, "Living the Experience" focuses on individuals who were seeking freedom, and on those who tirelessly and unselfishly participated in the Underground Railroad.

The spirituals throughout the reenactment are sung in homage to the creativity and the ability of Africans to use something ordinary to carry out extraordinary efforts.

The cast and staff of "Living the Experience" invite you to "live the experience" at

A SCENE FROM "LIVING THE EXPERIENCE."

the historic Bethel African Methodist Episcopal Church, located in ChurchTowne of Lancaster, Pennsylvania, where the pastors and congregation of old provided a safe house and a community for escaping Africans. Learn more about the reenactment by visiting the website: https://bethelamelancaster.com/ministries or calling 717-393-8379.

Israel so much that they could tell their Moses to go down to Egypt, a place of bondage—the plantation—to tell old Pharaoh—the old Massa—to let "my people" go.

The story and the song were also giving praise all the day long to the God who sits high, but looks low and fights the battle for the least, the last, and the lost.

At Bethel Harambee we are committed to singing the song that tells the story of an historically oppressed people. Because of their song and story they were able to say with conviction, "Before I'll be a slave I'll be buried in my grave and go home with my Lord and be free."

The beauty of these songs and stories is that they have no expiration date, they are never outmoded, and they work no matter the situation. When we look around today and see the plight of many African Americans, and think about the future, we believe that we need to learn the songs and the story. These songs

Bethel Harambee Historical Services produces the reenactment "Living the Experience" and provides space for the Leroy Taft and Mary Ella Hopkins Research and Study Center. The Hopkins Center fosters research about local African families, businesses, and homes, and the dissemination of stories from the African history of Lancaster. The Center has a growing collection of artifacts and documents, toward its goal of being a hub for African history that spans from Africa to the present by filling in answers about the time between.

and stories will help us hear that it was not the goodness of folk that brought us out of the miry clay, but the goodness of God.

In the past our story has not been told by us but by others. We have been allowed to sing the songs while others took the glory with a false story, the story of the deliverance of Africans in America. The true story is about how a good God, who is good all the time, did good things for folk in a no-good situation. The story is also about those folk who walked with God and who did so much with so little with so much against them. "If God be for us, who can be against us?" This story, for too long, has not been told.

I believe that the reason so many young African Americans are walking around in a fog, and so many older African Americans are walking in denial, is because they do not know the real story behind the song. Today in our churches we have turned to songs that have no historical meaning for us or for generations to come. And we no longer tell our story. We act as if nothing is happening to our people, all the while many of us are being taken captive, being placed in all types of bondage, and no longer determining our own future. These lost Africans are now singing songs that demean themselves, our mores, and our morals. They are convinced—because of where they were born and the environment in which they live—that there is no way out, except through means that do not bring deliverance, but rather the acceptance and celebration of bondage. To understand this is to listen to their songs that sing of no hope and deny a story of deliverance.

We believe that the hope of our future is in our past. The stories were the perspiration for our fight for freedom, and the songs were our inspiration. Our people lived what they sang about. They were not only dancers and dreamers, but they were workers and thinkers.

In the past these qualities worked against all odds and we became free. To stay free we need to live the life we sing about. We do not need

"Living the Experience," Bethel Harambee Historical Services, and the Hopkins Research and Study Center are all part of the effort to revive ChurchTowne, a community in Lancaster, Pennsylvania, where businesses, homes, and a one-room school once thrived. The goal is to offer ways for the people now living in this historic community to establish a strong economic, educational, evangelical, responsibly environmental, and enterprising base. This commitment comes from Bethel AME Church's past, and its current vision: to serve as Christ-centered, African-centered leadership for holistic community-building.

BETHEL AME CHURCH OF CHURCHTOWNE, LANCASTER, PENNSYLVANIA.

new songs; we just need to live our story while we sing our song. And it must be our story and our song if it is to work for our people.

When we sing our song and live our own story, others become inspired to seek freedom and live free. So it was during our sojourn in the past. As we sang and lived our story, women, in part because of our example, fought to be full citizens, and others began to demand their full rights as Americans. Our fight has helped to fulfill the American dream, the dream that states that all persons are created equal and are granted inalienable rights by God. Those who live for this dream, as Martin Luther King has said, are not rabble-rousers, but are American freedom-fighters.

Come sing with us our song and hear our story, and you will find that it is a miracle event within the miracle experiment called America.

Reverend Edward M. Bailey, is pastor of Bethel African Methodist Episcopal Church, ChurchTowne of Lancaster, Pennsylvania.

REVEREND BAILEY IN FRONT OF THE BETHEL AME CULTURAL CENTER,
HOME OF HARAMBEE HISTORICAL SERVICES AND THE HOPKINS
RESEARCH AND STUDY CENTER IN CHURCHTOWNE OF LANCASTER, PA.

INDEX

ABOUT THE AUTHOR

Phoebe M. Bailey was born to John Cornelius and Margaret Marie Bailey, the youngest of 15 children, in Huntington, Long Island, New York.

At the request of Bethel Harambee Historical Services, Phoebe helped to create *An African American Cookbook* as an extension of "Living the Experience Reenactment." The presentation is an African Christian's historical perspective of the enslaved Africans' investment and leadership in the quest for freedom and equality through means such as the African Methodist Episcopal Church and the Underground Railroad.

The Reverend Edward M. Bailey, Phoebe's brother, and the congregation of Bethel African Methodist Episcopal Church in Lancaster, Pennsylvania, continue to preserve and tell the stories of those Africans who have been ignored and not readily mentioned as part of traditional American history, and to restore and rebuild a community of promise.

For more information about Bethel Harambee Historical Services and "Living the Experience," call 717-393-8379 or visit https://bethelamelancaster.com/ministries.